RAISING TWO FISTS

RAISING TWO FISTS

STRUGGLES FOR BLACK CITIZENSHIP
IN MULTICULTURAL COLOMBIA

ROOSBELINDA CÁRDENAS

STANFORD UNIVERSITY PRESS
Stanford, California

Stanford University Press
Stanford, California

Printed in the United States of America on acid-free, archival-quality paper

Library of Congress Cataloging-in-Publication Data available on request.

Library of Congress Control Number: 2023947942

ISBN 9781503613799 (cloth)
ISBN 9781503635807 (paper)
ISBN 9781503635814 (ebook)

Cover design: David Fassett / Notch Design
Cover art: Esteban Jimenez Guerra
Typeset by Elliott Beard in Adobe Garamond Pro 10.5/15

CONTENTS

ACKNOWLEDGMENTS

IT IS A DIFFICULT TASK indeed to acknowledge and publicly thank those who have contributed to making this book possible. I want to begin by thanking the activists from the National Association of Displaced Afro-Colombians (AFRODES) and Process of Black Communities (PCN) whose work and lives not only inspired me to begin this project but whose steadfast friendship also accompanied me through a project that has now spanned more than fifteen years. I am in awe of their determination. In AFRODES's national office: Geiler Romaña, Eusebio Mosquera, Jattan Mazzot, Luz Marina Becerra, and Marino Córdoba. From PCN's national coordination team: Carlos Rosero, Francia Márquez, Charo Mina, Hernán Cortés, Eliana Rosero. From the Mira River Community Council—Anderson Orobio, Mailen Quiñones, and Lidoro Hurtado. And the community organizers in Soacha, in particular Aurora Casierra and the late Osías Quejada. There are many others who graciously gave me their time, shared their stories, welcomed me into their homes, and tolerated my incessant questions. Thank you.

There are a handful of people who introduced me to Colombia and a few more who were key in making it home. First, Juan Mejía and his beautiful extended family—the Mejías, the Boteros, and all their satellites. Sonia Serna, Diana Ojeda, and Julio Arias are the core of my Colombian chosen family. It is a gift to have known them through this project. I have also had the privilege of sharing with broader circles of scholars over the years who have extended their generosity and with whom I have collaborated in this and other projects.

Because the seeds of this project were planted when I was a master's student at the University of Texas at Austin, I benefited from the mentorship there of Charles Hale, Ted Gordon, João Costa Vargas, and Sharmila Rudrappa. Later, as a doctoral student at the University of California, Santa Cruz, and in my post-PhD professional career, I was also gifted the mentorship of Eduardo Restrepo, Bettina Ng'weno, Anna Tsing, Lisa Rofel, Susan Harding, Jonathan Fox, and most especially Mark Anderson and Julie Skurski.

I received funding from a number of organizations over the years: the Wenner Gren Foundation, the Social Science Research Council, the University of Texas, the University of California Regents, the University of California Mexus Program, the Consejo Nacional de Ciencia y Tecnología (CONACyT), the American Association of University Women, the Mellon Foundation's Sawyer Seminar, the Institute for Citizens and Scholars, and Hampshire College. Funding for this work was provided by a grant from the Office for the Advancement of Research at John Jay College.

There are many brilliant peers who have accompanied me on this journey, learning with me, sharing new resources, offering advice, reading drafts of my work, and commiserating along the way: Jennifer Goett, Keisha-Khan Perry, Mohan Ambikaipaker, Mariana Mora, Roberta Villalón, Courtney Morris, Jaime Alves, Bill Girard, Miel Alegre, Sandra Alvarez, and Rose Cohen. At Hampshire, I had colleagues who supported me to finish the book in all of the ways that "young" scholars need: sharing teaching and advising loads, advocating for junior faculty, and taking me out for meals and drinks. I want to especially thank Margaret Cerullo, Kara Lynch, Hiba Bou Akar, Lili Kim, Amy Jordan, and Jennifer Hamilton for their encouragement.

I wrote the bulk of this book from my home in New York City, where I moved in 2012. There, I found a community of amazing people—Maricruz, Sandralis, Sandri, Denisse, Roberta, Enrique, and their respective families—who sustained my work with food, love, and lots of much-needed music and dance breaks. The queen of that community is Janvieve Williams Comrie, who has been my partner in crime for many years and who, along with Ajamu

Baraka, Anthony Dest, and Tianna Paschel, has helped sustain my activism in support of racial justice in Colombia even from a distance.

Leigh Campoamor deserves a separate and unique paragraph in this long list of thank-yous. Leigh was my writing partner in the final years of writing this manuscript. She read endless iterations of this book, always offering insightful analysis as well as meticulous line edits! As if this were not enough, she introduced me to Sara Appel, who read and assessed the full manuscript, offering lucid advice to get to the finish line. Thank you, Leigh. It's been painful, but I have loved doing it with you.

And finally, my people in my other homes. To my family in Mexico, especially my mother, who trusted me when I told them I couldn't travel to see them, or that I had to miss a family event because I had "to work" even when the semester was out. My father didn't live long enough to see this book to its completion, but he has been present all these years *acompañándome*. To my partner, Esteban Jiménez, who patiently listened to my tribulations and waited until I finally pressed "send" on this manuscript. I also want to thank him for so lovingly creating the beautiful artwork for the cover. And finally, I think it is quite appropriate that my incredible daughter, Lucía—who was not quite a fully formed idea when I began this project and is now a hyperlucid teenage writer—is the first person to read and edit the epilogue of this book. Thank you for the edits and for being the fuel that drives everything I do. This book is for you, Lucía.

RAISING TWO FISTS

ATLANTIC OCEAN

PANAMA

VENEZUELA

COLOMBIA

PACIFIC
OCEAN

• BOGOTA

• BUENAVENTURA

• CALI

• TUMACO

BRAZIL

ECUADOR

PERU

COLOMBIA

- • Cities/Towns

- ——— International border

BLACK CITIZENSHIP
National Inclusion and Diasporic Belonging

"¡EL PUEBLO NO SE RINDE, CARAJO!"

On Saturday May 20, 2017, the city of Buenaventura—Colombia's blackest city on the Pacific Coast—was convulsing. The day before, a peaceful protest at which tens of thousands of people declared an indefinite general strike, had gone awry as armed men infiltrated the civilian ranks, instigating violence and triggering what the national media reprovingly described as out-of-control looting and rioting (*El Espectador* 2017c; *Semana* 2017a, 2017b). When talks between the national government and the civic strike's Organizing Committee broke down, the day's outcome became dismal: more than forty people detained, numerous civilians injured, a state-imposed curfew, and a prohibition on further protests (*El Espectador* 2017b).

Despite escalating government repression, on that Saturday morning Bonaverenses filled the streets for the fifth consecutive day, unequivocally declaring their city in a state of "social, economic, and ecological emergency" (personal communication, May 20, 2017; Proceso de Comunidades Negras 2017).[1] They wore white shirts and donned the national colors in flags, hats, and headbands, shouting, "¡El pueblo no se rinde, carajo!" (The people will not give up, damn it!), as one protester emotionally declared, to "show Colombia and the national government that Buenaventura *exists*" (personal

1

communication, May 20, 2017).[2] The government's hostile response was to increase the city's police and anti-riot units by more than five hundred men, including soldiers who surveyed the city from helicopters and gassed protesters from tanks.

This powerful mobilization put several ironies on display. Most glaring is that Buenaventura, an impoverished city of four hundred thousand inhabitants with no reliable potable water system or even second-tier hospital, is Colombia's largest port, the entry and exit point of outrageous economic wealth that circulates in legal and illegal markets.[3] How is it that a city from which 60 percent of Colombia's coffee exports are shipped suffers from a 68 percent unemployment rate (*El Espectador* 2017a; *Semana* 2017c)?[4] How is it that a maritime port at the mouth of the Dagua, Anchicayá, Calima, Cajambre, Yurumanguí, Naya, and San Juan rivers, all of which run across one of the wettest regions of the world, has daily water rations (*Semana* 2017c)?[5] Bonaverenses raised these questions loudly and clearly with their demands of basic social rights, such as access to potable water, employment, and education. But more than that, Bonaverenses demanded an end to a long history of plunder. Their signs, some of which read "Estamos cansados" (We are tired), were echoed by impromptu testimonies of people on the streets, who stated that Buenaventura was done being "a town where people come to plunder and where/for which nothing is done" (personal communication, May 20, 2017).[6] Videos, photos, and audio circulating on social media and in mainstream press outlets assured viewers everywhere that protesters would not relent until the government agreed to draft an economic development plan in which Bonaverenses had a voice and from which they reaped the benefits. Until then, they would continue to disrupt business as usual, halting the port's vast commercial activity with roadblocks and labor stoppages and generating massive economic costs for port entrepreneurs.[7]

A second irony is that when the protests in Buenaventura erupted, President Juan Manuel Santos was in Washington negotiating the US foreign-aid package for Colombia's postwar rebuilding. Following a four-year negotiation that formally ended Latin America's longest civil war in November 2016, Colombia had begun a long-awaited transition to peace. While President Santos was being internationally recognized for his work to bring peace to Colombia,[8] Buenaventura continued to be one of Colombia's—and the world's—deadliest places.[9] By the time of the civic strike in May 2017, the peace accords with the Revolutionary Armed Forces of Colombia (Fuerzas Revolucionarias Armadas de Colombia, or FARC), had been signed, and Bonaverenses, like the rest of their fellow Colombians, were eager to experience the long-awaited peace that Santos's government touted. Instead, in just the first three months after Colombia's peace accords, 21 community leaders across the Pacific Region received death threats, 819 people were displaced, and 5 were murdered (personal communication, May 20, 2017).[10]

A final irony has to do with the date of the protests. May 21 is the commemoration of Colombia's abolition of slavery, which since 2001 has been celebrated nationally as Día de la Afrocolombianidad (Day of Afro-Colombianness) marked by state-sponsored symposia, book launches, and extravagant cultural events such as gastronomic festivals, dance performances, film screenings, and concerts intended to put Afro-Colombians' national contributions and expressive culture on proud display (Cárdenas 2012). But rather than spend the day in celebratory events, Bonaverenses—89 percent of whom are self-identified Afro-descendants—commemorated the end of slavery on that first "peaceful" year in more than half a century by doing what they had been doing since before abolition: resisting state repression to insist that they, too, were entitled to full citizenship. To do this, they relied on one another and the communities of resistance they had built from their shared experiences of marginalization.[11] But they also relied on a larger community of allies that extended beyond the city, the region, and even Colombia. As they braved the militarized streets on that Sunday morning, the more than fifty thousand bodies on the streets of Buenaventura were joined in remote solidarity by their black brothers and sisters in Quibdó and Cali; in Panama and Brazil; in Washington, DC, and Chicago.[12]

Buenaventura's civic strike was an instance of African diasporic resistance, sustained by racial solidarity across the Americas. In Quibdó, another majority Afro-Colombian city in the Pacific Region where a civic strike had preceded Buenaventura's by five days, locals held a candlelight vigil on May 21. In Cali, a group of black women organized a concurrent protest outside city hall, calling for regional solidarity across the Pacific Region. Their signs used the popular line from Grammy-winning musical group ChocQuibTown's song "Somos Pacífico" while they chanted, "¡La vida no se vende, se ama y se defiende!" (Life should not be sold / it should be loved and defended). Black activists in Panama and Brazil joined in by using the hashtag #SomosUnSoloPueblo (We are one nation), which was a call to diasporic unity and a strong statement that black people everywhere are part of a single nation. And in the United States, members of the Congressional Black Caucus tweeted messages condemning the Colombian state's excessive use of force and calling citizens to protest outside the Colombian embassy in DC.[13]

As I followed the events unfolding in Buenaventura for weeks, I had a growing sense that there was something distinct and important about the civic strike. Initially, what captured my attention was the way Buenaventura strikers combined fury with lucid analysis. While I had seen Afro-Colombians mobilize for resources and labor rights, and against government corruption and corporate-caused environmental degradation, Buenaventura's strikers demanded all at once, and in doing so, they beautifully articulated an intersectional theory of structural racism. The seemingly disparate list of Bonaverenses' uncompromising demands was a concerted attack on the many ugly heads of the hydra that is antiblack racism. They denounced economic exploitation, social invisibilization, political marginalization, and the brutal disregard for black lives all in one breath. In a sense, the civic strike was a continuation of many other preceding struggles, an echo of prior voices. But by articulating these demands centrally as Afro-Colombians and members of the African diaspora, Buenaventura was also a loud call to racial justice. In its condensed and eloquent illustration of the mechanisms through which structural racism operates in Colombia today, Buenaventura was unique.

The intensity of Buenaventura's strike was also remarkable. Protesters flooded the streets for twenty-one consecutive days amid deepening government crackdown. With each passing day, the stakes seemed higher for all involved. The national press ran several daily stories on the civic strike, and although most mainstream international newspapers did not pick up the story, some progressive outlets abroad paid close attention.[14] As far as black mobilizations in Colombia had gone, Buenaventura's strike was on a different scale. But in addition to the scale, there was something else that seemed substantively different and that crystallized when I came across a striking photo published in one of Colombia's largest newspapers—*El Espectador*. At the foreground of the photo were two young women—one was cupping a hand around her mouth to amplify her voice and the other was holding a sign. Other people—whose faces are not visible—hold two signs that appear side by side at the center of the photo's frame. One of the signs reads "Chocó and Buenaventura Are Also Colombia"; while the other, which includes a drawing of a raised fist, reads "Pueblo negro en pie de lucha" (black people standing in struggle) followed by the hashtags #SoyBuenaventura (I am Buenaventura) and #SoyChocó (I am Chocó).[15] I was struck by the way the photo captured quite succinctly the distinctiveness that I had been struggling to articulate. The two signs put on display the protesters' use of a dual strategy, simultaneously demanding full citizenship rights as members of the nation-state (Colombia) while calling for members of a diasporic black nation (*pueblo negro*) to stand with them in struggle. Buenaventura was not only a protest of disenfranchised citizens clamoring for full inclusion, although it was that. Buenaventura was not only a call to black diasporic solidarity, although it was also that. Buenaventura was a crystal-clear and unapologetic example of a two-fisted black mobilization that demanded rights to national inclusion and made claims to diasporic belonging. This is what I call the struggle for Black Citizenship.

BLACK CITIZENSHIP IN A MULTICULTURAL NATION

I was not in Buenaventura during this historical uprising. I joined the rest of the international supporters from my home in New York, signing letters, circulating documents, and otherwise spreading the word. However, I have been following black mobilizations in Colombia for nearly twenty years, both from abroad and from up close during the five years that I lived in Bogotá and the decades during which I've visited regularly. I have accompanied and collaborated with two of Colombia's best-known black organizations—the National Association of Displaced Afro-Colombians (AFRODES) and the Process of Black Communities (PCN)—in their high-level work negotiating policy with the national government and in their more local and grassroots initiatives. I have visited villages and rural areas in the Pacific Region and have become acquainted with the struggles of Afro-Colombians in urban areas as well. Over the years, I have collaborated with black activists in Colombia as they shift their political strategies, adapt their discourses, and build new networks of support. This book is a description of that trajectory and a reflection on the limits and possibilities of the various political strategies that I've seen Afro-Colombians use in their struggles for justice, which centrally includes demanding rights to the state in the name of multiculturalism. It is also an ethnographic analysis of the multiple forms of violence that Afro-Colombians face today, evidencing how even in a multicultural state like Colombia, structural racism continues to condense historical and contemporary forms of violence that interlock and coproduce one another.

Scholars have been assessing the concrete impact of multicultural reforms across Latin America for at least a decade, trying to explain why in the current post-multicultural moment when black and indigenous people in the Americas have more rights than ever, they continue to be subjected to intense forms of racial violence. They have documented the curious coincidence of multicultural reforms and intensified extractivism across the region (Cárdenas 2012c; Hale 2005; Vélez-Torres 2014), noting how the impact of this increased competition for space and thirst for "natural resources" falls along gendered lines (Goett 2016; Morris 2016; Perry 2013; Smith 2016a) and both builds on and deepens the historical dispossession of black people in the Americas (Bledsoe and Wright 2019; McKittrick 2011; Mollett 2014; Perry 2013). This critical scholarship has outlined the contradictions and exclusions embedded in the liberal notion of citizenship itself (Holston 2009), which drives a wedge between first- and second-class citizens, who are separated by race and its enduring colonial hierarchies (Beltrán 2020; Reiter 2013; Smith 2016b). Scholars have also noted that in practice, the legal reforms brought about by multicultural recognition have been insufficient in effectively interrupting racism (Hooker 2020; Rahier 2020), and that in recruiting black and indigenous activists to work closely with the (neoliberal) state, multiculturalism poses serious risks of collusion and co-optation (see the contributions in Rahier 2012). Most importantly, some of these scholars have insightfully noted that multiculturalism—like the national ideology of the *mestizo* nation before it—has not precisely "failed" but rather was never designed to dismantle the structures that perpetuate racialized dispossession (Mollett 2016; Vergara-Figueroa 2017).

I build on this critical scholarship to advance a capacious vision of Black Citizenship as a pursuit that is not limited to the nation-state but is anchored in an African diasporic understanding of justice, which centers the care for *all* life and is so aptly captured by the phrase and concomitant movement "Black Lives Matter." This insight too is evidently built on the work of others, the great majority of whom are black women (Hernández Reyes 2019; Mollett 2021b; Morris 2012; Perry 2013; Smith 2017). As these scholars note, a diasporic vision of justice emerges from the lived experiences of violence that black people in the Americas have endured, and black women in particular exercise this vision through gendered strategies to survive and even thrive in the midst of multiple and enduring forms of violence. Still, despite their attention to violence, I echo these scholars in focusing less on black victimization itself and more on the ways in which black people harness the accumulated knowledge resulting from these painful and also joyful experiences to envision and put into practice more liberatory futures for all. This is what I call the pursuit of Black Citizenship.

Black Citizenship is thus an incomplete project whose outlines are sometimes clearer and sometimes remain obscured by the categories with which contemporary racial politics are bound—such as those defined by multiculturalism. In the end, my exploration in this book is hopeful, not as a naive celebration of a fait accompli but as a grounded appraisal of Black Citizenship's possibilities and an exercise in imagining new forms of anti-racism and freedom.

The Multicultural Conjuncture

The multicultural turn of the early 1990s, when states across Latin America began to recognize and legally enshrine differential cultural rights for Afro-descendants, was a critical point at which blackness became visible as a constituent, if still marginalized, element of the Colombian nation (Friedemann 1984; Paschel 2016).[16] Before then, black Colombians were ambiguously included in the nation as both racialized (nonmodern) others and fellow (modern) nationals (Restrepo 2004; Wade 1993). Although the pervasiveness of racism had spurred some of the first black mobilizations well before the multicultural turn, the imaginary of the Colombian nation as a product of racial intermixing known as *mestizaje*, which had been dominant since the middle of the twentieth century, tended to marginalize or discredit them.[17] Under the dominant logic of *mestizaje*, black Colombians were routinely interpellated into disadvantageous racial positions, while the public recognition of those processes of racialization and the denunciation of antiblack racism were nearly impossible.

This was the case until the multicultural turn that swept most of Latin America in the early 1990s. In Colombia, official multiculturalism amounted to designating the nation's ethnic others, that is, identifying allegedly coherent "communities" with "cultures" that were distinct from the dominant Euro-Andean *criollo* national culture (Restrepo 2004; Wade 1993).[18] In the case of Afro-Colombians, the most sweeping manifestation of state multiculturalism was the passage of Law 70 in 1993, which recognized Black Communities as culturally distinct and granted them specific rights, including the right to collective titling of their ancestral lands in the Pacific Region.[19] Afro-Colombians thus went from being primarily conceived of as individuals with citizenship rights commensurate with those of fellow nationals (in theory if not in practice) to being treated as collective subjects of special rights by virtue of possessing particular cultural characteristics. This recognition was modeled on indigenous activists' understanding of ethnic difference, which emphasized native people's autochthony and their collective history as a distinct *pueblo* (people).[20] The shift is noteworthy not only because of the profound differences in the ways that blackness was articulated before and after the onset of multiculturalism but also because this was the moment at which the mobilization of organized black politics burgeoned in Colombia. As Paschel (2016) has noted, it was at this point that political struggles began to be explicitly articulated as black struggles waged by black subjects.

Despite its promise to destabilize the notion of a homogeneous national subject and reveal the white supremacist foundations of *mestizaje*, the turn to multiculturalism has fallen short of delivering inclusive forms of citizenship for black and indigenous people. Several decades after the onset of multiculturalism, the overall balance of its political impact is at best lackluster and at worst perverse. As mentioned earlier, where its radical potential has not been seriously undermined in practice, multiculturalism has been co-opted or altogether retooled for ulterior ends (Hale 2005; Hooker 2020; Lehmann 2016; Rahier 2012; Van Cott 2000a). However, multiculturalism has also been productive in various senses. On the one hand, the sense of national renewal and racial reconciliation offered by multicultural reforms has proved productive for the maintenance of state legitimacy and its associated capitalist expansion. On the other hand, and despite its built-in limitations, Afro-Colombian activists have also found creative and sometimes counterintuitive ways to use multiculturalism to further their political agendas. For example, rather than remaining bound within the culturalist definition of blackness offered by official multicultural reforms, Afro-Colombians have expanded the narrow spaces of multicultural recognition to demand a national reckoning with antiblack racism.

Throughout the book, I assess the political outcomes of this state-led multicultural rights regime, focusing on the political possibilities created by and for Afro-Colombians since the 1990s until the present. While undoubtedly the outcome is far from triumphant, I am still interested in analyzing how multiculturalism has unfolded over the past three decades in Colombia. By looking at both its foretold limitations and its unexpected entanglements, I don't foreclose the possibility of radical political emergences. To be clear, multiculturalism has not been a very fertile terrain for black freedom, but in it Afro-Colombians have cultivated political visions that hold the promise of future flourishings.

Rights Are Not Enough

This book analyzes struggles for Black Citizenship on the ground—that is, Afro-Colombians' organized deployment of a dual strategy for simultaneous national inclusion and African diasporic belonging. I use the term *citizenship* robustly to indicate (1) the legal guarantee of civil, political, and social rights; (2) active participation in political institutions; and (3) membership in a political community that furnishes a sense of identity. By folding in an uncompromising black political perspective, the activists whom I follow in this book are furthering a complex vision of citizenship that accounts for the historical particularities of Afro-descendants' experience. It is a vision that is both grounded in the territorial contours of the Colombian nation-state and diasporic in scope.

As analysts and activists, we often imagine nation and diaspora as an either-or choice, and there is much at risk in doing so. On one end of this false dichotomy, we risk remaining discursively trapped within the borders of the nation-state and its authority to sanction rights both when trying to understand the structures that reproduce inequalities and when imagining alternative futures. At the other end, we risk arriving at a foregone conclusion that justice for black people is simply impossible within the existent global configuration, which to a large extent continues to rely on state-based recognition of rights. In the first case, we remain unable or unwilling to see that the tools with which we fight for racial justice are limited because they are the master's tools (Lorde 1984). In the second case, while lucidly aware of the structural impossibility of entirely undoing injustice with rights-based claims, we risk retrenching to a paralyzing state of cynical critique.

I focus on rights and citizenship because these were the terms of the struggles that I repeatedly encountered in spaces of black politics in Colombia. Certainly, justice can be pursued through myriad routes that exceed, escape, or eschew a liberal, state-centric focus on rights. But the struggle for rights and the insistence on inclusion in the Colombian nation as full but differentiated citizens centrally preoccupied the activists with whom I conducted this research, and as such I take it seriously. Rather than offer a theoretical elaboration of these concepts, I take them as categories to be ethnographically explored. Which communities of belonging are black activists claiming in their struggles for ethnic rights, differential reparations, and peace? How do they understand and remake the relationship between black identity, citizenship rights, and the Colombian nation?

Rights-based struggles are both necessary and inherently incapable of fully addressing the multiple forms of violence that Afro-Colombians face today. They are ineffective because they rely on an institution—the Colombian nation-state—that is heir to settler colonialism and whose very ideological foundation is premised on the maintenance of white supremacy for the recognition, implementation, and protection of those very rights. In noting this, I follow the small but powerful scholarship that has recently paid attention to settler-colonial dynamics in Latin America (Castellanos 2017; Loperena 2017; Mollett 2021a; Speed 2017; Ybarra 2018). Like these scholars, I draw attention to the continental continuities of settler colonialism, which have remained obscured because of our insistence on contrasting Latin American racial formations to those of the United States (and Canada) (Mollett 2021a). Rather than see the two as contrasts, I follow the suggestion that Latin America "should be included in the general history of the global expansion of white settler populations from all over Europe" (Gott 2007, 270).

And yet struggles for rights are a pragmatic resource that Afro-Colombians do in fact utilize—sometimes to effectively undermine inequality (see Agudelo 2005; Asher 2009; Escobar 2008; Oslender 2016; Paschel 2016; Vergara-Figueroa 2017). This book illustrates this tension as it is navigated by Afro-Colombians who are engaged in various kinds of struggles, both in organized politics and in their daily lives. Organized Afro-Colombians—whether activists or not—do not limit their strategies of survival and subversion to claims that are legible to or dependent on the state. Instead, they participate in rights-based struggles while also carrying out numerous daily actions that protect their integrity and build the conditions to live flourishing lives without requiring state sanction. This is well illustrated by what Goett (2016) identifies as black cultural practices and vernacular ways of being that function as "powerful sources of oppositional agency" (9). In both these daily practices and organized political interventions, an awareness and strategic deployment of African diasporic belonging and practices of solidarity are key.

A Diasporic Imperative: Against the Politics of Death

The dual strategy that I call Black Citizenship became starkly apparent in Buenaventura, where Afro-Colombians' demands for basic citizenship rights and denunciation of structural racism bore fruit only after twenty-one days of a fierce struggle with very high costs for demonstrators: one person killed, dozens wounded by live ammunition, and hundreds arrested and severely affected by tear gas (Democracy Now! 2017). After an initial stalemate, various breakdowns in talks, and a final forty-hour meeting between government negotiators and the civic strike's Organizing Committee, both parties signed an agreement.[21] Bonaverenses such as community leader Hamington Valencia celebrated the agreement enthusiastically, hopeful at the promise of fully participating in civil and social life, and proud to have "honor[ed] [their] heroic ancestors who had survived insult, cruelty, and servitude" against "the structural inequities shaped by exclusion, racism, and voracious capitalism" with their strike (Hamington Valencia Viveros, posted on social media, June 6, 2017). Afro-Colombians were joined in this celebration by voices in the diaspora who sent African proverbs and *ashe*, while reiterating their commitment to bear witness as the implementation of the agreements unfolded.[22] Although Bonaverenses were keenly aware of the hard work that lay ahead in holding the Colombian government accountable, the general mood following the end of the strike was triumphant, and Afro-Colombian activists were emboldened by the abundant expressions of international solidarity that poured in. As Charo Mina Rojas, a prominent activist from a major black organization put it, the struggle was not over but its weight was lessened by the feeling that it was shared by black people everywhere: "This is a time for moving from fraternal solidarity to broader movement building with common agendas for the liberation and self-determination of black people. We are one people. My struggle is your struggle" (Latin American and Caribbean Solidarity Network 2017).

In anticipation of the difficult journey ahead, the strikers remained organized in citizen councils to oversee implementation of the agreements. As expected, the limitations of rights-based struggles were soon confirmed by the government's continued breaches and foot-dragging, and Bonaverenses' optimism quickly turned to frustration as they realized once more that the state's promise to extend basic civil rights was no panacea. But the sobering reminder that rights are insufficient in protecting black life struck with full force a few months later when Temístocles Machado, a local community activist and leader of the civic strike, was murdered in cold blood just as the citizen councils gathered in January 2018 to assess the progress made on the implementation of the government's agreements.

Temístocles had been granted protective measures by Colombia's National Protection Unit (UNP) for a short period during the civic strike. These limited measures entitled him to carry a special cell phone and a bulletproof vest, but they were removed soon after the strike ended. Although more visible strike leaders had received more robust protection measures, Temístocles was made particularly vulnerable by a visit from the Centro Nacional de Memoria Histórica (National Center of Historic Memory)—a government agency charged with documenting human rights violations committed during Colombia's long civil war. The center intended to digitize an impressive file that Temístocles had compiled over the years documenting land disputes in the area and about which he had received numerous threats. In fact, Don Temis—as he was affectionately known—had been very vocal in denouncing public-private collusion to carry out development projects that displaced black residents from now-coveted oceanfront neighborhoods in Buenaventura. His file documented the numerous and violent methods that allegedly politically unaligned armed men—like those who shot him—used to intimidate, displace, and silence community members (Verdad Abierta 2018). Knowing that he treaded in dangerous waters, Don Temis sought out renewed protective measures and even met with Colombia's vice attorney general just a few days before he was murdered. In the end, although the evidence he had collected was safeguarded, Temístocles's life was not.

Following Temístocles's assassination, voices rose again far and wide denouncing untimely death and demanding justice in the struggle to protect black lives. In New York City, the *Amsterdam News* heeded Afro-Colombians' request for "an outcry from the African Diaspora" (Carrillo 2018), while in Buenaventura members of the civic strike's Organizing Committee boldly reminded their fellow Colombians that they would prevail, chanting "Por nuestros muertos, ¡ni un minuto de silencio!" (For our dead, not a minute of silence) (personal communication, January 21, 2018).[23] Temístocles's death, as well as the response that followed from black people across the Americas, suggests that the pursuit of Black Citizenship is sutured together by a diasporic thread, which I identify as the struggle against the politics of death. These politics include projects to displace, disenfranchise, criminalize, and otherwise annihilate life in all its expressions—both human and nonhuman. Of course, Afro-pessimist scholars both inside and outside of Latin America have long paid attention to untimely death as a structuring characteristic of the black experience (Alves 2020; Hartman 1997; Wilderson 2010; Sexton

2008; Vargas 2018), and this book is heir to their insights. At the same time, I focus less on the overdetermined experience of blackness as social death that these authors describe to explore the ways in which Afro-Colombians push against these deadly forces—however (un)successfully. Furthermore, given the context of a prolonged and crude civil war, the Colombian case offers an exceptionally clear opportunity to analyze how the multiple forces of death unfurl both in their daily insidiousness and in their gruesome spectacles. By the same token, by following Afro-Colombian activists' daily lives and organized responses to these deadly forces, I hope to glean valuable lessons to transform, as the environmental and anti-racist activist Francia Márquez insists, the politics of death into a politics of life.

WAR AND PEACE IN COLOMBIA

This book covers the period from the early 1980s to the present. During that period, I trace the emergence and solidification of state multiculturalism, the institutionalization and deepening of a neoliberal national development project, and a series of (seemingly) dramatic shifts in the dynamics of Colombia's civil war. In terms of the landscape of electoral politics, Colombia has a long history of alternating power between the liberal and conservative parties, both of which remained aligned with neoliberal economic agendas and (nominally) open to multicultural reforms during the period I analyze.[24] The arrival of Álvaro Uribe to the presidency in 2002, however, changed this landscape considerably. On the one hand, Uribe and his legacy known as *uribismo* deepened government commitment to neoliberalism, further exacerbating racial, gender, and economic inequality in Colombia. On the other hand, Uribe and his cronies radically redirected the course of the civil war. In addition to halting prior administrations' attempts at a negotiated end to the war, Uribe adopted a *mano dura* (strong-arm) approach determined to eradicate the remaining guerrillas—the Revolutionary Armed Forces of Colombia (FARC, by its Spanish acronym) and the National Liberation Army (ELN)—at any cost. Coupled with his now-documented alliance with paramilitary groups that waged a ravaging dirty war against armed dissidents and civilians alike, Uribe's *mano dura* resulted in a dramatic intensification of the conflict during his two terms in office, which ended in 2010. Shortly after Uribe's departure from office, President Santos resumed negotiations with the FARC and succeeded in signing a peace accord in 2016. The story of Colombia's civil war is, of course, much more complicated than this cursory summary describes. Throughout the book, I trace the vicissitudes of the war and the peace negotiation process in detail, as well as the alleged "postwar" period, paying particular attention to its impact on the Afro-Colombian population. Here, I pause briefly to provide a bird's-eye view of Colombia's bloody battlegrounds.

Colombia's civil war is the longest armed conflict in the Western Hemisphere. Although it is difficult to pinpoint when it started, analysts often identify 1948—when the popular presidential candidate Jorge Eliécer Gaitán was murdered—as the beginning of the war and point to the government's signing of the 2016 peace accords with the FARC as its end. While useful in demarcating the most recent cycle of political violence in Colombia, these bookends fail to capture the complex dynamics of the war—its oscillating intensity, its fluctuating geographies, and the numerous actors (both national and international) that have directly and indirectly shaped it. My purpose in this section is not to make sense of this complexity or to make a direct contribution to the robust literature on the war.[25] Instead, I glean the insights of some of these analyses to better understand the context in which Afro-Colombian struggles have unfolded over the past three decades.

Gaitán's murder in 1948 unleashed a period of intense partisan violence known in Colombian historiography as La Violencia. This bloody period was poorly resolved through a power-sharing agreement between leaders of the Liberal and Conservative Parties known as the National Front (Frente Nacional), designed to alternate their respective candidates in the presidency. Some analysts have suggested that the National Front created a closed political system overseen by a tight elite, which, rather than ending the violence, paradoxically created the conditions for its subsequent phases (Leal Buitrago 1986; Pécaut 1988; Sánchez 1992). This helps explain the emergence of Colombia's oldest and largest leftist guerrilla group, the FARC, which traces its origins to *campesino* self-defense forces that predated La Violencia.[26] In the 1950s, these poorly trained groups went from being dispersed armed enclaves to adopting a Marxist platform with a strong agrarian component, and by 1964 they had declared themselves an insurgent army.[27]

The success of the Cuban Revolution inspired and aided, in some cases, the emergence of the next generation of guerrilla groups in Colombia. This was the case with Colombia's second-largest guerrilla group, the ELN, which was also linked to the liberation theology movement that inspired members of the Catholic Church across Latin America to adopt "a preferential option for the poor" (Gutiérrez 1988). While many of the groups that emerged during this period laid down their arms in the 1980s—including the Movimiento 19 de Abril, or M-19, whose members were targeted for assassination after they went through an amnesty to form the Unión Patriótica Party—the ELN survives to date.

Through the 1980s and 1990s, as both the FARC and the ELN continued to grow thanks in part to their increased involvement in illicit activities, the military employed a strategy of containment. This involved waging low-intensity warfare while limiting open combat. A corollary of this strategy has been the use of paramilitary forces that work covertly with the military in counterinsurgency operations. This was made possible by the prior existence of extreme-right militias; they were created as vigilante groups to protect the interests of large-scale capitalists and to eradicate leftist guerrillas. During the 1990s, these groups emerged as a united and mighty armed group known as the United Self-Defense Forces of Colombia (Autodefensas Unidas de Colombia, or AUC). Specifically, the leaders of the paramilitary group known as Autodefensas Campesinas de Córdoba y Urabá (ACCU), which had been operating in the northernmost portion of the Pacific Coast since the 1980s, promoted the creation and alliance of paramilitary groups throughout the country and in 1997 formally consolidated into a nationwide coalition.[28] While the stated purpose of the AUC was military in nature, it is well documented that the group was involved in very lucrative capital-generating endeavors. These included both the illicit coca economy and large-scale development projects such as oil-palm plantations and mining—sometimes through covert alliances with entrepreneurs and government officials.[29] After securing its stronghold through both economic power and terror-inducing tactics in the northwestern region of the country, the AUC coalition grew and expanded across the entire national territory.

The conflict was also deepened by US foreign policy in Colombia, which exchanged direct aid for diplomatic and military allegiance. Most significantly, in 1999 Colombia's president Andrés Pastrana and US president Bill Clinton signed a collaborative agreement known as Plan Colombia. Although this was presented as a comprehensive aid package that included institutional, social, and economic development, its allotment for military assistance and training oscillated between 76 percent and 99 percent of the total (Tate 2007). This figure peaked in the year 2000, when the US government destined $765 million for the war against drugs and counterinsurgency in a single year. With this robust financial and military backup from the US government, the Colombian army escalated its attack against the drug trade and associated illegal armed groups. The emergence of organized paramilitarism in conjunction with the state-sanctioned military escalation spurred by Plan Colombia significantly changed the dynamics of Colombia's civil war and escalated the competition for territorial dominance nationwide. The result was a period of intensified conflict that enveloped the entire country, folding in areas like the Pacific Region, which had remained on the margins of the war's geographies until then.

While some of the figures associated with the war—like forced displacement and massacres—peaked in the early 2000s, armed violence in Colombia has not meaningfully abated in the past twenty years. This has unfortunately continued to be the case even after the signing of the peace accords in 2016. President Duque's administration, which immediately followed the signing of the accords, lacked the political will to implement them, leaving the underlying causes of Colombia's conflict largely unchanged. In some cases, in fact—as is the case with the number of human rights activists murdered, which I outline in chapter 4—the violence has actually increased. Despite a remarkable negotiation process and a globally celebrated document that outlines a robust plan for national renewal, a distinct environment of peace is not yet fully palpable in Colombia. Since the signing of the peace accords, new dissident groups have emerged, old ones have morphed into seemingly novel criminal configurations, and the politics of death continue unabated.

THE RESEARCH FIELDS
Organized Politics

This book's inquiry is centered on political projects and processes of subject formation. The first is defined by the space of organized politics, which is made up of a number of organizations that explicitly identify as black and mobilize political projects on that basis. This is an uneven terrain composed of highly dissimilar organizations with broadly differing political objectives and trajectories. It is therefore important to carefully describe the organizations I worked with and to make explicit the reasons for these collaborations.

My fieldwork closely followed the political work of two of Colombia's largest black organizations: the Process of Black Communities (Proceso de Comunidades Negras, or PCN), and the National Association of Displaced Afro-Colombians (Asociación Nacional de Afrocolombianos Desplazados, or AFRODES). PCN was created within the context of the multicultural turn of the early 1990s. Initially called the Organization of Black Communities (or OCN by its Spanish abbreviation), a coalition of students and intellectuals from the southwestern Pacific Region challenged socioeconomic inequality and sought to further black cultural recognition. Over time, OCN followed the lead of local *campesino* organizations—such as the Asociación Campesina Integral del Atrato (ACIA)—that were fighting for land and livelihoods in rural areas and adopted a two-pronged vision that centered on respect for black cultural difference and territorial autonomy.[30] Today, PCN is an umbrella organization that groups numerous ethno-territorial organizations of various scales nationwide. PCN has been at the center of many academic investigations (Escobar 2008; Asher 2009; Oslender 2008; Agudelo 2005) that analyze the work of the organization at the national level. Although I have collaborated with PCN's national coordination team for many years, my fieldwork focused primarily on one of the organization's local affiliates, namely the Consejo Comunitario del Bajo Mira y Frontera, Community Council of the Lower Mira River, which I refer to in short as the Bajo Mira. The Bajo Mira is a rural Black Community of approximately two hundred thousand *campesinos* living on the lower portion of the Mira River, which flows into the Pacific Ocean and stretches to the international border with Ecuador.

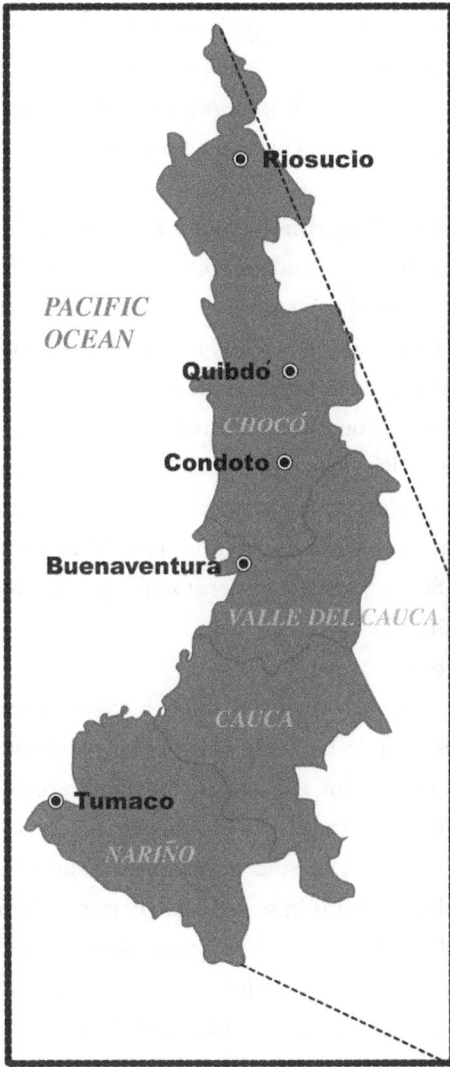

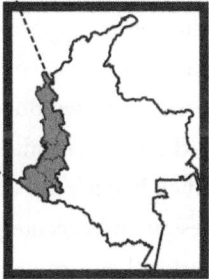

PACIFIC REGION

⦿ Cities/Towns

Community councils are an important site of black politics because they are the autonomous governing units that were designated by Law 70 as the seat for Black Communities. They are therefore the main authority that oversees environmental management of territories as well as the local seat for civil, political, and juridical functions. Also, it is important to note that the establishment of community councils is a precondition for collective land titling under Law 70.

Although the political work of the Bajo Mira follows many of the main tenets of PCN, the council's focus, strategies, and scale of action are significantly different from its parent organization. First, the Bajo Mira is a direct product of the implementation of Law 70. In this sense, it is not a grassroots organization that emerged spontaneously but rather an outgrowth of PCN's intentional organizing work. Second, although some of its members are well-seasoned activists who participate in PCN's national and international activities, most of them are local *campesinos* whose political trajectories began with their participation in the creation of the community council and the land-titling process. The Bajo Mira is a local ethno-territorial organization concerned primarily with improving the life conditions of its constituency and protecting its now-titled territory.

Like PCN, AFRODES is an umbrella organization with 124 affiliates nationwide. However, its affiliates include not only black ethno-territorial organizations (e.g., community councils) but also associations of internally displaced people (IDPs) whose members are primarily (though not exclusively) black. Because the group's focus is on the forced displacement of Afro-Colombians, its field of political action is in some senses narrower than PCNs. In practice, however, AFRODES has become an outspoken political actor on many matters related to Afro-Colombian rights. Although I am familiar with the work of several of its affiliates nationwide, my fieldwork centered on its two Bogotá offices, one of which is now defunct. The first of these is the national office, which I refer to simply as AFRODES.[31] The national office is made up of an elected board and occasionally hires consultants to design and execute projects and draft policy proposals to negotiate with the national government. Its political work consists primarily of lobbying high-level government offices, but the organization dedicates much of its time to grant writing and training delegates in its affiliate organizations on human rights protection.

The second office with which I did fieldwork is ABCUN, which stands for AFRODES Bogotá-Cundinamarca. This was AFRODES's regional office, which was explicitly created to attend to the urgent needs of black IDPs who arrived in the capital. The office closed in 2014 mostly due to interpersonal conflicts among the local leaders. Technically, ABCUN was located not in Bogotá, but in Soacha, the impoverished municipality to the south of Bogotá where thousands of IDPs have relocated. ABCUN was a grassroots organization, like its parent organization was at the outset. Both its affiliates and the members of its board were self-identified black IDPs—sometimes with no prior political experience—who arrived in Bogotá from every corner of Colombia. ABCUN's work was focused on soliciting and disbursing emergency humanitarian aid, which required routinely negotiating with city-level government offices dealing specifically with forced displacement. However, it also acquired a reputation as a cultural organization that worked to preserve, transmit, and represent Afro-Colombian traditions for younger generations and for non-black *bogotanos* unfamiliar with the Colombian Pacific's cultural wealth. To this end, ABCUN sponsored a dance troupe, a traditional music school, and a women's handcrafts collective, and its members were regularly invited to participate in events to showcase "Afro-Colombian culture."[32]

Together, these four organizations—PCN, Bajo Mira, AFRODES, and ABCUN—make up a small patch of the complex and variegated landscape of black organized politics in Colombia. Since the multicultural turn, black organizations of all scales and political affiliations have sprouted in every corner of Colombia, making it impossible to generalize about black organizations or even identify a coherent black movement. I focus on AFRODES, PCN, and their respective affiliates—ABCUN and Bajo Mira—for three basic reasons. First, along with other national-level organizations—such as Movimiento Cimarrón and the National Conference of Afro-Colombian Organizations (CNOA)—AFRODES and PCN are two of the most visible, reputable, and politically active black organizations in Colombia today. In addition, PCN and AFRODES sustain an active international lobbying campaign, making them an ideal site to trace the making of African diasporic alliances.[33] Finally, because of their work's respective emphasis on territory and forced displacement, PCN and AFRODES—and in particular their local affiliates—are excellent sites to observe grounded practices of placemaking as well as the changing role of ethnicity and anti-racism in emergent articulations of blackness.

Subject Formation

The political disputes that play out in the space of organized politics have tangible effects on discourses of blackness, which in turn have an impact on the daily experiences and practices of subjects who identify as black. This space of subjectivities constitutes the second focus of my analysis. Before Colombia's multicultural turn, which was the product of a protracted dispute over the meanings of cultural difference and the designation of cultural others, people seldom imagined blackness as a *cultural* diacritic, or marker of difference. Today, the ethnic definition of blackness is ubiquitous and has become common sense. As a result, people who identify as black now regularly imagine and produce themselves as culturally different from the Euro-Andean dominant cultural matrix. But this relationship also operates in the inverse direction, when individuals or groups extrapolate from the daily experiences that they undergo in a disarticulated fashion and turn them into the substance of broader political struggles. The relationship between these two registers of analysis—subject formation and political projects—travels in both directions.

Because my research field is made up of organizations and their members, it could be said that this is an ethnography of activists or of a social movement. However, I do not think that these categories adequately describe my approach. Saying that this is an ethnography of activists is too narrow, whereas claiming that it is an ethnography of a social movement is an overstatement. What I do is provide an analysis of specific mobilizations, trying not to divorce activists from their various forms of activism and looking at both activists' personal trajectories and the ways that these trajectories congeal in particular political projects. Stylistically, as well as analytically, this implies tacking back and forth between critical analyses of activists' biographies and their organizations' work as a way of highlighting the two-directional impact of the two registers.

This approach helps explain why certain discourses of blackness circulate more than others, how they do or do not resonate with people's daily experiences, and how these experiences in turn shape organized politics. I see this as an attempt to move beyond simply taking what organizations do and say they do at face value, which has been a recurrent problem in analyses of social movements (see Wolford, 2010). It is also a way of fleshing out the category "activist" by underscoring the uneven participation, hierarchical positions, and varied experiences of differently positioned actors that are shaped by race, class, region, gender, and sexuality. For example, a majority of the activists whose lives and work I describe in detail are women. In addition to recognizing black women's leadership, I reflect on the gendered inequalities that these women navigate both inside their organizations and in the social and political circles that they travel in more broadly.

This method has limitations that must be made explicit. First, this is not an ethnography of a community, a coherent social movement, or even a particular organization. It does not outline a neat collectivity of sorts, nor does it trace the quotidian experiences of people in a delimited space, literal or figurative. The uneven experiences and patchy activisms that I trace are too dispersed to be attributable to a collectivity. Second, because I mostly collected and analyzed the experiences of people who participated to varying degrees in this patchy social movement, this book does not adequately reflect the realities of "ordinary" people, those not affiliated with political organizations. However, my back-and-forth approach between ethnography and biography, and between organizations and their people, seeks to question this very divide between activists and "ordinary" people.

Black Organizations

When I began fieldwork, in the early 2000s, doing research of and with black organizations in Colombia made sense for several reasons. As I explained earlier, the first visible articulation of blackness as a politicized subjectivity in Colombia emerged in the context of the multicultural turn of the early 1990s (Paschel 2016). In a way, the multicultural turn was an unprecedented opening for Afro-Colombians to enter state-controlled spaces where public policy issues surrounding ethnicity and territory were negotiated. At this time, the government created numerous mechanisms for the formal participation of Afro-Colombians, so long as they followed the rules of the multicultural game, which required their official recognition and registration within a newly created office inside the Ministry of Interior. As a result, the number of Afro-Colombian organizations and legally recognized Black Communities mushroomed in the late 1990s. Thus, formally recognized organizations became a very important site around which much of the political effervescence around blackness in Colombia concentrated.

At the same time, that effervescence was accompanied by domestication. The concentration of political activity within formally recognized Afro-Colombian organizations significantly reduced the dynamism of civil society groups that had been doing more autonomous political work, albeit in a more disperse manner.[34] In many cases, the same people who had been formally working as members of theater collectives, labor unions, or peasant organizations joined or created these new Afro-Colombian organizations, either reconfiguring their existing organizations or leaving them by the wayside entirely. Furthermore, as I have noted elsewhere, the invitation to participate in state-controlled spaces often entailed the risk of co-optation (Cárdenas 2012b). Because the organizations that I follow in this book emerged in the context of this political opening, they have had to navigate the tricky field of state-controlled multicultural politics. In some cases, the people and causes that they pursue have maintained an autonomous vision of black politics, while in others they have aligned themselves with what has become the multicultural status quo. Rather than cast an a priori judgment on these decisions, I hope that the ethnographic description I provide renders enough detail for the reader to assess the political choices made by individuals and organizations.

ON POSITIONALITY AND ACTIVIST SCHOLARSHIP

My research practice is heir to a genealogy of scholarship that does not purport to simply interpret the world but rather seeks to contribute to social justice and liberation. This is a choice that actively affects the kinds of questions that researchers ask. Because the motivation for undertaking this kind of research is not an abstract pursuit of knowledge, but rather is driven by the urgent questions emergent in social reality, I use theory, as Stuart Hall (1997, 42) beautifully said, as "a detour on the way to something more important." In other words, for activist scholars the purpose of a deep engagement with social theory and the academic debates of the day is ultimately political. This is a stronger claim than the now widely (though not universally) accepted tenet in the social sciences that all knowledge is politically situated (Haraway 1988). Rather than a mere recognition of the impossibility of producing objective knowledge, this practice candidly and unapologetically discloses the researcher's political positions and then proceeds to design a methodology that is aligned with the real-world motivations that drive the research. I follow scholars who have brilliantly shown that engaged scholarship actually produces richer, more complex knowledge that stands the test of rigor precisely because of its deep engagement with social reality (Craven and Davis 2013; Goldstein 2014). As Hale (2008, 12) states in defense of activist research's rigor: "Given the collaborative character of activist research projects, getting it wrong means not only unfavorable reviews from academic peers or a delay in one's promotion schedule, but much more seriously, data and analysis that could harm or mislead our allies." In all, in addition to being transparent about their political motivations, activist social scientists have made a strong case for the epistemological value of engaged research (see Harding 2005; Hill Collins 2000; Nembhard 2008).

This type of research is not without its difficulties and contradictions. In fact, some of the very foundations that give activist research its strengths are also the source of tensions. For example, although the commitment to remain accountable to the researched communities can function as a litmus test for scholarly rigor, activist researchers must also navigate the sometimes competing, if not altogether antagonistic, priorities and timelines of academic production and political action. Perhaps thornier still is the matter of being in a position of relative privilege as a researcher while trying to contribute to the dismantling of structures of inequality with research itself. This contradiction has long been remarked on most lucidly by scholars who have been marginalized from hegemonic academic spaces and who have been dismissed precisely for allegedly lacking the rigor obtained by "objectivity." In the case of the United States, black and Third World feminists have consistently laid bare the ways in which the customary practices of knowledge production reproduce structures of racial, gendered, sexual, and economic inequality (Harrison 2011; Combahee River Collective 1977). How, then, do we pursue a decolonizing agenda from within the colonial space of academic production?

This question becomes all the more salient when we consider the other dimensions of inequality that emerge in research encounters—differences across race, class, gender, sexuality, and nationality, to name a few. In wrestling with this question, black and Third World feminists have also led the way. Their call is to not only ask, "Research for whom?" but also to ask, "Research by whom"? Together, these questions entail a critical analysis of the relationships we engage in as researchers. They urge us to ask all the difficult questions and to remain in struggle—not only as political allies with the communities with whom we carry out research but also in struggle with our own (un) earned privileges as researchers. I recall here the nuanced and powerful work of Keisha-Khan Perry in her book *Black Women against the Land Grab*, where she reflects on the multiple dimensions of her commonalities and differences with the women with whom she carried out research in Salvador, Bahia. As a black woman and an anthropologist with an institutional affiliation to a US academic institution, Perry recognizes the geopolitical differences between herself and her interlocutors but also identifies African diasporic solidarity as the steadfast foundation of her political motivations. As a white Mexican researching Afro-Colombian political mobilizations, a thorough reckoning with my positionality is in order.

At Home and in Struggle

Colombia is a place I call home. Although I was born and raised in Guadalajara, Mexico, I have deep roots that have tied me personally and professionally to Colombia since the mid-1990s. My interest in and commitment to anti-racism is a result of this trajectory. By the early 2000s, I had been visiting family in Colombia for some years and was pursuing a master's degree in Latin American studies in the United States.[35] The experience of dislocation accompanied by my professors' instruction in critical race theory and Latin American history prompted a deep reflection on my positionality as a Latina in the United States and as a white Mexican at home. As I learned to navigate racial politics in the United States, I became much more aware of the virulent racism that permeated the spaces I had grown up in and continued to visit each year, whether for personal or professional reasons. In a sense, discovering myself as an Other in the United States triggered an awareness of my racial privilege at home—while simultaneously my sense of home had extended beyond Mexico to include Colombia and Latin America more broadly. This experience of seeing in a new light what I had been previously impervious to animated in me a political conviction to make visible and denounce racism in those places with which I was most familiar. As a white Mexican whose past and future are intimately tied to various parts of Latin America, I pursue this work as deeply personal and therefore fiercely political. Living in struggle against racism is for me the only ethical way of living in a white body.[36]

I don't recall the exact date of my first encounter with forced displacement in Colombia. It must have been during a family visit in 1999, when I saw dozens of makeshift tents in a busy downtown area and heard *bogotanos* comment about the growing numbers of *desplazados* and the government's incompetence in managing the emergency.[37] I do recall that it was in 2002 when I learned of the work of Geiler Romaña, who was then the standing president of AFRODES.[38] At the time, I was developing a research project on the intersection of anti-racist and labor organizing among domestic workers in Bahia, Brazil, and I was immersed in Marxist texts and critical analyses of race in Latin America. While I continued with the project in Brazil, I felt a growing need to bring my work as an anthropologist closer to home and decided to shift my field site to Colombia, where I had begun laying down new roots. That is, I began to turn my fieldwork into homework.

I moved to Colombia in 2004 and began volunteering regularly at AFRODES and occasionally with PCN. Over the course of the following year, I developed a long-term research project in collaboration with the two organizations' leadership. At the time, the *compañeros* at PCN were very concerned with the status of Black Communities that had been forcefully confined by the escalating armed violence.[39] Although there seemed to be increased recognition of forced displacement, few people were talking about confinement as an attendant form of deterritorialization. When I spoke to them about codesigning a research project that served their political agenda, they suggested that I visit the Lower Mira River to begin documenting the impact of the war on that Black Community. The folks at AFRODES, however, were busy facilitating emergency aid for their constituents in Bogotá, which consisted of recent arrivals of black families from all over the Pacific Region. Given that I was based in the city, I immediately took to working in the areas where the organization's constituents were clustered, attending meetings, doing population surveys, maintaining their website, and regularly visiting with families of IDPs. That was my initial political engagement with both organizations, which has grown and morphed over the years.

When I returned to the United States to pursue a doctorate in cultural anthropology, I did so with a clear purpose to expose antiblack racism at home and a commitment to research methods that unapologetically embraced a political objective. I had been trained in activist anthropology at the University of Texas at Austin and was prepared to defend my political choices to my critics. I was encouraged by the knowledge that the model of the impartial researcher had been rendered obsolete within anthropology and that the discipline's "crisis of representation" had long upended our false certainties and revealed the colonial foundations of our anthropological gaze. Thus, as anthropologists, it was only logical to question our epistemological standpoints and to begin constructing new ways of producing knowledge. As an activist-anthropologist-in-training, I worked closely with leaders of PCN and AFRODES to identify research goals and select research sites. I shared the findings of my research with them at several points. In the summer of 2013, a year after completing my dissertation, I held several workshops to share my findings with activists from ABCUN, the Lower Mira River Community Council, and the national boards of AFRODES and PCN. Their responses to what I offered ranged. In some cases, like with the members of the Lower Mira River Community Council, there was a clear resistance to the analyses I presented. In particular, the members of the community council stood strongly by their decision to continue pursuing "sustainable development" initiatives—such as carbon capture through management of their forests— despite my cautions about how these projects dovetailed with greenwashed neoliberal agendas. In other cases, their responses were more unambiguously enthusiastic. In my meetings with national leaders from AFRODES and PCN, for example, participants were receptive and offered incisive contributions and generous corrections to my analyses. They also shared with me an invigorating feeling generated by my research. I recall very clearly when, after one such meeting, Luz Marina Becerra reflected on the profound value of "having your life's work laid out like that in front of you." I believe that those meetings and workshops were an important opportunity to socialize and recalibrate my analyses while honoring the tireless work of these activists. Later, I shared drafts of the chapters that were heavily biographical with the women whose lives I describe in the book. Although I provided Spanish versions of the texts, they never engaged directly with them. I surmise that they didn't have the time to read such lengthy academic texts. However, I take our continuing friendships and political collaborations as an indication of their endorsement of my analyses, and I am grateful for their enduring trust and generosity.

The challenges of pursuing activist research have proved endless. There have been numerous moments in which I have had to navigate difficult waters and many more instances in which I have surely committed blunders I am not even aware of. This was the case, for example, whenever I had to account for the gaps or irregularities in the "official" stories people told me—when interviewing them, for example—and the details I knew to be true because of my personal relationship to them. In reconstructing people's stories of victimization in particular, I was committed to remaining loyal to what people recounted while also aware of the constructed nature of all narratives. As a witness of this process of storytelling, I wrestled with the complexities of listening to and relaying widely divergent stories and the process through which their narrators produce themselves as victims, sometimes unwittingly and sometimes deliberately. I kept asking myself, How do I stress the constructedness of their narratives without casting doubt on the reality of their suffering? How do I push back against the easy reification of categories such as "victim" and "perpetrator" while remaining vigilant about the political stakes involved in doing so? The answers were never straightforward and often involved treading ground only to go back to reevaluate my choices. My compass in making these choices were the people whose lives I write about;

I regularly returned to share my thoughts and ask for feedback, and I have continued forging close relationships with many of them. This is the political field in which I carried out the research for this book: at the interstices of the passionately personal and the rigorously critical, where it becomes transparently evident that the knowledge that we produce as scholars deeply matters.

OUTLINE OF THIS BOOK

Overall, this book identifies three struggles for Black Citizenship: Black Territories, differential reparations, and black peace. I trace how these struggles have changed and sometimes overlapped over time and document how they are mobilized by diverse sets of political actors for different purposes. I show that these struggles are always intense sites of contention not only between black activists and the state but also in the cultural terrain of discourse and subjectivities. While the book covers ample ground—from Tumaco to Bogotá and from the 1980s to the present moment—my analysis always returns to Black Citizenship as a pragmatic strategy used by organized Afro-Colombians to undo contemporary inequalities and historical structures of violence.

I begin with an analysis of the movement for the defense of Black Territories, whose beginning I locate in the 1980s. This moment was characterized by a nascent discourse of ethnic rights for Afro-Colombians, which was modeled on globally recognized indigenous movements. The mobilization was centrally focused on securing collective land rights to protect rural Black Communities from ever-encroaching forms of extractivism, such as mining, logging, and large-scale agro-industry. During this period, Afro-Colombians demanded that the national government recognize and protect their right to be a separate people. To do so, they asserted their historical cohesiveness as a group different from the Euro-Andean majority while demanding state protection commensurate with that extended to their fellow Colombians. Although they did not explicitly utilize the language of African diasporic belonging, they insisted on black cultural and historical difference and claimed that difference as the very foundation of their demands for special state protection.

Chapter 1 analyzes this process to defend Black Territories in ethnographic detail by looking at the collective land-titling process on the Lower Mira

River, where local *campesinos* felt the pressure of extractive and agricultural industries intensify in the early 1990s. Using interviews with members of the local governing body, residents, and national PCN activists, I reconstruct the making of this Black Community. I show how local *campesinos* on the Mira River took up the language of ethnic difference and made recourse to the watershed 1993 piece of multicultural legislation known as the Blackness Law (Law 70) to safeguard their livelihoods—which consisted mostly of subsistence hunting, fishing, and farming. Throughout the chapter I trace both the diasporic resonances and the demand for national inclusion that undergird the pursuit of black territorial rights. While exposing the incongruities of multicultural rights with black people's territoriality in practice, I also explore how the members of this Black Community use multiculturalism to actualize their historically grounded visions of Black Citizenship.

I then describe how the changing geographies of Colombia's war thrust Black Communities into the cross fire in the late 1990s, forcefully displacing astounding numbers of Afro-Colombians from their newly titled lands. I rely on my interlocutors' life stories to illustrate the harrowing effects of the war on internally displaced people. While my focus is on the intimate aspects of the lives of Afro-Colombian IDPs, I also show more broadly how the spectacular violence of this period fundamentally disrupted the incipient project of Black Territoriality that had just started to bear fruit across the Pacific Region.

Nonetheless, I do not focus on loss. Instead, chapter 2 focuses on the creation of a new political strategy that built on the discourse of ethnic rights to make demands for differential reparations for Afro-Colombian war victims. In the early 2000s, an emergent discourse of victimization became entangled with that of ethnic rights and strengthened by a growing attention to antiblack racism. Although black activists' rising interest in denouncing racism was due in part to their increased participation in African diasporic spaces such as the 2001 World Conference against Racism, in Durban, South Africa, I contend that it was also due to black IDPs' everyday encounters with crude forms of inter-personal racism at their sites of arrival—in white-*mestizo* dominated places like Bogotá, where they became a hypervisible minority. Together, these experiences—of racial solidarity in the diaspora and intensified racism at home—triggered a process of racial becoming. As a result, black activists intentionally added open denunciations of racism to what had previously been a narrower focus on cultural and territorial rights for Afro-Colombians.

Adding further analysis to the struggle for differential war reparations, chapter 3 compares this pursuit to the diasporic movement for historical reparations. I briefly outline the histories of each and then examine their political trajectories in the particular context of Colombia's "postwar." I argue that while timely and powerful, the pursuit of differential war reparations for Afro-Colombians has dangerously tethered blackness to victimization in a nearsighted way. I focus on the limitations of relying on the hypervisibilization of contemporary suffering as the justification for basic rights, thereby exposing the dangers of conflating war reparations with full citizenship. In contrast, I present the powerful logic undergirding diasporic movements for historical reparations for slavery and the slave trade. While explicit demands for historical reparations are still incipient in Colombia, I show that the work that some black activists have been doing for decades to explicitly link war victimization to historical victimization has laid the groundwork for a robust pursuit of reparations. Rather than see struggles for citizenship, which are bound in demands to nation-states, as an impediment to historical reparations, which are decolonial and diasporic in nature, I argue that in Colombia, the two are intertwined and may even dovetail. In fact, for Afro-Colombian activists working at the intersection of multicultural rights and war reparations, the experience of the war has further crystalized the relationship between present and past injustices, providing a robust foundation from which to expand the terms of their demands from the conjunctural to the structural, from the contemporary to the historical, and from the national to the diasporic.

In the final chapter, I analyze Afro-Colombian mobilizations following the most intense moments of armed violence in the Pacific. I look at how Afro-Colombian activists have recrafted strategies that were created in a moment of crisis to respond to spectacular forms of violence—such as forced displacement, massacres, and death threats—to address antiblack violence not as contingent but as quotidian and structural. I focus on the formal transition between times of war and times of peace to evidence the systematic nature of antiblack violence, laying bare the ways in which Colombia's formal peace process flies in the face of the sustained attacks on black lives through poverty, marginalization, and outright physical violence, which have not just continued unabated but have actually intensified over time.

I locate the beginning of this alleged transition to peace in 2011, when disparate government emergency responses established more stable institutions dedicated to the implementation of reparations and restitutions for war victims. For this reason, I take the passage of the Victims' Law (Law 1448) in 2011 as the beginning of a final and ongoing example of the pursuit of Black Citizenship, with which Afro-Colombians strive to ensure their insertion as both fellow Colombians with stakes in rebuilding the postwar nation and as transnational subjects whose histories and interests surpass the nation-state's borders.

Chapter 4 traces several of the political strategies that Afro-Colombian activists have crafted in the midst of the ongoing implementation of the peace accords. I show that some initiatives are designed to occupy the spaces opened up by the state in the context of the negotiations. In doing this, Afro-Colombian activists continue to demand the insertion of various forms of racial and ethnic redress into national (and often color-blind) visions of peace. Such is the case of the Consejo Nacional de Paz (CONPA, or National Council for Peace) and the drafting of an "ethnic chapter" that was included in the final version of the peace accords. At the same time, I outline a more expansive definition of peace, which is understood not simply as an end to armed conflict but as anti-genocide. This vision of peace, which seeks to eliminate all forces of death is grounded in Black Communities' ancestral cultivation of the care for life and is best exemplified by the life and work of Francia Márquez, a fierce grassroots organizer who was recently elected vice president as part of Colombia's first-ever left-wing ticket to win the presidency.[40]

I lean on the work of Afro-pessimists and black optimists alike to analyze the notion of black peace as anti-genocide and to shed light on the fact that the struggle against premature death and precarious life is a constant across the diaspora. Not coincidentally, there are deep resonances between Márquez's insistence on a politics of life and the Black Lives Matter movement's struggles against black death. Together, I see Afro-Colombians' various strategies to forge peace within, outside, and against the state as a multipronged effort to harness the opportunities afforded by the national process of transitional justice for the establishment of more permanent mechanisms for black justice. Like previous iterations of struggles for Black Citizenship, this one entails a simultaneous participation in the remaking of the nation-state and a projection of a diasporic vision of peace that centrally challenges antiblackness as a global phenomenon.

CHAPTER 1

BLACK TERRITORIALITY
Cultivating Ethnic Rights

"THIS TERRITORY IS IN DANGER"

On a late September afternoon in 1994, Aroldo and a small group of other residents of Bocas de Guabal, a small village on the Mira River in Colombia's littoral border with Ecuador, held a meeting to discuss the rapid rate at which their community's mangroves were being destroyed. Mangroves were being exploited for the construction and leather-tanning industries, with dire consequences for locals' livelihoods. For example, when the mangroves were cut, *concheras*, women who made a living collecting shellfish, lost their only source of income. But in addition to being an important source of money, mangroves were essential components of locals' well-being. During a conversation that we had in 2009, Aroldo explained the mangroves' importance to me in detail. He described them as "daycare centers" where baby fish remained safe until they were large enough to swim in the river without being eaten by larger fish, and as "little houses" where crabs laid their eggs and made their homes. The disappearance of mangroves was a significant threat to locals' source of sustenance. Also, a few families who lived on the river's mouth had lost their houses when the Pacific Ocean's waves, no longer contained by the mangroves' powerful barrier, beat against the village's residential areas.

35

That afternoon the atmosphere was tense. Because some people benefited considerably from the commercialization of the mangrove wood and bark, they opposed a ban on its exploitation. But the consequences of indiscriminate exploitation were too ominous to be ignored. The purpose of the meeting, therefore, was to reach a consensus in which commercial mangrove exploitation was not entirely prohibited but rather carefully managed. Of course, this was easier said than done. On the one hand, Bocas de Guabal residents were familiar with predatory capitalism. Everyone remembered how the *chanul* (*Sacoglottis procera*), an exotic tree that is a coveted source of export-quality timber, had entirely disappeared following the entrance to the area of foreign timber companies. On the other hand, they were tired of living so precariously. In a region with little to no formal state presence—no health services, education, electrification, sewage services, or drinking water—and no stable sources of employment, the possibility of exploiting mangroves for a small profit was undoubtedly attractive. The situation that they tried to resolve that afternoon was not new. The problem of how to create and sustain livelihoods that are abundant but not voracious, and that can respond to locals' needs and aspirations, was a long-standing preoccupation of *mireños*.[1] This problem was compounded by the fact that *mireños* live in a very promising area for capital reproduction, and they had therefore confronted repeated attempts to place local people, plants and animals in exploitative relations with others and elsewheres. Until that day, however, the inhabitants of Bocas de Guabal had not had a concrete political tool with which to confront this problem.

In the midst of the exchange, the attendants heard the humming of a motorboat approaching. Fernando, a native of Bocas de Guabal, disembarked. He was accompanied by Juan Manuel, a man from Tumaco—the region's urban hub—who aspired to a seat in the city council. Fernando and Juan Manuel had struck a deal that benefited them both. Because Juan Manuel wanted visibility with potential voters, he benefited from being accompanied by Fernando—a native *guabaleño* who was well known as a respectable local committed to their communities' well-being. Although he was not invested in Juan Manuel's political campaign, Fernando accepted riding in his boat to spread the news regarding the recent passage of Law 70—Colombia's landmark "Blackness Law," which in 1993 had granted ethnic and territorial rights to rural, riverine communities along the Pacific Basin. For several years, Fernando had been a militant with one of Colombia's best-known black organizations—Process of Black Communities (PCN)—working for collective land titling and other ethnic rights for Black Communities. For Aroldo—who had become a well-known community leader himself by the time he recounted this story in 2009—this was a memorable meeting during which he first heard the word *territory* to refer to his village, to his farm, to the mangroves, and to the forest where he had hunted and cut wood his entire life. Fernando's message that day, as Aroldo recalled it fifteen years later, was straightforward and captivating:

> "*Muchachos*, this territory is in danger." [Fernando] explained the issue of large companies, how they kept advancing, and he told us that collective titling of all the territory was a strategy to mitigate the impacts of their advance and that then we would have to make some internal rules so that each of us respected the space as it was defined. Well, back then he didn't give us much detail, he simply said, "This is good. We are a part of this process that is stretching all the way from Chocó to Nariño. Further down the road you will get acquainted with the work that we've been doing in order to get President Gaviria to sign this law."

In 2003, ten years after the passage of the law, the people of Bocas de Guabal, along with fifty-three other villages of the Lower Mira River, received a collective title for more than forty-six thousand hectares of land. Although the work of lobbying the government to pass the law had been completed when they first heard the word *territory* in 1994, delimiting and protecting their own territory was not an easy task. First, they had to create a community council, a local government body that had been especially created for Black Communities following Law 70. This involved the difficult work of spreading the word up and down the river, mobilizing with little to no resources, and pressuring the state to finally grant them a collective land title. Despite all these difficulties, every person that I spoke with about the titling process recalled it as a period of remarkable political effervescence and hopeful enthusiasm. When I asked the protagonists why everyone had been so enthusiastic, they all agreed on the reason, but as usual, Aroldo put it most

COLOMBIA

Collective land titles of

Black Communities 2021

eloquently: "[Because] it was a current issue. It was not a made-up thing; it was something that was in fact happening in Buenaventura, in Chocó, in Cauca, and Tumaco was not an exception. We were losing our land through loans, sales, and also through invasion. . . . So people of course felt very touched by the message of the need to get the territory back, or at least protect what was left of it. . . . This is why people were so committed."

Law 70 gained currency among the eleven thousand inhabitants of the Lower Mira River because they saw it as a promising tool with which to protect their territories. It provided them with a language with which to speak and be heard about the felling of the forests, the destruction of the mangroves, and local communities' own complex participation in these processes. The language of the law made sense to them because it was literally grounded in their livelihoods and life experiences. In particular, it resonated with their affective and effective attachment to localized notions of place—their river, their farm, their village, and their region, which spread across the national border into Ecuador. For them, this was the meaning of the term *territory*.

Although a great deal has been written analyzing Law 70 and Colombia's multicultural turn as an unprecedented conjuncture,[2] I want to focus less on its novelty and more on the histories of the *longue durée* that made the recognition of ethnic and territorial rights for Black Communities possible. I argue that although the threat to the mangroves might appear new, and *mireños'* chosen political response innovative, both the threat and the suggested strategy resonated with locals' historical experiences as Afro-descendants on the one hand and as marginalized citizens struggling to insert themselves fully into the Colombian nation on the other. As such, I look at the work to make and defend Black Territories as an example of the fight for Black Citizenship, that is, of the demand for inclusion in the nation and the simultaneous assertion of belonging to an African diasporic community.

The struggle to make and defend Black Territories is both old and new. On the one hand, the processes of racialized dispossession and black creativity that made and sustained local communities of belonging such as the ones along the Mira River have long histories. Over time, *mireños* have built a sense of place and community that is expansive and flexible while resolutely rooted and cohesive (Feld and Basso 1996; Oslender 2008b). This sense of place and belonging carries diasporic resonances that derive from the *longue durée* of their lived experience as Afro-descendants in the Americas (Gilroy 1995; Goett 2016; Hart 2006). For *mireños*—as for other Black Communities along the Pacific Region and the continent more broadly—the arrival of the development machine in the form of commercial logging in the 1990s was but an extension of the model of white, European modernity that seeks to exterminate, incorporate, or marginalize subjects that don't fit its logic. It was a dynamic that they were intimately acquainted with. While the specific threat to the mangroves may have indeed been new, the recurrent attempt to place people, plants, and animals in exploitative relations with one another was as old as *mireños'* ancestors' presence on those lands.

On the other hand, the specific use of the language of ethnic and territorial rights—as a Black Community—that was mobilized by *campesinos* along the Pacific Region and became audible to the Colombian state in the 1990s, was indeed novel, and its impact shouldn't be underestimated. But the very traction that it gathered among black *campesinos* along the Colombian Pacific was in fact due to its historical sedimentation. Fernando's suggestion that local *campesinos'* "traditional production practices" could provide the basis from which to launch a strategy against mangrove destruction likely resonated not only with *mireños'* current conundrum but also with the stories that they had heard from their parents and grandparents.

Ultimately, I am driven to ask whether and to what extent ethnic and territorial rights—or the defense of Black Territories—have fulfilled the promise they held for the people of the Mira River. I use ethnographic observation and the intimate stories of *mireños'* lives to explore the extent to which the strategy to make and defend Black Territories has been successful. I take the criteria for success from black activists and members of this Black Community themselves, who insist on the importance of maintaining sufficient political autonomy from the Colombian state to craft livelihoods that prioritize their communities' needs and aspirations while demanding its full protection to guarantee their rights as citizens. I let the ethnographic description do the critical work of evincing when there is reason to celebrate and when there is reason for concern. Of course, this is not an innocent distinction. In the end, the underpinning criteria that guide my descriptions are best captured by Stuart Hall's statement regarding the usefulness of multicultural politics at large. For Hall (2001, 141), the multicultural question is useful only insofar as it is capable of meeting "the double demand for greater equality and social justice *and* for the recognition of difference and cultural diversity. Or, to put the problem more colloquially, the determination of minority populations to have their cake and eat it" (emphasis added).

MAKING BLACK TERRITORIES
Diasporic Resonances

> Ocupación colectiva: Es el asentamiento histórico y ancestral de comunidades negras en tierras para su uso colectivo, que constituyen su hábitat, y sobre los cuales desarrollan en la actualidad sus prácticas tradicionales de producción. [Collective occupation: The historical and ancestral settlement of Black Communities on lands for collective use, which constitute their habitat and on which they carry out their traditional production practices in the present moment.]
> —*Law 70 (1993)*

In its rigid understanding of ancestrality as settledness, the concept in Law 70 of collective occupation differs significantly from *mireños'* own sense of place and logic of ancestrality, which privilege mobility and flexibility. And yet the very idea that they belonged to a Black Community that was anchored in place and shared a common history and livelihood practices made sense to *mireños*—and to other black *campesinos* like them who lived in riverine communities along the Pacific Region of Colombia. Law 70 and its multicultural logic gained currency among the inhabitants of the Mira River because it contained African diasporic resonances to which they were attuned. The law provided new language to address the old and ongoing problem of racialized dispossession and was articulated with locals' sedimented practices of making place and community. In its ability to evoke collective memories of continuous exploitation and incite deep emotions of black solidarity, Law 70 carried diasporic resonances that locals were particularly sensitive to, which partly explains its allure to *mireños* and its success as a regional and national organizing strategy.

Even if they did not make explicit connections to Africa, slavery, or the Middle Passage, the very modality by which *mireños* have created their sense of place and belonging is diasporic. It is diasporic because it is always-already entangled with histories of racialized dispossession, because it is itinerant and dislocated, because it expands across national boundaries, and because it creates networks of symbolic and biological kinship that are spread far and wide. *Mireños'* understandings of kinship, place, and ancestry reveal a deep diasporic logic that posits an unequivocal sense of belonging that is more predicated on routes than roots. And although this conflicts with the Colombian government's rigid notions of belonging that are reliant on an isomorphic relation between places, people, and "their cultures" (Gupta and Ferguson 2008), it resonates with *mireños'* contemporary experiences and deep histories.

These diasporic resonances are not memories of paradise lost, nor are *mireños'* deep recollections of solidarity romantic tales of resistance. On the Mira River there was never an innocent past when Maroon communities built autonomous lives harmoniously or when "free peasants" cultivated life-styles outside of exploitative relations with others and elsewheres. Rather, the life histories of *mireños'* ancestors were always entangled with slave gangs, foreign markets, and extractive economies (Jaramillo Buenaventura 2018; Taussig 1987). Thus, I write against the flattened idea that *mireños* have always stood outside of or against these projects of exploitation. Rather, the diasporic resonance that I refer to is a sometimes subtle but always embodied awareness of *mireños'* complex insertion into enduring structures of oppression—not always critically outside it or heroically against it. This resonance is an important part of the groundwork that allowed for Law 70 and its multicultural logic to take root on the Mira River.

Cultivating Ancestral Rootedness

The ancestors of the current inhabitants of the major rivers around the city of Tumaco migrated from the nearby mining areas of Barbacoas and Iscuandé at the end of the nineteenth century.[3] After emancipation in 1851, gold mining, which was the economic mainstay of the area, went into sharp decline as a result of the increase in the price of labor and a substantial depletion of the mineral. At the beginning of the twentieth century following a bloody war— La Guerra de los Mil Días—that caused people to flee from the neighboring Cauca region, these migrations of both free and enslaved former mine workers intensified, prompting further movement from the foothills of the mountains in southwestern Colombia to the coastal areas of the Pacific Region. Thus, by the 1920s, Tumaco was the major urban center in the southwestern coastal region, and in recognition of its importance as such, the national government began the construction of the railroad that would eventually connect this port town to the departmental capital of Pasto (Agier et al. 1999; Leal 2004)

However, the majority of the region's population settled dispersedly along the coast and its rivers, looking for places to survive in small groups. One of the preferred riverbanks for these early migrants was that of the Mira River, which provided fertile lands for subsistence agriculture; a mangrove forest abundant in game, shellfish, and lumber; and easy access to both marine and freshwater fishing. In strict geographical terms, the Mira River is quite close to the port of Tumaco, a mere nine miles from the most proximate edge. But the social distance between this rural, riverine area and the urban center in Tumaco is uneven and varies depending on the subject, timing, and purpose of the travel.

To get from the city of Tumaco to the villages that line the banks of the Mira River, there are several options. The first is to take a motorboat from the southernmost tip of the bay into the open sea and toward the Ecuadorian border, to the mouth of the river at Congal. The second option is to take a bus or a taxi from downtown Tumaco down the main highway to the unpaved road that connects it to the right bank of the lower river; then one must wait at the edge of the highway for a car or a motorcycle willing to drive the short but dusty stretch to La Boca Toma. The third option is fully paved. It involves driving down the main highway further inland and then turning right onto a side road that ends at Peña Colorada, a village on the middle portion of the river. This last bit of the road, which is significantly better than the one to La Boca Toma, is maintained not by the departmental or national government but by the oil-palm plantations that line the left bank of the river and need a reliable way to get their product out for sale. Elsewhere, I write about these plantations and their impact on Black Territoriality at length (Cárdenas 2012c).

Since my first visit to the Mira River in 2007, I have taken all three routes. But even though the river stretches for more than twenty-five miles past Peña Colorada and then into Ecuadorian territory for over sixty miles more, I have always stayed on the lower portion of the river. The reason for this is straightforward. Peña Colorada is the last village included in the collective land title that was granted to the Community Council of the Lower Mira River—which I refer to as *Bajo Mira* for short—in 2003. And this particular community council is affiliated with the PCN, one of the most important national-level black ethno-territorial organizations in Colombia, with which I have collaborated since that same year. When I refer to the Bajo Mira, I am only referring to a portion of the Mira River's total course—from Peña Colorada to the mouth of the river at Congal. This portion is intelligible today as an ethno-territorial unit—a Black Community—as a result of a set of historical and geographical factors that range from the material practices of local *campesinos* to the global market's demands for local goods; from national disputes over land tenure to the negotiations surrounding the demarcation of the Colombia-Ecuador border. I cannot do justice to these histories here, but I do want to pause long enough to acknowledge them (Hoffman 2002). And therefore to draw attention to the fact that the Bajo Mira, as a collective territory of Black Communities, is a human-natural assemblage whose conditions of possibility emerged only in the past thirty or so years.

Aroldo, one of the oldest and most active members of the Bajo Mira's community council, was born in a village on the banks of a nearby river also in the department of Nariño. Because he was born with a rare disease that disabled his speech, his parents relentlessly sought a cure for him until they found a miraculous spring on the Ecuadorian side of the border. Aroldo and his siblings therefore grew up in the Ecuadorian province of Esmeraldas, where his father labored as a day worker in large farms and his mother tended to their numerous children. As a young man he "got a woman" and started working as a logger to sustain his new household, which included his common-law wife and her two young children.[4] After a couple of years, he and his wife separated, but he continued working for the same logging company, which eventually sent him back to the Colombian side of the *guandal* forest.[5]

The company, which was based in a small town along the Tumaco-Pasto highway, sent its temporary workers out far and wide to search for commercial lumber. This is how Aroldo became familiar with the timbered wealth of the lowland forested region and eventually arrived to the Mira River. During one of his logging trips there he met a young woman whom he liked, and he returned to woo her until she eventually agreed to become his wife. Because Cindy, his second wife, had been born on the Mira River, she inherited a good-sized farm that the two of them began to work together. Aroldo continued his intermittent work cutting timber and with the cash from his wages and the crops from their land they raised their eight children.

Although technically a native *guabaleña*, Cindy had no living kin in the village of Bocas de Guabal. When she was a young girl her parents sent all of her siblings to Ecuador, where one of her uncles lived, so they could go to school. Although she very much wanted to go, her mother didn't let her because she was a sickly child who suffered from chronic stomach pains. So Cindy stayed behind and lived with her mother and father in Bocas de Guabal until she married Aroldo in the 1980s. Although she regularly visits one of her sisters who now lives in Tumaco, none of her siblings ever moved back to their birth village. Today, Cindy's status as a native *guabaleña* is actually reinforced by her marriage to Aroldo, who is known and respected along the river's villages as a hardworking *campesino* (peasant), a fellow *vecino* (neighbor), and a committed *compañero* (partner in struggle) who works on behalf of the rights of the Bajo Mira's communities.

Milena Hurtado is another *guabaleña* who is known far and wide for her steadfast commitment to the community council's political work. Like Aroldo, she arrived at the Mira River as an adult and became a *guabaleña* as a result of her marriage to a local man. Although she was born in the city of Tumaco, she spent many years in Cuenca, a city in Ecuador's southern highlands. When Milena was ten years old, her mother gave her away to a nun who agreed to look after her. Although the nun was sent to Italy soon after, she left Milena with her sister, Estela, who Milena still refers to as her *mamita*. When Milena narrated her childhood and early teenage memories to me, I was particularly struck by the matter-of-factness with which she recounted repeated experiences of sexual and gendered violence. For the most part, she recalled this period of her life fondly and offhandedly mentioned that, after her *mamita* Estela's son tried to rape her, she embarked on a long journey that eventually took her back to Tumaco. Then she continued her story. After leaving her *mamita* Estela's house, she washed dishes in a small hotel in Cuenca. Then, she was a domestic worker in Cali. After that, she made her way back to Tumaco, where she reunited with her birth mother and siblings. But the family reunification went sour when her sister's husband raped her and her mother blamed her for it. Because she was no longer welcome in her sister's house, Milena rented a small room from an elderly acquaintance in town. It was then that she met Edilson, a quiet *campesino*, who convinced her to move with him to the Bajo Mira, where his mother had a farm that they could work together.

Milena's nonchalance in her recollection of gendered and sexual forms of violence suggests the extent to which they are normalized, not only in her own memory but more generally in the social settings she described. I return to reflect on this gendered dynamic later in the chapter, but here, I wish to note that, as Milena's story attests, experiences of mobility, rootedness, and belonging are also deeply marked by gendered differences between men and women.

The matter of ancestral occupation on the Bajo Mira is a complex one. In some cases, such as those of Aroldo and Milena, a person's legitimacy as a native is conferred after he or she proves a commitment to the community through marriage, residence, or work. Genealogy and birthplace can certainly play an important role as well, but they are neither sufficient nor determinant. As the stories above reveal, one can be born in one place and claim native status in another. And one's affiliation to a locality can also change throughout the course of one's life. The case of Don Abel is quite telling in this respect. In 2010, after learning that all the official documentation on the Bajo Mira's collective land-titling process had been lost, I collected the life stories of nine of the community council's founders in an effort to reconstruct this recent history. I interviewed Don Abel, a sixty-seven-year-old man who was living in one of Tumaco's poorest neighborhoods and began by asking him when and where he had been born. When he responded that he was born on the Río Mejicano, another nearby river that I knew had its own community council and collective land title, I responded, "Oh, so you are not from the Mira River." My statement didn't make much sense to Don Abel, who corrected me quite matter-of-factly: "No. I *am* from the Mira River. Because I am here; because this is where I went through the *proceso*; and this is where I still am part of the process, on the Bajo Mira."

By *proceso*, Don Abel was referring to the organizing work that resulted in the conferral of forty-six thousand hectares of land to be collectively held by the members of the Bajo Mira's community council.[6] He was also indirectly referring to Law 70, the 1993 piece of legislation that granted Black Communities on Colombia's Pacific River Basin collective cultural and territorial rights. But most concretely, he was recalling a period of remarkable political effervescence along the Mira River, which resulted in the creation of the Bajo Mira's community council in 1998 and in the issuance of its collective land title in 2003. Certainly, the two processes—the national lobbying that resulted in the passage of the law and the local organizing effort that put it into practice—are closely related, but they are not identical. When he mentioned *el proceso*, Don Abel was signaling the concrete practices that designated some people (and not others) as members of the Bajo Mira's community council and delineated the borders of its associated collective territory.

The process involved the designation of "natives" whose legitimacy, according to the law, depended not only on their indigeneity and ancestrality— that is, on proof of their historical occupation of the area—but also on their blackness. In fact, according to the law, the two markers of belonging are inextricable from each other. To be recognized as black, one has to belong to a rural, riverine, community.[7] And conversely, to aspire to a collective land title, the rural riverine dwellers of the Pacific Basin must prove that they possess particular cultural characteristics that identify them as a distinct ethnic group. Only then can they be recognized as members of a Black Community with rights to collective property. In practice, these turn out to be thorny issues. As will become evident, it is difficult to designate natives in a place where people's histories of occupations reveal high levels of mobility. Similarly, it is difficult to identify a definitive criterion—birthplace, residence, or self-identification—to distinguish a person as "from" the Bajo Mira.

The matter of belonging to (or being excluded from) a given community entails significant stakes. In the case of Don Abel and the Black Community of the Bajo Mira, the most obvious stakes involved his continued access to the lands that were eventually titled to the community council. Following this logic, one could interpret his resolute identification as a *mireño* as strategic, intended to legitimate his seemingly questionable status as a native. But in fact, the opposite is true. It is not that Don Abel was desperately trying to validate an unusual situation; rather, it simply did not occur to him (or to others) that being born on another river constituted an impediment to being considered a native. This is because, rather than being an anomaly, physical mobility and sustained relationships with others elsewhere are the norm on the Mira River. Fluidity, itinerancy, and expansiveness characterize the trajectories of people, places, and relationships. In fact, as Jaramillo Buenaventura, who worked among Black Communities in the Northern Cauca region notes in his ethnographic work, mobility is the norm, and constitutes a way to create bonds between and within places (Jaramillo Buenaventura 2018).

This is also apparent when we look ethnographically at another key axis of belonging: kinship. Like notions of ancestrality, kinship bonds, though strong, are neither rigid nor determinant. In her ethnographic account of the region, for example, Hoffman (2007) shows that being related to the founding families of a given village can confer an individual significant status, but it does not unambiguously translate into political or economic power. Moreover, kinship can be determined by consanguinity or by symbolic affiliations. An individual can become so thoroughly assimilated into a family through marriage as to take on that family's last name, and can subsequently be entirely disengaged from them, take on a different name, and move to another river. Unlike in other parts of Colombia where "notable" last names are fiercely policed and genealogies rigorously kept (at least in theory), on the southern Pacific last names are loosely interpreted as approximate indications of kinship. Thus, people who share the same last name often treat each other "as if" they were blood relatives, with no need to verify the consanguineous basis of their relationship.

This expansive and flexible use of kinship is also reflected by the common practice of calling peers *primo* or *prima* (cousin) and elders *tío* or *tía* (uncle

or aunt) irrespective of consanguinity. In fact, the two sets of terms are analogous and their only difference is generational. *Primo* or *prima* and *tío* or
tía therefore signal a recognition of sameness, which varies according to the
situation. Thus, two *campesinas* from the Bajo Mira who run into each other
in downtown Tumaco might use it to address one another. Or two fellow
tumaqueñas who sell goods in neighboring stalls in a market in Cali might do
the same every morning. Or finally, a black urban youth from the nearby port
city of Buenaventura might call a quiet *tumaqueño* at a bar in Bogotá *primo*
upon meeting him. In each of these cases the assumed sameness is different,
ranging from scales of geographic proximity, "we are from the same river" or
"we are both from the Pacific Coast," to an unspoken acknowledgment of
racial sameness, or "we are black." Or, they might substitute the term *primo*
or *prima* with *paisano* or *paisana*, another sign of affiliation that can be loosely
translated as "countryman" or "countrywoman" and refers to a shared geographic space, but it can also be used to signal racial sameness.

In all these cases, the explicit use of a relationship marker invokes a community of belonging. It also implicitly parcels out insiders from outsiders—
people who are not from a given river; people who are not from the Pacific
Region; or more broadly, people who are not black. None of this is surprising.
But what I find remarkable is the fact that the same term can be used with
so much versatility and stability at the same time. In all these cases there is
indeed a community that is being signaled. But in each case the relationships
that define that community are different, making it unclear whether they
indicate the existence of various, discrete communities or of a single one with
porous and unstable boundaries. What remains constant, however, is their
use as a racial marker of sameness.

Places, too, are simultaneously fixed and variable. The importance of the
finca, or farm, is perhaps the most illustrative example of this. On the one
hand, settledness in a particular place—such as a given river—is signaled by
the act of clearing an area of the forest to turn it into a *finca*. Thus, before
one can work a farm, one must "make" it—literally convert it into an agricultural space. The difference between the wilderness and an agricultural area is
understood as a matter of degrees, and it fluctuates highly. People designate
different levels of wildness that range from *monte bravo* (wild forest) to *monte*

alzado (worked forest) and *monte biche* (half-grown forest). Agricultural areas are also heterogeneous and highly mobile. In addition to the *finca*, whose location in space can shift over time, people keep *zoteas*, which are herb gardens that are maintained next to the household in old canoes, and *colinos*, which are single-crop parcels usually designated for plantains. Furthermore, farmers continually build mobility into each of these agricultural patches by actively soliciting seeds and cuttings from a wide network of kin and friends. Thus, the farm itself is both the epitome of settledness and an exemplification of mobility, which again suggests that when the time came to build "territory," mobility was already built into it (Cohen 2010).

When recalling his arrival to the Mira River, for example, Don Abel described the moment in which he "made his farm" as the biographical marker of masculine adulthood and stability. After his childhood on the Río Mejicano and early teenage years on the Río Chagüí, he spent his youth cutting lumber in Ecuador. Don Abel recalled those years as a carefree period in which he liked to chase adventure and did not hesitate to get on a boat, join a group of fellow travelers, or follow a new boss to unknown destinations. Like Aroldo, the timber routes eventually took Don Abel back across the border to Colombia, and in his early twenties he started working for a timber contractor who lived in San Lorenzo (Ecuador) but had business in Nariño: "I worked with him for a while and then I worked with another man, who took me to Sagumbita (on the Mira River), and that was when I stayed and made my farm. . . . That was the beginning of my stability. That was when we started working to make [build] the village [*hacer el pueblo*]. Before that, there was no school; there was nothing there. There was just the forest and a few houses, and people survived with just their plantains. They would exchange the plantain for fish and that's how they lived. There was nothing there."

Although the farm (*finca*) and the village (*pueblo*) are important markers of stability, neither is fixed in time or space. It is undoubtedly important to have a *finca*, to turn a portion of the forest into an agricultural patch of land and designate it as one's own. Furthermore, the moment and geographical place in which one decides to do so is of consequence because it produces one as a local, as a resident and fellow *campesino* or *campesina* of a concrete place such as the Bajo Mira. But the physical location of the *finca* and the village can change. Any given *campesino* or *campesina* can work a *finca* for several years and then clear a new patch of land elsewhere. They can alternate work on both *fincas* or phase one out and let it turn to forest again. Then, they might decide to clear it again.[8] Even the village, the place marker that one might imagine as the paradigmatic example of settledness, is often transient and mobile. Like Don Abel reveals, in a single lifetime one might help create a village and see others disappear, all the while maintaining a firm sense of rootedness in a given place.

Such widespread patterns of mobility are also evident in the life stories of those who were born, raised, and live on the Mira River today and who seemingly fit the settled model of ancestrality written into Law 70. When I interviewed him in 2010, Don Claudio was the oldest living founder of the community council. He and his wife were both born on the Mira River, and two of his sons were active members of the community council's board. Although two of his daughters moved to Cali at a young age (twelve and fourteen, respectively), he still has many children and grandchildren in the Bajo Mira. He is, by all measures, a local and a respected elder. And still, his own trajectories, as well as those of his ancestors, reveal a great deal of itinerancy. When he was a young boy, his mother moved to Ecuador with her second husband and all of Don Claudio's siblings, making him the oldest member of his family to live on the Mira River after his father's death. Like most other men (and some women as well) on the Bajo Mira, he spent a good portion of his youth traveling. This practice, which people refer to as "walking" (*andar*), is in some senses a rite of passage, an important biographical marker that separates childhood from adulthood.[9] Walking refers to living an itinerant life, although in Don Claudio's case, traveling came after "making a farm," it still constituted a central aspect of his adult life. Thus, although life on his *finca* was plentiful and pleasant (*sabrosa*),[10] when he was a young man he took to traveling to Ecuador: "My little business was doing well and so I took to traveling, drinking, and wandering." Again, I wish to note that there is a gendered difference in men's and women's ability to move and in the conditions under which they do so. While many of the men I spoke to recalled their years of walking with great nostalgia, the women's narratives of mobility were often constrained, determined by others, or marked by experiences of gendered and sexual violence.

My ethnographic exploration of the Lower Mira River shows a fluid reality where people, places, and the relationships between them do not follow the dichotomous logic described by categories such as "native" versus "outsider," "resident" versus "traveler," "transient" versus "permanent." And yet every single one of the people whose trajectories I have described was unequivocal about "being from" the Bajo Mira. Rather than referring to an immemorial rootedness, *mireños* claim ancestry and belonging—to both a specific place and a community—through expansive practices of itinerancy. In fact, that mobility is an essential part of building community because it creates connections through social relations such as work and kinship. Working on the *finca*, rowing on the river, wandering through their region, and raising families across villages on both sides of the border provided an array of intimate experiences that made their territory intelligible because it was tangible. Those experiences are the substance of *mireños'* attachment to place and a critical reason the concept of territory was compelling and capable of mobilizing them as a Black Community.

The Promise of National Inclusion

In adapting their local practices to the language of ethnic difference embedded in Law 70, members of Black Communities across the Pacific Region were making a resolute statement about their right to be included within the nation and reconfiguring Colombia's structures of alterity in significant ways. Thus, Afro-Colombians' embrace of multicultural rights is the second prong of their pursuit of Black Citizenship, which insists on black particularity even as it claims equality with fellow Colombians. Ethnic blackness became entrenched as the dominant articulation of blackness in recent history because it simultaneously addressed the political interests of black organizations and of the Colombian state. For the latter, it was an expedient way to regain much of the political credibility that had been lost in the prior decades due to the armed conflict, to rationalize many of the nation's previously uninventoried lands, and to jump on the multicultural bandwagon that was spreading across Latin America to continue presenting Colombia as a modern nation on the world stage (Van Cott 2000b). Additionally, ethnic blackness and the passage of Law 70 were also the result of a complex political alignment that brought together state and international interests. Paschel (2016) refers to this as a multicultural alignment whose conditions of possibility were facilitated by the emergence of an international "ethno-racial field."

For members of Black Communities themselves, the motivation is worth exploring at length. At a most immediate level, ethnic blackness was an efficacious means to halt the speed at which large capital and state development initiatives were encroaching on lands that had been historically inhabited by black Colombians. It was a way to protect territories, like the Bajo Mira, which were in danger. But it was more than that. Ethnic blackness was embraced by *mireños* and other black *campesinos* living along the riverine areas of the Colombian Pacific because it was a way of asserting a right to difference that resonated with their diasporic experiences while resolutely anchoring themselves in place *as Colombians*. In other words, it was a means to pursue Black Citizenship.

The question becomes why and how Afro-Colombians imagine themselves as members of the Colombian nation and continue to demand full inclusion as fellow (if different) citizens. My argument is informed by two bodies of literature. The first of these is the critical literature (Gutmann 1993; Hooker 2005b; Kymlicka 1996; Povinelli 2007) that sees multicultural recognition as the new face of liberal citizenship, which promises equality and full citizenship for all but remains anchored in its foundational exclusions and racial hierarchies. From this perspective, despite its gesture toward embracing racial and ethnic difference—rather than annihilating it—the multicultural nation cannot but reaffirm white supremacy and maintain unequal relations of power. The second literature is on settler colonialism (Jacobson 1999; Saito 2015; Wolfe 2006), which, though not often used to analyze Latin American national formations, allows me to see black and indigenous difference in the same analytical framework and to explore their decolonial possibilities.

The main insight from the first body of literature—that the multicultural nation reaffirms colonial exclusions—becomes clearer when we look at the particularities of Latin American national formations and the place of blackness within them.[11] It is important to recall that, unlike their European counterparts and later postcolonial nations in Asia and Africa, early nationalisms in Latin America were not born of grassroots popular movements. Instead, they were led by creole (*criollo*) elite groups of landowners, who, allied with a somewhat smaller number of merchants and professionals, sought to wrestle power from their peninsular brethren while keeping subaltern political mobilizations at bay (Anderson 1983).[12] As such, the postcolonial vicissitudes of blackness begin at the heart of a creole nation-building project that was caught in a conundrum. On the one hand, creoles sought to keep intact relations of bondage and dependence between themselves and the black and indigenous masses. On the other, given that the enemy of republican independence was the royalist camp of Spaniards and Portuguese, creoles had to cultivate a sense of horizontal camaraderie with their racialized others in order for the imagined community of the nation to become politically viable (Holt 1995). As if this tension were not sufficient, creole nations also had to contend for a respectable (i.e., whitened) position in the world political system. As a result, nationalist visions were as much influenced by the pressures of internal social conflicts as by the lingering specter of European colonialism and the growing menace of American imperialism.

The shifting place of blackness within creole nations—such as Colombia—must therefore grapple with the contradictions inherent in this attempt to maintain the powers of the Euro-descendant elite while building a seemingly "horizontal comradeship" with black and indigenous people. To navigate this tension, nationalist visions have negotiated the place of blackness by making recourse to a set of dichotomies—inclusion and exclusion, sameness and difference, visibility and invisibility. At times, blackness has occupied a definite place on either end of these dichotomies: black people are either included or excluded as fellow nationals, visible or invisible as subaltern subjects. More remarkably, however, nationalist formations have sought out compromises between their elite and popular objectives by producing seemingly contradictory combinations of these dichotomies, for example, by offering cultural inclusion but denying political participation.

The main lesson from the critical analysis of the liberal nation is therefore that the dream of a horizontal comradeship of *colombianos*—the use of masculine gender here is deliberate—cannot coexist with the maintenance of colonial racial hierarchies, which was the driving impulse behind creole nationalism to begin with. Thus, the place of blackness (and other racial categories of otherness) within Latin American nations simply cannot be one of equality. Put differently, the postcolonial creole nation is not a promising repository for dreams of black justice.

If national inclusion holds an empty promise of equality for black subjects, how do we explain Afro-Colombians' resolute pursuit of ethnic rights and national inclusion? The Gramscian framework of hegemony is helpful in evidencing the nuanced dynamic between dominance, resistance, and consent that is unfolding here (Gordon 1998; Hanchard 1998). On the one hand, the concept of racial hegemony allows me to take Afro-Colombians' dreams of national inclusion seriously, not simply as an expression of false consciousness. On the other hand, because its focus is on the terrain of struggle, racial hegemony helps explain the stubborn permanence of white supremacy. But while the notion of hegemony is useful to explain instances in which black subjects act in ways that go counter to their class interests, it does not in itself explain their steadfast attachment to cultural difference and territory. To do so, I turn to the literature on settler colonialism. While seldom used to explain racialized nationalisms in Latin America, the concept of settler colonialism is quite useful to understand black claims to a nativelike status in Colombia.

Perhaps most important, thinking about the Colombian nation as a settler-colonial project allows me to examine the creation of the triad settler, native, slave (and the attendant racial categories of "white," "indigenous," and "black") as part of a single structure while being attentive to their respective roles in decolonization.[13] The main insight I draw on is that settler colonialism "is characterized by a persistent drive to ultimately supersede the conditions of its operation" (Veracini 2011, 3). In Veracini's words, "whereas colonialism *reinforces* the distinction between colony and metropole, settler colonialism *erases* it" (3). Accordingly, the struggle against settler colonialism (decolonization) must aim to keep the distinction ongoing. This means upending the illusion of a well-integrated horizontal community of brethren and instead finding ways to reinscribe the differences between each of the components of the triad of settler, native, slave. In this particular case, decolonizing would amount to undermining the myth of a harmonious multiracial and pluriethnic Colombia by insisting on black and indigenous difference through their sheer survival as *others*. This is not the same as incorporation through recognition, which is the project behind state-led multiculturalism to perpetuate settler control through reconciliation, and the management and neutralization of difference. For the colonized, surviving as black or indigenous has the potential of undermining the most fundamental characteristic of settler colonialism: the assertion that the difference between the settler and its others has been superseded through the magical alchemy of the nation.

While it is important to recognize that the relative positions of blackness and indigeneity within Colombia's structures of alterity are not identical, I do suggest that Afro-Colombians' insistence on ethnic difference is a manifestation of a decolonial impulse. For members of Black Communities, the struggle to *be* different (read, *ethnicity*) and to secure a place (read, *territory*) in which to exercise that difference (read, *autonomy*) has decolonizing potential and should not simply be read as a reaffirmation of the empty promise of equality under the creole national project (of settler colonialism).[14] Because it is asserted within the context of the settler nation, the embrace of black ethnic difference is indeed contradictory, and as I show in the rest of this chapter, its results are not unambiguous. However, Afro-Colombians' claim to national inclusion as ethnic others is not only a multicultural accommodation; it is also a challenge to the settler-colonial project's primary objective, which is to subsume the difference between settler and its others under the illusion of commensurability.

DEFENDING BLACK TERRITORIES

In the rest of this chapter I show the concrete realities of Black Territoriality ethnographically. Rather than provide a broad and comprehensive analysis of Black Territoriality in the abstract, I sketch a detailed description of *mireños'* grounded experiences as they carry on with their lives and defend their territory. My intent is to examine what ethnic and territorial rights have come to mean for the people of the Bajo Mira in practice, and I do so using their own terms. I explore the complex and contradictory ways in which the law and its multicultural logic are appropriated and accommodated—sometimes smoothly and other times awkwardly, sometimes advantageously, and other times ineffectively—into local histories, landscapes, and identities. On the Mira River, multicultural rights have been both a gift and a limitation, and these are precisely the outlines of a complexity that I hope to sketch.

Grounded Meanings

During one of my visits to the Bajo Mira in 2009 the community council was carrying out a series of food security workshops in all of the river's forty-three villages. The project was a joint effort of the US Agency for International Development's operator MIDAS (which stands for "More Investment in Alternative Sustainable Development" in Spanish) and the national government. Specifically, it was a program called Red de Seguridad Alimentaria (Food Security Network, or ReSa) being carried out by Acción Social—the now-defunct, gigantic government office in charge of poverty alleviation and the management of all international aid monies that I describe in detail in chapter 3. Alexander, then president of the community council's board, suggested that we join the workshops so I could become better acquainted with their work.

Territorio (territory) was the term that Alexander used when he invited me to join the workshops and made one of the community council's motorboats available for that purpose. His choice of term was a direct result of his participation in "the process." Before the passage of Law 70 and the ethnic organizing that took place in the region, most *mireños* did not refer to the forests, rivers, and mangroves in which they lived, farmed, fished, and gathered goods as their territory. But people like Alexander, who had attended numerous meetings and workshops with other affiliates of PCN—the oldest and staunchest national-level ethno-territorial organization—had come to use the term regularly to refer to several overlapping concepts.

At its most concrete level, territory referred to the forty-six thousand hectares of land that had been demarcated as the collective property of the Bajo Mira's "historical inhabitants," a term employed in the text of Law 70 to refer to Black Communities. Thus, Alexander used it when explaining that, "to get financial support for this food security program, MIDAS and Acción Social require that we eradicate all of the *territory*'s coca plants." The term would also be used in accordance with PCN's definition, which refers to a set of symbolic and material relations that include but also exceed the concept of land. It is often used in the phrase "defense of territory," and when asked to explain it, PCN activists say that territory exceeds land in two senses. First, it includes other material elements of the ecosystem such as the subsoil, the rivers, the oceans, and the skies (see Escobar 2008). Second, it includes intangible elements such as spirits of ancestors and other nonhumans, ritual grounds, and historical sites that are essential for the cultural reproduction of the community. Most specifically, in Colombia the term is always-already ethnicized, eliciting the association between blackness and rootedness that was solidified by the process surrounding Law 70. *Territory* has become a term of common sense (in the Gramscian sense), unreflexively used and routinely taken for granted to signal the allegedly natural relationship of being black, having a distinctive culture, and being settled in a given place. Thus, it has become a platitude to say that black people have or belong in collective territories, just like indigenous people have or belong in reservations (*resguardos*).

At the ReSa workshop on that early September morning, Alexander used the term in its most comprehensive sense. Perhaps he was hyperconscious of my meddlesome presence; perhaps he was taking advantage of the rare opportunity to attend a village meeting to extol people to participate more directly in the community council's activities. Over the twelve years of its existence, the community council had seen a steady decrease in locals' participation, and unsurprisingly, Alexander was adamant about reinforcing a sense of appropriation among the workshop's attendants. He wanted to inspire them to feel entitled to their territory. Despite his youth—he was only twenty-nine at the time—Alexander delivered a pontificating speech that used the official language of ethnic difference masterfully. He referred to the community's ancestors, to their traditional practices, and to their blackness. He was, by all measures, employing the ethnic definition of blackness that had become naturalized by then: "When you see us [board members] on the community council's motorboat, you shouldn't think that this work or this struggle is only ours. This *territory* belongs to all of us; to all of us who *feel black*." To this, an elderly man who had been sitting quietly in the back of the room added in a confident voice: "and who cultivate the land." This comment stood out for me as an important moment in which the various meanings of blackness and belonging were evidenced. While Alexander was trying to emphasize the community members' blackness as a territorial (an implicitly ethnic) identity, for this man the most salient commonality that the people of the Bajo Mira shared was the fact that they cultivated the land. In other words, while "territory" and "feeling black" addressed some of his daily experiences and aspirations, they did not fully describe the reasons he attended the meeting that day. On their own, blackness and territory were not sufficient motivators to create the sense of belonging that Alexander wanted to instill in him and the rest of the workshop's attendants.

I recount this anecdote to show that, although the official language of multiculturalism—which combined ethnic difference and territoriality—has become the dominant discourse to define and legitimate Black Communities as recipients of rights, multiple other notions of blackness, territory, and belonging continue to exist along the Mira River. In the following sections, I trace some of the practices that inform these other notions because they capture the challenges that *mireños* face and express their aspirations for the future in terms that are not constrained by the law's uncritical celebration of (biological and cultural) diversity and ancestral tradition, or by its rigid notions of identity and territory.

As will become evident, *mireños* continue to search for ways that engage others (both human and nonhuman) in nonexploitative ways, even as they participate in capitalist markets—through both coercion and consent. Theirs is therefore not a triumphant struggle against capital but a sometimes tragic sometimes valiant entanglement with it—an embrace and a refusal, an allure and an entrapment. And yet, amid the seemingly relentless voracity of capitalist relations, I am struck by the fierce endurance of other kinds of relationships, which are marked by attentive care and mutual flourishing rather than solely driven by the pursuit of profit. Although *love* is not a term that is often used critically in discussions about territoriality, I employ it here to describe locals' continued efforts to cultivate and preserve such nonexploitative relationships in the midst of persistent extractivism.[15]

Further, when we examine local appropriations of Black Territoriality ethnographically, we see that *mireños'* notions of well-being exceed the opposition of tradition and development written into Law 70 and its multi-cultural logic. Rather than choose "traditional production practices" as the appropriately black and only route to prosperity, *mireños'* grounded notions of well-being challenge Law 70's implicit allotment of a "savage slot" for Black Communities (Trouillot 2002, 2003). They want both the protection of the state with its extension of basic civil rights and the autonomy to make and defend black lives as they see fit. In other words, they want Black Citizenship. In what follows I let emic concepts, which have been silenced or otherwise obscured by state multiculturalism, surface in the hopes of both harnessing the opportunities ushered in by the multicultural turn and dreaming bigger dreams than state-sanctioned rights to difference.

Love

Bocas de Guabal, Aroldo's village of a few dozen families, sits on the bank of a quiet side stream that eventually hits the river mouth and the last village of the Bajo Mira, Congal. Because Congal is so far away and therefore an expensive destination, Aroldo offered to take people there whenever he had sufficient gasoline. From his village, the trip was less than an hour long and of exceeding beauty and calm. One late afternoon, after a busy day in Tumaco amid smoky buses and loud motorcycles, Aroldo and I rode out to Congal with his daughter, Aura, to drop off Doña Estela, a resident of Congal, and her two kids. The sun had set while we were still on the river's main course and by the time we turned into Guabal, it was completely dark. Perhaps the combination of elements—the crisp night, the tentative moonlight, the foreboding lightning—made me feel particularly contemplative, almost melancholic. I think Aroldo felt the same way, because he started to speak in a beautiful narrative style, not overly poetic, but certainly nostalgic. He spoke in a soothing voice and reduced the motor's roar to a hum to tell me about "the way things were."

He told me that on that stream, *sábalos*, one of locals' favorite fish, used to be so plentiful that they jumped from the water in swarms to feed on mosquitos. He recalled seeing *babillas* (small caimans), *tortugas* (turtles), and iguanas resting on the shore. He began to list the types of fish that people caught in those waters but was interrupted by a rustling inside the boat. Doña Estela had been carrying a small animal inside a plastic bag on her lap, and it had suddenly jumped onto the bottom of the boat. There was laughter and excitement as Aroldo used his flashlight to find it. He picked it up, cupped it in his hands while he took a close look at it, and after only a few seconds declared, "It's an anteater." The small, furry animal did not have the long nose characteristic of my own idea of what anteaters look like. Perhaps that's why Doña Estela looked dubious, although she confessed that she herself had no idea what it was. She told us that her daughter had found it while they waited for a boat to take them home, and she thought it looked lost and should be taken back to its habitat. Aroldo continued as he sat back down to steer the boat: "It's small, but it's an adult. It got scared with the lightning. Those little guys disappear during thunderstorms. No matter how tightly you keep them at night, they find a way to escape. If there is thunder tonight that little guy will not be there in the morning. I'm not quite sure what the mystery is with that *animalito*."

And so the conversation went on, Doña Estela, her kids, Aura, and I listened attentively. But as we turned onto a new stream we saw one of the lumber rafts (which are locally known as *chorizos*) that loggers build to transport wood, floating in front of us.[16] Aroldo's face went blank as the *chorizo* floated slowly by the side of our motorboat. He shook his head and went quiet for a couple of minutes. I knew that the community council's internal rules had prohibited commercial logging. I also knew that the council had signed a contract with MIDAS for a forest conservation project that required the commitment to abstain from logging. In exchange, the community council received an annual pay in kind per hectare of "conserved forest."[17] As the community council's legal representative, Aroldo was obviously concerned about jeopardizing the contract, but his biggest preoccupation was not liability; it was the forest. Doña Estela could tell that Aroldo was distressed and she immediately assured him that it was not people from Congal who did it. After giving her a brief lesson on the economics of illegal and legal lumber extraction, Aroldo said: "The problem, and the main difference between now and before, is that now they are cutting trees that are too small. They will cut any tiny *palo*." He held up his index finger to show how thinly people were willing to cut down tree trunks. "They don't let the forest recover. This pace is not sustainable; it is devastating."

Doña Estela insisted. She was sure that it was people from other villages who came down to Congal to cut wood and sell it despite the internal prohibition. I wasn't sure if she was trying to comfort him, but in any case, it was too late. Aroldo was already lost in his memories of abundance and his lament of devastation. He told us about how people starting using dynamite for fishing. He explained the difference in destruction inflicted by various fishing technologies: the *atarraya*, the *trasmallo*, the *chinchorro*, even *barbasco*, a local vine used to poison and collect fish on river creeks.[18] Slowly, as he once again became immersed in joyful recollections of plentiful fishing and living in and from the forest, his mood lifted. Then the air turned salty, and as the outlines of Congal surfaced—a few lights, a makeshift dock, and two heavily armed soldiers guarding the entrance—the atmosphere changed. Aroldo turned off the motor, and we hopped out of the boat and into a makeshift military post where we were casually questioned. Although I was unaccustomed to these kinds of encounters in other villages, everyone around me proceeded matter-of-factly as Aroldo (falsely) explained that I was an "expert" working with the community council on the implementation of a food security project. Then, Don Hugo, another elder who had participated in "the process," gave me a quick but exhaustive tour of the densely populated village.

On the way back to Guabal we talked about politics. The conversation was sparked by the visit to Congal, which Aroldo assured me was a major site of all kinds of contraband traffic. From Congal, one could walk to Ecuador in only forty-five minutes or embark on a deadly boat ride to the United States on the open waters of the Pacific. This is why the army patrolled the village night and day. This is why they had asked for my ID and inquired about my business there. This is also why the army had recently found the abandoned bodies of fourteen young women strewn in the forest surrounding the village. This is why the paramilitaries had set a training base in the neighboring villages of Terán and Milagros in 2000. And this is why the majority of the residents of Milagros fled, and the village disappeared.

Like most conversations about politics, the topics were volatile, and so we quickly went from cocaine and arms traffic to President Obama. And when we were in the middle of a joint exegesis about Obama's foreign policy on Latin America, Aroldo hushed me. He turned off the motor and quietly paddled to the other side of the river. He quickly fetched his machete and whacked a large fish gasping for air on the top of the head. Then we waited in silence for the fish's body to float back up to the surface so we could take it back with us for dinner. While we waited, he told me it was a *cubo*, a tasty saltwater fish that he hadn't eaten in a long time and was very excited to bring home with him. But the fish's body didn't surface that night, so we headed back to his house empty-handed and disappointed. That night before going to bed we ate a plate of white rice, boiled green plantains, and canned tuna, which we washed down with a warm cup of powdered milk that Aroldo's wife, Cindy, had flavored with instant coffee and heaps of refined sugar. When I got up the next morning, I saw Aroldo putting on his rubber boots to head out into the *monte* (forest) with the party of technicians who had come from Bogotá to monitor the forest conservation project. I was still rubbing my eyes when he pointed to the back of the house, where Cindy was busy gutting and scaling the fish, which he had fetched and found at sunrise.

I recall this day in detail because it captures well several aspects of the lived experience of Black Territoriality in terms that are neither constrained nor exhausted by the state's multicultural logic. First, there are the deep memories of abundant livelihoods that depended on the river and forest but did not push those resources beyond their capacity for replenishment. According to Aroldo, the challenge to maintain such interdependent relationships has become only more difficult over time, despite governmental interventions to preserve biodiversity and nongovernmental organizations' conservation initiatives. This is because there are increasing incentives for locals to cut trees, dynamite the river, and participate in the perverse networks of crime that sustain contraband across borders. The challenge turns to irony, when—unable to take home a single fish to eat—we dine on canned tuna and powdered chocolate in a region that is known worldwide for its vast riverine systems and exceptional cacao.

In the face of this constant threat, Aroldo's resolute dedication to his territory is apparent in his intimate knowledge of its critters, his careful observation of the river and the forest, and his commitment to defend a way of life that he feels privileged to have grown up and thrived in. In the midst of intensified militarization and compounded environmental devastation, Aroldo maintains a clear vision that defends Black Territories not as pristine biodiverse areas, or as museums that preserve "traditional productive practices," but as complex landscapes—composed of people, plants, and animals—where all can lead flourishing lives and die in dignity. I use the word *love* to describe this set of practices, which do not result from a static preservation of tradition or an essential cultural trait of Black Communities. Rather, they are daily practices that cultivate care, pay close attention, and build intimate knowledge of others—both human and nonhuman.

Well-Being

To wager an assessment of the successes and failures of Black Territoriality in practice, I explore my interlocutors' dreams and aspirations for the future and search for clues as to whether the implementation of Law 70 has moved them closer to fulfilling those dreams. In doing so, I recall the words of Farah Griffin (2003, 77), who suggests that we should measure "the success of social movements . . . by the status of brown and black girls." Although she was looking at a vastly different social movement—the Cuban Revolution—Griffin's suggestion that we center the experience of our society's most vulnerable and disenfranchised remains a useful guide to measure success. The stories in this section attempt to do precisely that—center the stories of the women and girls of the Bajo Mira as they articulate their (sometimes unfulfilled) dreams and strategies for attaining them. To glean what well-being means to them, I ask what the future looks like in their eyes and what Colombia's multicultural society offers them today.[19]

During one of my attempts to keep up with the team of forest conservation monitors as they recorded tree measurements, I slipped off a tree's roots and landed on my back. Although I managed to walk the rest of the way and complete the day's activities with the men, when we returned to Guabal, Aroldo asked Milena—his neighbor and fellow community organizer—to make sure that my limp was nothing serious. When she saw my bruised backside, Milena smiled and told me to take my clothes off. She made me a sitz bath and stroked the bruises with herb bunches. Then, she handed me a bottle of an herbal concoction that she kept atop her plastic wardrobe cabinet. When I asked if she had prepared it herself, she pulled out an entire assortment of bottles that she used in her work as a midwife (*partera*). Milena had delivered so many babies that she had lost count of them. I had recently gone through childbirth myself, so we had an animated conversation about birthing. She told me that most of her own children were delivered by another *partera* from across the river but that she had given birth to two of them on her own. When I asked what happened when there were complications, she said that in those cases women were taken to Tumaco. But she also admitted that sometimes women died during or soon after childbirth, and sometimes their babies didn't make it either.

Although she was confident in her own curing abilities, she lamented the near-complete absence of health services on the river. In her view, it was not only possible but also would be ideal to combine local healing knowledges with a decent medical infrastructure and basic public health services. She told me that there were a total of four health clinics along the Bajo Mira, which were intended to serve a population of approximately two hundred thousand. One of them had only recently been built following the intense lobbying of a former secretary of the community council's board, Felipe Landázuri. Felipe had been a community health officer in his home village of Candelilla de la Mar and had managed to have a well-equipped clinic built there. But in June 2008, he was taken from his home by paramilitary soldiers and murdered.[20] "After his death," Milena said, "the health clinic fell apart." The other three had suffered severe damage during the floods of 2009, and she couldn't tell me whether they had been properly repaired because she had never used their services.

We had been sitting on the floor, under a single light bulb that cast a dim light on her bedroom, and suddenly the whole house went dark. The generator that kept the bulb on had run out of gas. Unmoved, Milena immediately called out for Daisy, her only daughter, and sent her to fetch some candles from the neighbor's shop. "Tell him I'll pay him back later," she said, and then apologized for the darkness in her home. After she helped me dry myself in the pitch black, we walked out into the kitchen to wait for the candles. Although she was only sixteen at the time, Daisy was already a tall and shapely woman of exceptional beauty. She often joined the conversations between her mother and me by sitting quietly next to us, but she rarely intervened. That night, as her mother was busy frying several pieces of *tatabra* (peccary) for dinner, I asked her about school.

At sixteen, Daisy had only recently finished the fifth grade and hoped to keep going to school past the elementary level soon. Milena explained that the local school in Guabal was only an elementary school and that the closest middle and high school was in Congal. Although Congal was only forty-five minutes away, no one in Guabal or other neighboring villages could afford to pay for the gas needed to send their kids back and forth every day, so most people who had relatives or acquaintances in Tumaco sent them off to attend high school there. In addition, the school in Congal suffered the chronic dearth of teachers and resources that most schools along the river faced. This scarcity was not new for the people of the Bajo Mira, but it was something that they hoped to overcome. In fact, many had placed their hopes on "the process," thinking that the chronic education issue might be solved once they had a legal territory and a locally based authority. The community council had in fact made an attempt to intervene, but given that there were no discretionary funds to spend, the council was always forced to negotiate with the municipality or with the international cooperation organizations that funded such projects.[21] In the end, although the council managed to get funding to build several new schools, it couldn't keep the schools properly staffed. The problem was deep-seated and structural. Locals did not have the needed certificates to teach in village schools. And those who went to Tumaco to get the credentials seldom returned to the river, choosing instead to pursue urban livelihoods.

As a makeshift solution to this problem, Milena, like most other parents in the Bajo Mira, was thinking of sending Daisy to live with an in-law in Tumaco. But she also had bigger plans. She and her husband had bought a lot in the city and were hoping to build a small house there with wood from the forest. Then, she could do what many mothers did and move there temporarily while her daughter finished high school. Like those other mothers, she was motivated by the dream of economic improvement that education promised. If Daisy finished high school, she might be able to get a job, move to the city, and go home to Guabal once in a while to visit. But Milena was also motivated by fear. After we finished eating and Daisy had left, she told me in confidence that one of the paramilitary soldiers that was stationed in Guabal had been stopping by to ask to speak to Daisy. Milena had ignored his requests and had forbidden Daisy to speak to any of them, but she knew that she could keep him at bay for only so long.

Everyone in Guabal knew that Victoria, a local woman in her midtwenties, had been raped by one of those same paramilitary soldiers. When her father found out, he sent her away to Tumaco, where she gave birth to a boy prematurely before returning to the river. A couple of months before the rape, Victoria's mother had told me a story that revealed much about her hopes for her seven daughters and that acquired added meaning in light of my learning about the event. She told me that when Victoria turned fourteen, she started itching to make money and asked her for permission to work in Tumaco, and Victoria had responded enthusiastically by finding her a job cleaning and cooking for an acquaintance. She had hoped that by getting a job, Victoria could avoid following in her oldest sister's footsteps. Rosa, who was twenty-six, had married a local man when she was still a teenager and was, according to her mother, the unhappy mother of five. But Victoria's father, who was an active participant in "the process," opposed Victoria's employment. As soon as he found out that Victoria was doing domestic work in Tumaco, he went to fetch her to bring her back to the river. Exasperated, he told his wife that he had dedicated his entire life defending the territory in which he raised his children so that they could be free, so that they could avoid the enslavement of paid employment. When she told me this story, Victoria's mother repeated the word *enslavement* and dwelled on it. Then she pointed to her daughter Rosa's house on the other side of the river and looked at me, "But isn't *that* the same thing?"

Victoria's and Milena's dreams and their persistent struggles to attain them are telling for several reasons. First, they elucidate the promises of citizenship that remain unfulfilled even after the formal extension of multicultural rights in their communities. Milena dreams of adequate health care for pregnant women to complement her midwifery practice. She dreams of a viable way for her daughter to complete her basic education and for a setting in which she can grow up free from the threat of coercive sexual relations and gendered violence. Victoria dreams of a means to dignified employment, a route to financial autonomy to escape the "enslavement" of domestic work and compulsory motherhood. Unlike multiculturalism's logics, their notions of well-being and their hopes for their own and their daughter's futures do not oppose tradition to development. Milena wants electricity, running water, proper transportation, and the freedom to cultivate her plot of land as she wishes. Victoria's dreams seem to be similarly constrained by the spurious choice between tradition and development. On the one hand, there is the offer of a "traditional" rural life, which, according to her mother, condemns women to domestic subjugation and perpetual poverty. On the other hand, there is the possibility of pursuing a "modern" urban dream, which for her father was tantamount to the nightmare of proletarian existence.

I outline this false dichotomy to stress that local concepts of well-being do not align with those outlined by Law 70 or its multicultural logic, which uncritically celebrates conservation and tradition. If that is as far as our political imaginations can go, we might be condemned to a false choice between the commitment to defend nonexploitative relationships with others and the rightful desire to live well (*vivir sabroso*) and die with dignity. But isn't it possible to dream of both? Following Stuart Hall, isn't it possible for Afro-Colombians to have their cake and it too?

An Imperfect Victory
Traditional Production Practices

> Prácticas tradicionales de producción: Son las actividades y técnicas agrícolas, mineras, de extracción forestal, pecuarias, de caza, pesca y recolección de productos naturales en general, que han utilizado consuetudinariamente las comunidades negras para garantizar la conservación de la vida y el desarrollo autosostenible. [Traditional production practices: The techniques and activities of agriculture, mining, forest extraction, cattle farming, hunting, fishing, and natural product gathering in general that Black Communities have customarily used for the conservation of life and sustainable development.]
> —*Ley 70 (1993)*

The first time I attended the food security workshops funded by USAID, Alexander and I arrived just in time for the participants' group presentations. There were four groups, each of which had a poster board to explain how each of the steps of corn and bean cultivation was "traditionally" done, including adaptation of the terrain, cultivation methods, fertilization, and harvest. Andrés, the workshop facilitator, was a tentative eighteen-year-old from a nearby village who had recently received his degree as *técnico agronómo* in Tumaco, which is roughly equivalent to a US associate's degree in agronomy. He sat quietly as each of the groups, composed of four or five well-seasoned *campesinos*, described how they selected an adequate plot of land, cleared the brush, cut the trees down, and then strewed the seeds. Then, he stood up and drew on the whiteboard, saying: "Well, the main difference is that *these people* do not want us to strew the seeds. *They* want us to cultivate in rows. Corn seeds should be planted one by one, five centimeters deep and twenty centimeters apart. There should also be a distance of eighty centimeters between each row. Beans, on the other hand, should be planted in perfect squares of forty centimeters by forty centimeters. It is also important to place stakes so that this shrub species, which is called *calima*, can wrap itself around it." He then proceeded to give the participants a lesson on organic fertilizers such as tree leaves, cacao peels, and plantain shoots. He explained that they contained nitrates, phosphorus, and potassium, which were rich nutrients for the crops. He also outlined, quite mechanically, a set of natural pest control methods, which ranged from making scarecrows to preparing a concoction of organic pesticides. Then, he ended by saying, "*These people* don't want us to abandon our manual ways, they just want us to combine our knowledge [with theirs]. *They* don't want us to use chemicals, so we have to use compostables."

After the workshop ended, everyone was treated to lunch in the village school. I sat down with Andrés, Alexander, and the other two workshop facilitators, a local *campesina* and a *tumaqueña* social worker. I asked many questions, which they patiently listened to. Why was the project giving out bean and corn seeds in communities that didn't consume beans and corn? Why not plantain and rice? How did they balance the injunctions of the project sponsors—USAID and Acción Social—with local agricultural practices? Were the *campesinos* actually changing their cultivation methods to meet the sponsors' demands? But most important, why was it necessary to teach farmers how to farm? Alexander, who had spent many hours listening to my incessant questions, answered all with a single sentence, "*Compañera,* the entire purpose of these workshops is to recover traditional cultivation practices that were lost due to the use of illicit crops." I knew enough about illicit crops and substitution programs to know what he meant. It didn't really matter that locals didn't eat very much corn and didn't care for beans. What mattered was that they were offered alternative means to generate income so that the war on drugs wasn't seen as a violent eradication program but a sensitive reeducation intervention, and even an economically just measure. It was highly unlikely that in the ten years since the entrance of coca in the region in the early 2000s people had forgotten how to cultivate foodstuffs, but aid organizations had to perform a pedagogy of *campesino* rehabilitation, whereby former "criminals" were made into docile farmers.[22] The alleged priority of this program—and its associated forest conservation, governance, and environmental management programs—was therefore to lure local *campesinos* from coca cultivation. The rest were collateral benefits.

The topic of coca cultivation on the Bajo Mira was unpredictable. Sometimes when coca was mentioned, people spoke in a hushed voice or denied it outright. Other times, people candidly spoke about cultivating it, processing it, or occasionally harvesting it for a day's pay (which is commonly referred to as *raspar*). They would share with me the details of how they got involved with it. The stories were all quite similar. First, a handful of *paisas*—the local term to refer to white outsiders—had given them free imported seeds and handed them a generous advance payment. Then, they came back to collect the bulks of leaves and promptly paid the remaining balance. It was a perfect commodity chain. Or as Aroldo put it, "Coca came in a full package: the seed, the money, the technology, the market, and the protection strategy."

But the honeymoon didn't last long. *Campesinos* were then taught to make cocaine paste in makeshift labs in the forest and were required to sell in that form rather than as leaves. The problem with this shift was that it made the transaction highly time-sensitive because the quality of cocaine powder is inversely related to the age of the paste from which it is processed. And since the "coca package" came with an exclusive sale "contract" enforced by violence, farmers sat on a steadily decreasing income until their sole buyers showed up. Local *campesinos* knew that any attempt to sell to other buyers would most likely result in death. Sometimes buyers would use time as leverage to pay farmers extremely low prices, well below the going market rates. Sometimes the delay was due to armed combat with other buyers, or to having to wait for the right moment to collect their product. It was clear that coca cultivation was not just a smooth commodity chain; it was a major driving force behind Colombia's civil war.

On the Bajo Mira, after a four- or five-year coca bonanza in the early 2000s, things started spinning out of control. As a local elder put it, "Coca was the master that came and radically changed everything." He continued:

> Everyone started getting money. People who had never held more than one hundred thousand pesos [approximately US$55) in their hand all of a sudden were getting five million [$2,800]. People weren't ready for that; they went crazy. If a guy drank *charuco*, he started drinking whiskey. If he owned a wooden canoe, he bought a boat and a two hundred [horsepower] motor. And when his neighbor saw that, well, he wanted the same thing. And then the buyer would say to him, "Go ahead, I'll give you the seed." And that neighbor was no longer aiming to get five million; he now wanted ten million. And that's how this time bomb was built.

Then, around 2004, the aerial fumigations that were being were carried out in the upper portion of the Mira River started moving toward the coast. But despite the incessant showers of Roundup (glyphosate), in 2008, Tumaco was still the Colombian municipality with the largest concentration of coca cultivation. "The master" was resilient; much more so than other crops; much more so than the forest, the rivers, and *campesinos* themselves.

The Colombian government, aided by the US government's military muscle, seemed determined to exterminate coca in nearby Nariño. Or so they said.[23] Just a few years earlier they had eradicated coca in the neighboring department of Putumayo with robust funding from Plan Colombia.[24] But the costs had been extremely high, and their draconian measures, which had gotten a lot of bad press, were an open secret. In fact, a USAID officer who I interviewed in Tumaco once bluntly admitted, "In Putumayo we [USAID] came in like it was Afghanistan. *We were* the government. The governor would call *us* before he made any decisions." In the case of Nariño, following the disaster in Putumayo, the government had to proceed with greater care.

It needed substitution programs for illicit crops and could no longer simply come in with helicopters like "Afghanistan." USAID and the Colombian government needed social and economic programs in their eradication plans. Call it food security. Call it forest conservation. Call it strengthening the local governance bodies of Afro-descendant communities.

By 2010 local *campesinos* reported that coca cultivation in the Bajo Mira was "in a coma." Official figures on total cultivation area in the municipality of Tumaco show that expansion was contained between 2008 and 2012.[25] At that moment, the stupor was evident, but the question of how coca cultivation had been folded into the "traditional production practices" of this Black Community remained ambiguous. What exactly can be identified as traditional and accordingly rescued when local practices are so deeply entangled with the capitalist imperative to produce profit? And still, how do we activate mechanisms to minimize harm and pursue love and well-being instead? My ethnographic observations reveal that multicultural recognition has amounted to an imperfect victory in attaining these ideals. While the imperative for Black Communities to preserve traditional production practices afforded local *campesinos* an expedient legal means to protect their forests and rivers from third parties interested in extracting their territory's resources, it did not shield them from a disadvantageous transformation of their livelihoods. When examining the grounded practice of Black Territoriality, it is evident that national and international attempts at rehabilitating local economies—framed in the logic of multiculturalism—have been misguided and insufficient. Crop substitution programs reveal a deep disregard for local practices by purporting to "teach" *campesinos* what they already know and imposing "expert" knowledges and even a choice of crops on them. Moreover, these projects—informed as they are by multicultural rights—demand that *mireños* maintain said traditional practices to retain their legitimacy as ethnic subjects. Thus, rather than protect local livelihoods, Law 70 placed local *campesinos* in a double bind to remain "traditional" in the face of relentless extractive pressures. In the end, the entry of coca into the Bajo Mira exacted a double displacement—first through the eradication of local crops and then through the imposition of foreign ones in the name of ancestral tradition.

Autonomy

> Una comunidad negra podrá constituirse en Consejo
> Comunitario, que como persona jurídica ejerce la máxima
> autoridad de administración interna dentro de las Tierras
> de las Comunidades Negras, de acuerdo con los mandatos
> constitucionales y legales que lo rigen y los demás que le asigne
> el sistema de derecho propio de cada comunidad. [A Black
> Community can become a Community Council, which as a
> juridical entity exercises the maximum authority of internal
> administration inside the Lands of Black Communities,
> according to the constitutional and legal mandates that govern it
> and to whichever others are assigned to it by each community's
> common laws.]
>
> —*Decree 1745 (1995)*

The legal language that outlines the implementation of multicultural rights for Black Communities is promising in its intended devolution of power to local authorities, who in theory are free to oversee the internal administration of community matters and the observation of their customary laws. If successful, this would amount to an expression of Black Citizenship in which each community would retain enough sovereignty to carve out its own path to well-being while being guaranteed civil rights and state protection from external violence. In the language of multiculturalism, this is referred to as *autonomy* and stubbornly defended by black activists in their negotiations with the state, as well as by members of Black Communities attempting to exercise their territorial rights in their everyday lives.[26] As I show here, in practice autonomy has amounted to a partial victory. While it has furnished community councils—the maximum authority inside Black Communities—with concrete tools to negotiate with third parties (including the national government) to gain access to resources and to protect their own interests, the promise of autonomy has not fundamentally shifted Black Communities' position vis-à-vis these external actors who continue to intervene in their territories. Put bluntly, the law created a new administrative unit that the national government, nongovernmental organizations, and the private sector must all contend with, but because it did not alter the fundamental structures of power, community councils remain subordinate to others whose interests do not necessary dovetail with their own.

When I first attempted to reconstruct the history of the land-titling process, I spent some time at the community council's office in Tumaco. I had already been told that all the documents that had been presented to meet the government's requirements for collective titling—maps, community census data, local histories—had been lost in a flood in 2009, but I nonetheless insisted on going through the office files in hopes of finding some hidden treasure. During one of those unfruitful morning office sessions, Aroldo invited me to step away from the files and join a meeting that the board was holding with a representative of the UN's Food and Agriculture Organization (FAO). The matter at hand was a food distribution program that the FAO and the UN's World Food Programme (WFP) were jointly carrying out in the area. The program was not exclusive to the Bajo Mira, but there was particular interest in covering that area because, since the 2009 floods, the Bajo Mira was being carefully observed by humanitarian aid and emergency relief organizations globally.

Because it was designed to address current and future food scarcity, the program was delivering food and seedlings for edible crops, namely plantain and cacao. Ernesto, the FAO representative, explained that they had allocated a total of two hundred thousand seedlings for the Bajo Mira to be distributed to a total of five hundred families. He also explained that 60 percent of the seedlings would be purchased, and the rest would be produced by the project itself. Finally, he explained that the project's terms of reference restricted the FAO's purchases of "vegetable material" (i.e., seeds and seedlings) to sellers that had been certified by the Colombian Institute of Agriculture and Livestock (ICA, by its Spanish abbreviation).

When Ernesto finished, Armando, the board's treasurer, was visibly irritated. He got up from his seat and paced around the room. What followed was a long and tense negotiation in which Armando proceeded in a carefully organized and politically savvy manner. He began with the matter of the seedlings to be purchased. According to Armando, during a prior meeting, another FAO representative had committed to purchasing 30 percent of all the seedlings from the community council, irrespective of the fact that they were not certified by the ICA.[27] Ernesto resisted and made a final offer of 10 percent of the cacao seedlings and 30 percent of the plantain seedlings. But he immediately bargained on the sale price, arguing that the FAO's purchasing power was dramatically diminished because of the steady decrease of the US dollar exchange rate.[28]

Armando continued with the issue of the beneficiaries. The community council had given the FAO its most updated lists of the Bajo Mira's inhabitants to keep adequate records of the distribution. But instead of using the community council's lists, the FAO had been using other lists that MIDAS had put together. The inconsistency caused considerable confusion. At a logistic level, it made it extremely difficult to keep track of who was receiving what and to ensure equity. Because most projects did not cover the total population of the Bajo Mira, the board constantly attempted to cobble various projects together to even things out. Although it seemed like a purely technical issue, Armando explained, this was a delicate matter with deep political consequences. Because the community council was in charge of announcing when and where distributions would occur, the council was the effective face of the donations. In other words, most beneficiaries thought the community council, not the FAO, was *the* donor. This was a double-edged sword. On the hand, it provided an opportunity for the community council to build up its popularity as a generous "internal administrative authority" that looked after its constituency. But if the distributions didn't go as planned—if they were inequitable or unreliable—the council's reputation was at stake.

The argument surrounding the lists sparked a broader discussion about the community council's effective role in the project. Was the FAO simply using the community council's information infrastructure? Was the FAO riding on the credibility that the community council had carefully built over the years? Would the FAO jeopardize that credibility? For Armando, the crux of the problem was that the community council was not a full and equal participant in the project's implementation. The community council had been awkwardly inserted as the official face of the project but had no effective say in how it was actually carried out. At this point, Norberto, the board's secretary, intervened. He told Ernesto that by circumventing the community council's authority, the FAO had effectively forgone the possibility of working with

the council *as partners*. He then proceeded to list all the resources and connections that the community council had access to, laying out an inventory
of their assets. When Ernesto attempted to explain why the FAO had used
MIDAS's lists Armando burst into an exasperated but polished monologue:

> This community council has existed for twelve years. Every three years we
> hold a general assembly at which our board members are elected. *This is a*
> *democratic ethno-territorial organization with clear political objectives.* We do
> not exist simply to execute projects. Therefore, we must have absolute clarity
> on what the political consequences of our involvement in any given project
> can be. Otherwise, we can end up harming the process. It is very important
> for people to see that we keep our word, that's the only way that we can
> preserve our credibility. We are not like the municipal government, which
> simply imposes decisions on its constituents. The community council is a
> democratic organization. We need to consult both internally with the board
> and with the communities themselves before we make decisions.

After this, Ernesto became more conceding. Another contentious issue
had been the total number of beneficiaries that the FAO had contemplated.
To balance out its internal accounting of beneficiaries, the community council
had been pushing the FAO to add another 180 families to its roster. Although
Ernesto had been reluctant to commit himself to increasing the number of
beneficiaries throughout the meeting, all of a sudden, he loosened up. And
once the balance had shifted a bit, Armando and Norberto pounced on him.
They demanded resources to set up an experimental garden of cacao variet-
ies. Then they pushed Ernesto to admit that the certification from the ICA
could be circumvented and to commit to purchasing more seedlings from
them. They negotiated a set amount of money that the community council
would be given to pay for gasoline. Finally, they addressed what they saw as a
structural problem that ailed most of the projects funded by the international
cooperation. In general, projects contemplated paying salaries only to people
who were certified *técnicos* (technicians), and they saw this as both financially
and politically unjust. On the one hand, the money allocated for experts
always ended up going to people in Tumaco or, worse yet, in Bogotá. On the
other hand, it was an insult to local knowledges, which evidenced that the

respect for traditional practices and knowledges was mostly lip service and never intended to be compensated financially. Overall, the hiring of *técnicos* was a structural mechanism that perpetuated the privileging of the same people—white, educated, outsiders—while failing to recognize the members of the community council as integral producers of essential knowledge.

After Ernesto left, the board members stayed on to comment on the meeting. They seemed satisfied with the outcome. Comparatively speaking, the balance had shifted in their favor. And yet I couldn't help but doubt whether what had just happened could in fact be interpreted as a victory. Certainly, they had defended their role as *the* legitimate internal authority of the Bajo Mira. This was a right granted to them by Law 70 and not an insignificant source of political leverage. But had they actually placed themselves in a more advantageous position of power? Were they actually exercising the autonomy promised by the state? As I listened to their complacent narration of the events, I scribbled my own thoughts silently in my notebook: "In my view, they are highly dependent on international cooperation monies to cover their most basic operative costs. They rarely participate directly in project design and implementation. They are usually paid in kind and seldom given the opportunity to manage monies themselves. With so many structural deficiencies, what political decisions can they effectively enact? On the Mira River, gasoline is the minimal condition of possibility required to do politics."

This tug-of-war between members of the community council's board and external actors seeking to implement various kinds of projects inside the Bajo Mira's territory was a scene that I have witnessed on numerous occasions over the years. While the FAO's presence and attempts to steer negotiations to its advantage is not surprising, there are a few other aspects of this story that are noteworthy. First, the mere fact that the Colombian government did not adequately respond to the humanitarian crisis following the floods says volumes about the state's political will to improve life conditions in the region. At the same time, the community council's ability to truly exercise its legally conferred authority to manage internal administrative affairs is seriously constrained. Unlike indigenous *resguardos* or municipalities, Black Communities do not receive cash transfers from the national government to use as discretionary funds. Therefore, they remain beholden to third parties for access to monies to cover the basic costs of running a government office. What autonomy can we speak of when the community council's maximum authority must constantly haggle with outsiders simply to ensure that its reputation with its own constituency be maintained?

Further, as the scene above reveals, *mireños* have been unable to turn local resources—human and nonhuman—into effective means that confer them with the power to make decisions about their own lives. This, I contend, is a manifestation of the permanence of colonial relations at various scales—regional, national, and global. The FAO's inability or unwillingness to hire and compensate "traditional" experts accordingly is a stark reminder of the permanence of colonial structures in which local knowledges are systematically undervalued, if not unrecognized, except rhetorically. This is also a sobering reminder of the fundamental impossibility of attaining racial justice within the bounds of a settler-colonial state, which constantly tries to paper over relations of inequality with the facade of horizontal camaraderie. Even when successful, the pursuit of Black Citizenship has amounted to only an imperfect victory.

A CANALETE

"A canalete"

> Un saludo de bienvenida
> y un abrazo de llegada
> Estamos todos los negros
> luchando la misma causa
> Si esta lucha no se diera
> ¿qué sucedería?
> Se acabarían las montañas
> y terminaría nuestra vida
> Los negros del Litoral
> Pacífico colombiano
> Vivimos en esta tierra
> que nuestros abuelos dejaron
> Aquí fue que ellos vivieron

y la conservaron

No la comprometieron

Porque nosotros quedamos

A welcoming greeting

And a hug upon arrival

All us negros are here

Fighting for the same cause

If this struggle didn't take place

What would happen?

The mountains would disappear

And our life would end

We, the negros of the littoral

On the Colombian Pacific

Live on this land

That our grandparents left

This is where they lived

And they conserved it

And they didn't compromise it

Because we are still here

        —*Song of the Bajo Mira Community Council*

The wooden oar, or *canalete*, is ubiquitous on the Bajo Mira. Although many people now have motorboats, the *canalete* continues to be an indispensable household item. In addition to its material importance, it has also acquired broader meaning as one of the paradigmatic symbols of the Colombian Pacific's Black Communities. This is probably because the *canalete* condenses many of the characteristics of blackness that Law 70 sanctioned: rural, riverine, and traditional. Perhaps for this reason, I became highly suspicious of the romantic ways it was used at the many meetings of black organizations that I have attended over the years. It seemed to me that the *canalete* and its associated act of rowing had become overinterpreted and abused in evocations of blackness in Colombia. In some ways, I too condensed my own interpretive biases on the *canalete*. The countless times that I had seen the image of a black person rowing on the sublime waters of a peaceful river on the covers of books, reports, films, and websites uncritically reproducing the discourse of Law 70 had produced a near-total saturation in me. Over time, I became incapable of interpreting it as anything other than the official language of multiculturalism, and its evocation repeatedly produced a feeling of frustration in me. Was it not possible to imagine and mobilize blackness in ways that were not constrained by the rigidities of ethnicity and its attendant rurality, traditionalism, and geographic settledness?

Unsurprisingly, as I reread and coded field notes, interviews, and documents, the *canalete* refused to disappear. At first, I ignored it, convinced that its proliferation in my research materials was simply a confirmation of its tired usage and symbolic emptiness. But after a while, I was forced to reconsider it. This became particularly apparent in my attempt to reconstruct the history of the Bajo Mira's titling process by interviewing its most active participants. After combing through every single one of those interviews, it became clear to me that I had to take its repeated mention seriously. In my interviewees' accounts, the *canalete* was not being used as an ossified symbol of rurality and tradition or as an uncritical recitation of official multiculturalism. Instead, the protagonists of the Bajo Mira's collective land-titling process used the phrase *íbamos a canalete* to illustrate the high level of enthusiasm that accompanied *el proceso*. In translation, the phrase means "we rowed to get there." But they used it both literally and figuratively to transmit to me how unique that period of organizing for land titles had been. The overall idea, which I heard repeatedly, was that the collective land-titling process had been a moment of unique political effervescence for the communities of the Bajo Mira; people were so deeply committed to the process that they were willing to row up river for hours just to attend a meeting. The act of going *a canalete* was shorthand to illustrate the intensity of the hopes and desires that moved them.

There was an additional moral value implicit in the phrase. When people referred to the *canalete* they did so in opposition to the motorboat, which also carried a set of associated ideas. The motorboat was directly associated with progress, development, and modernization, which, though positive in some senses, was also regarded with a good deal of suspicion by some. Unlike the *canalete*, the motorboat required gasoline, which in turn made people reliant on money. This necessity of entering the cash economy suggested both dependence on external actors and the risk of falling prey to crime or corruption. The desire for gasoline—whether by individual community members or the community council itself—drove people to become entangled with licit and illicit actions and transactions. It motivated people to cultivate coca, become subservient to donors, and collaborate with armed actors. It was therefore seen as a symbol of moral degradation and the erosion of autonomy. By opposition, the *canalete* was attached to dignity. The dignity of economic, political, and social independence. The dignity of moral righteousness. And perhaps for the first time in many people's lives, the dignity of being black. For if the *canalete* had become representative of the official language of multiculturalism, it was also a carrier of *mireños'* own values, which were implicitly held up against the corruptive power of capital.

These associations, which had emerged in individual interviews, were collectively reiterated during a group meeting that I organized for the purpose of reconstructing the history of the titling process. The meeting gathered seven of the people who had actively participated in the process. Although some of them still worked with the community council, others had become distanced from the process, and so the meeting served as an occasion for old friends to meet again. Admittedly, the very nature of the meeting may have been responsible for the fact that the conversation that day was permeated with nostalgia. But even if taken with a grain of salt, with the full awareness that memory can be deceiving, the collective remembrances that I gathered that day deserve to be interpreted as more than just a propensity to romanticize the past. That day, perhaps inevitably, the memory of traveling *a canalete* was invoked once more by the founders of collective council:

> People felt deeply moved by the idea of protecting their territory, or what was left of it. Back then, the main problems were not the guerrilla or the *paras* [paramilitaries], so the main thing that motivated people was how to improve their conditions of life. Well, they thought that if we organized, we might be able to carry out projects to assist our communities and then maybe one day we might be able to buy a little motorboat. So people said, "OK, let's do it," and they would row harder. And sometimes the river had grown from

one village to the next, but if a meeting had already been called there people were committed to making it, so if someone had a canoe we would row. And other times we couldn't get there on a canoe, so we had to walk. And then if the river got big again we had to swim, and even if the water came up to our navels, we'd keep going until we made it to our destination. We would hold our meeting and then head back *a canalete*.

What is the point of deconstructing the ethnic and territorial understanding of blackness and its attendant set of multicultural rights—of pointing out its rigidities, its limitations, and its problematic presuppositions—if not to evaluate its political promise? In the end, multicultural rights and the defense of Black Territories are useful insofar as they are capable of facilitating the attainment of those same dreams that moved people to travel their river *a canalete*.

CHAPTER 2

DIFFERENTIAL REPARATIONS

Uprooting and Emplacement

"AND THAT'S WHEN EVERYTHING CHANGED"

María Elena is the second youngest of fifteen siblings. When she was growing up in Condoto,[1] Chocó, her parents had two plots of land, one that they designated for foodstuff cultivation and the other for mining. On their *finca*, or farm, they grew plantains, bananas, cassava, *chontaduro* (palm fruit), and fruit trees. During the harvest seasons, which María Elena remembers as plentiful, people from town would come to buy their surplus. They raised pigs, goats, and chickens in the patio behind their house, mostly for subsistence, although they also ate *guagua* (paca), *tatabra* (peccary), *chucha* (opossum), and armadillos that were abundant for hunting and a wide variety of freshwater fish that they caught in the river. On their mine they scraped, stirred, and washed soil until they had a rich sediment of gold and platinum that they sold to local traders on the weekends. María Elena's mother birthed fifteen children total, but only ten survived past infancy. With the food from the farm and the money from the mine, María Elena's parents fed their ten children and sent all of them to school.

When María Elena was young, people referred to *guerrilleros* as *chusma* ("riffraff" or "rabble"), and she remembers that every time they came into town, grown-ups told their children to hide under their beds "because the bad guys had arrived." The FARC, Colombia's largest guerrilla group, had been intermittently present in her hometown of Condoto since the 1980s, and people were used to seeing them come and go. Back then, she recalls: "They drifted in and out. They would arrive, take a stroll around town, do what they had to do and then go back to their *monte*."[2] But over the years as they settled in the Chocó's rivers' towns and villages, their relationship with the townsfolk began to change. María Elena recalls the presence of the *guerrilla* during her childhood less like an occupation and more like a *convivencia* (co-existence). She even holds that "people were fond of them" (*la gente les tenía cariño*): "In a sense people started to live with them, and really, back then they didn't massacre people the way they are doing now. The guerrilla was kind of like an authority, something like that, because in some towns there was no police. . . . If there were any conflicts between families or people of the same town, they would act as mediators. They were the ones who solved those conflicts." At the same time, there was undoubtedly a coercive dimension of *guerrilleros'* relationship with locals, a situation facilitated by their weapons. María Elena recalled: "They also made demands on people. They'd keep the best part of people's harvest and since they were armed . . . nobody could say no." Because the *guerrilleros* were the only group of *armados* with a significant presence in the area at the time, there was a relative sense of calm.[3] However, their disruption of everyday life and their intervention in local structures of authority should not be overlooked.

This was the situation until the mid-1990s, when María Elena finished high school and met Daniel, a young man from the distant town of Barba-coas. Daniel was working for a mining company that had him traveling back and forth between the southwestern department of Nariño and Chocó. The two of them fell in love and soon after had a son. At the time, María Elena's extended family started splitting their time between Condoto and Santa Bar-bara, a small village four hours away on the San Juan River, where one of her sisters had a common-law husband who owned a large plot of land. Because Luis, her brother-in-law, simply could not work the land on his own, María Elena, her husband, and her siblings spent a good deal of time on Luis's *finca* mining, farming, swimming, and drinking beer (sometimes with the resident *guerrilleros*) in a small bar that he had set up on his property. With the *finca's* profits, Luis bought a small boat, which he used for personal transport and to make extra money taking people up and down the river. But in 1997, a few months after María Elena's son turned three, "everything changed": "Then the paramilitaries arrived, *and that's when everything changed.* . . . There were a lot of them, when they came into town. First they arrived in Condoto and started massacring people. They started carrying out selective murders, which was very uncommon in town. That never used to happen. There would be one or two dead people every morning. Everyone was bewildered, terrified with fear. After that, the paramilitaries settled in the rivers and brought their lists."[4] The lists María Elena is referring to were put together by local informants who were paid to finger alleged guerrilla sympathizers and collaborators. To make money or avoid being signaled themselves, locals identified people who came in contact with *guerrilleros*: shop owners who sold them goods, neighbors who let them stay in their house, farmers who gave them a goat or a pig, boat drivers who transported them. Sitting in her apartment in Bogotá more than ten years after the fact, María Elena took a long pause before she continued telling me how everything had changed:

> They would come into houses and get people. Sometimes people would be eating and they'd say, "Finish your meal 'cause we're gonna kill you." A person who's eating and is told that they're gonna be killed, who would keep eating? So they would pull them out of the house and tell them to say good-bye and they wouldn't care if people were screaming, if the wife or the children were kneeling, begging, they didn't care about anything. They would simply take them out and say, "Dig your hole right there, dig your hole." And the person would dig their own hole, would stand next to it and they would shoot them right there and watch them fall in the hole, then they'd barely kick a little dirt in with their foot. Then they started to kill motorboat drivers. And my brother-in-law had a motorboat.

One day in late March, when they were heading to her brother-in-law's farm, María Elena and her family noticed that the small bar on his property had been razed. They immediately knew they had to flee. They didn't turn the boat around to go back to Condoto. Instead, they kept going down the San Juan River and headed for Istmina, a larger town where they could hide out while they carved out an emergency plan. After only a week, they decided to go to Bogotá, because two of María Elena's brothers who had moved there to go to college had stable jobs and apartments where the extended family could stay until things in Condoto cooled down. But María Elena never went back.

María Elena's story can be seen as a paradigmatic example of how thousands of members of Black Communities became internally displaced people (IDPs) in the late 1990s and 2000s. However, following the work of Aurora Vergara-Figueroa (2017), I take a critical look at the very category "IDP" and the theoretical premises that undergird it. As Vergara-Figueroa notes, the massive scholarship produced in the field of migration studies in general and Colombian displacement specifically to address the so-called IDP crisis has suffered from a fundamental shortcoming. In essence, because it lacks historical depth in its analysis, this scholarship depicts violent events like massacres and mass displacements as isolated instances divorced from the long history of racialized dispossession that African descendants in the Americas have suffered. Instead, it explains Afro-Colombian displacement exclusively as the result of the armed conflict, failing to situate the spectacular violence of the contemporary moment within the *longue durée* histories of enslavement, colonialism, and capitalist dispossession.

In addition to failing to produce adequate policy responses for refugees and IDPs, the dominant framework described here reproduces colonial logics, which blame "fragile states" for the global crisis of forced displacements. This singling out of fragile states, which are primarily in Africa, Latin America, and Southeast Asia, in turn justifies contemporary iterations of civilizing missions, allegedly intended to "save" these predominantly black and brown populations from themselves. What this logic obviates, of course, is that the coincidence of the global map of forced displacements with the so-called darker races of the world—as W. E. B. Du Bois called them—is not fortuitous but rather a product of history.

Rather than seeing María Elena's experience as a product of an "internal war" in a "Third World country," Vergara-Figueroa urges us to see experiences like hers as part of a cyclical process of deracination and diasporization that Afro-descendants have been subjected to since the transatlantic slave trade. Following the work of the Afro-Colombian historian Santiago Arboleda (2004, 2007), Vergara-Figueroa proposes the term deracination (*destierro*) to better understand the historical complexity of experiences like María Elena's.[5] Unlike displacement, which is seen as an anomaly, deracination is fully understood as systematic. For Arboleda, *destierro* entails an irreversible and irreparable uprooting. Its impact is the violent disintegration of uprooted societies and the loss of their ancestral knowledge. Furthermore, he describes *destierro* as a phenomenon of prolonged historical projection that has its origins in colonial domination. But despite urging us to reckon with the full weight of deracination, neither Arboleda nor Vergara-Figueroa see only destruction in these cycles of violence. Following the work of other diaspora theorists like Agustín Laó-Montes and Kim Butler, Vergara-Figueroa lingers on the moments along the cycle of deracination in which Afro-Colombians have actively reterritorialized themselves and built a collective project of diasporic affinity.

In this chapter, I analyze María Elena's experiences after her forced displacement from Condoto as an example of *destierro*. Although I continue to use the terms *desplazado*, *forced displacement*, and *IDP* as emic categories when they are used by people on the ground, what I describe here is a cycle of uprooting and emplacement. I do not see the spectacular violence that prompted her departure from her native Condoto as a "new" phenomenon, as some analysts have claimed.[6] Rather, I contextualize it as a particular moment in the long history of racialized violence lived by Afro-Colombians. María Elena's assertion that "everything changed" when the paramilitaries arrived in her hometown should be read with a historical understanding of Afro-Colombians' *longue durée* encounters with *armados* and other sources of institutional violence. This shift should not be interpreted as a radical rupture in which violence unexplainably appeared on the Pacific, but as a fulcrum between its two main expressions: everyday and spectacular. What occurred in the 1990s along the Colombian Pacific was a transformation of the primary manifestations of violence from everyday forms of dispossession predicated on structural racism to spectacular displays of human suffering and trauma wrought by *los armados*. The two should be understood in tandem, not as fundamentally different but as intrinsically related.

By paying simultaneous attention to everyday and spectacular forms of violence, I focus not only on destruction but also on the generative power of experiences of *destierro*. While ethnographies of violence tend to approach violence primarily as a force of destruction and rupture (Ghassem-Fachandi 2009; Nordstrom and Robben 1995), I follow Lamia Moghnieh (2017, 26) in analyzing it also as a social life force "that transforms and reconfigures subjectivities, suffering and place." Moghnieh points out that in contexts where violence is not only encountered in spectacular events but also "lived in" every day both as an experience and as anticipation, it is critical to "investigate the social and political possibilities emergent from violence, while also accounting for its detrimental effects" (25). This involves breaking away from understanding violence through a trauma-resistance binary to lay bare the multiple textures of human suffering while also exploring the productive potentials of living in and encountering violence. In the case of uprooted Afro-Colombians, this involves an attention to what is produced in the midst of all the trauma and destruction. Thus, I do not only denounce loss but also actively document important political emergences that have followed the experience of *destierro*.

María Elena's story of uprooting is instructive for several reasons. On the one hand, it is a typical case that illustrates the vicissitudes that many Afro-Colombians uprooted from the Pacific Region face when they arrive in cities like Bogotá with relatively small black populations. Similar to thousands of other Afro-Colombians from primarily black regions of the country, María Elena's experience of uprooting was accompanied by new experiences of interpersonal racism, which triggered in her a complex process of political becoming. After her arrival in Bogotá, in the process of "becoming an IDP," María Elena also became black in new and more racially conscious ways.

On the other hand, María Elena's story is useful because it is not at all typical. María Elena is now a high-profile activist who from 2009 to 2012 served as president of AFRODES, the National Association of Displaced Afro-Colombians, an organization that has become one of the most visible interlocutors on black politics in Colombia.[7] Precisely because hers is an exceptional case of a person who mobilized her personal experiences toward a clear political end, it can tell us about how activists' individual trajectories congeal into concrete political projects. Additionally, María Elena's position as a prominent activist serves as an entry point to analyze the political work of AFRODES. Her story runs parallel to the organization's creation and its speedy ascent to become one of Colombia's most visible black organizations. Together, these two registers of analysis—biographical and organizational— allow me to ethnographically trace the emergence of the struggle for differential (war) reparations and to analyze its continuities with and departures from the pursuit of ethnic rights, which preceded it.[8]

Together, María Elena's life story and political trajectory offer a paradigmatic example of how uprooted Afro-Colombians' encounters with interpersonal racism can trigger the production of new black subjectivities. When aggregated, these experiences have had a considerable impact on Colombia's formations of blackness and on the landscape of Afro-Colombian politics. Over the past two decades, these initially disperse experiences have become articulated into a rather coherent political project, which I identify as the struggle for differential (war) reparations. In essence, this struggle demands that the Colombian government design specific programs for Afro-Colombians in its duty to provide emergency aid and reparations to war victims. Although this political project is profoundly embedded in the multicultural logic of the 1990s—which identified Afro-Colombians as ethnic and collective subjects of rights—it also expanded its logic by drawing attention to structural racism in more direct and vigorous ways. As a result, the massive uprooting of Afro-Colombians from their collective territories has changed both the contours of organized black politics and the place of blackness within Colombia's structures of alterity. I identify this struggle for differential reparations as an example of the recurrent pursuit of Black Citizenship that I trace throughout this book. In the case of war reparations, like other political struggles I discuss, Afro-Colombians are demanding full protection and accountability from the state while asserting their cultural and racial difference.

SHIFTING BATTLEGROUNDS

Across the Pacific Region, the war entered in full force in the late 1990s. While the dynamics were different in the northern and southern parts of the region, by the turn of the twenty-first century, the geographies of the war had fully enveloped the area where the largest concentration of Afro-Colombians has historically lived. In the southern Pacific, the onslaught of spectacular violence was spurred by the drug war in the neighboring department of Putumayo. Because Putumayo had established itself as one of the areas with the highest density of coca-leaf cultivation in Colombia, the armed forces made a particularly brutal entrance there, pushing out civilians and armed groups alike. Many of those who left Putumayo fled to neighboring Nariño, where they reestablished their coca cultivation and illicit armed activities. Nariño and the southern Pacific Coast in general were fertile ground not only for coca cultivation but also for military expansion more broadly because of the easy access they offered to major ports such as Buenaventura and Tumaco, where cocaine could be easily shipped north.

In the northern Pacific, beginning with the department of Chocó, the shift had begun a few years earlier. There, the paramilitary organization known as Autodefensas Unidas de Colombia (AUC), began its nationwide expansion in the late 1990s. After securing an economic and military strong-hold in Córdoba and Urabá (on the northern Caribbean coast) for over a decade, the AUC became a nationwide coalition in 1997 and began unfurling a national terror campaign with the stated intent of exterminating left-wing *guerrillas* and all others that they deemed enemies of "national progress." It is now well known that the AUCs entered into tacit partnerships with the government to carry out extralegal attacks on dissident groups while profiting from the expansion of both licit and illicit industries that capitalized on the war. Furthermore, the consolidation and expansion of the AUC, as a robustly funded armed group, significantly altered the dynamics of the war, expanding battlefields to new areas and increasing armed competition over territory. As both the military and other armed groups sought to establish command over key trading posts for drug and arms traffic and over land on which to establish profitable activities to fund the war, the Pacific Region, which had thus far remained outside of the battle zones, was abruptly folded into the war (Restrepo 2005; see also Oslender 2008; Wouters 2002; Escobar 2008). Although the shift was the result of a complex nationwide process that had been brewing for some time, the changes for Black Communities were so profound and swift that they appeared to happen overnight. Some observers pinpoint the beginning of this transformation with great precision to the night of December 20, 1996, when paramilitary troops opened fire on the town of Riosucio, in northern Chocó (Oslender 2008).[9]

Razing

In the 1990s, the area around Riosucio, Chocó, which had been used by the FARC as a resting and settlement area for more than twenty years, became a coveted point for development projects and strategic military control. Paramilitary fronts that had a stronghold in Antioquia and Córdoba advanced into the northwestern part of Chocó to initiate a battle for territorial control against the FARC. After the infamous paramilitary attack of December 1996, the inhabitants of Riosucio's rivers lived through a bloodshed that lasted several months. First, the AUC's men of the Elmer Cárdenas Bloc, led by Freddy Rendón Herrera (a.k.a. El Alemán), opened fire on *guerrilleros* and civilians alike. A few weeks later, the FARC counterattacked. In response, the Colombian army surrounded the area, implemented entry and exit controls, and initiated a search operation. Finally, the general in charge of the army's Seventeenth Brigade, Rito Alejo del Río, gave the order to initiate Operation Genesis, four days of relentless aerial, land, and water attacks—by members of the army and "civilians" in fatigues allegedly protecting locals from the FARC. By February 1997, the balance in Riosucio consisted of dozens of murdered *campesinos*, burnt houses, dead animals, trampled farmlands, and the ineffable memory of a group of armed men playing soccer with the head of Marino López Mena—a local *campesino*.

In the months following Operation Genesis, eighteen thousand of the twenty-seven thousand inhabitants of Riosucio fled. This mass exodus was to that point the largest forced displacement in Colombian history. Some left in organized caravans that managed to break through the army's cordon. Others left in smaller groups of incomplete families, neighbors, and lifelong friends who kept one another company through the journey to Quibdó, Pavarandó, or Turbo. Many of those who stayed were singled out as *guerrilla* collaborators and given twenty-four hours to leave under penalty of death. Although later that year several national and international organizations oversaw escorted mass returns to the region, Riosucio has not been the same since. As its name suggests, Operation Genesis was successful in razing the old Riosucio to the ground.[10]

The onslaught that began in Riosucio and spread throughout the Pacific Region closely followed the triumphant moment of Black Territoriality marked by the passage of Law 70 and the political effervescence that collective land titling had stirred.[11] By the end of the 1990s, the celebratory mood that had reigned on the Pacific turned sour. Members of newly recognized Black Communities were being forcefully displaced by the thousands; black activists were being systematically silenced through intimidation or selective murder; collective territories were being emptied of their rightful owners and used as military training grounds, coca plantations, war trenches, or contraband trade centers. The forests and rivers that had provided mining and farming grounds for thousands of families like María Elena's had become battlegrounds.

Emplacement

Given the irruption of violence on the Pacific and its accompanying mass displacements, it is urgent to ask what has happened to the articulation of black ethnic identity and territoriality that took root and became recognized by the state in the 1990s. Did the most recent wave of spectacular violence across the Pacific Region raze the project of Black Territories to the ground? Furthermore, if we recall that Black Territoriality had carved out a clear physical and symbolic place for Black Communities within the Colombian nation, has the blow to that territoriality caused members of Black Communities to lose their place within Colombia as black political subjects?

Answering these questions requires undoing two common sense ideas: that physical permanence is the same as emplacement (Chu 2006) and that uprootedness is an unnatural state of being (Malkki 1995). Rather than assume that forced displacement has necessarily disarticulated Afro-Colombians' ethnic identity and territorial rooting, my analysis explores the extent to which this experience has led to new black subjectivities and political projects. Using Massey's (1994) extroverted definition of places, which sees them not as bounded areas but as axes in complex network of social relations, it becomes clear that after being uprooted, Afro-Colombians have newly emplaced themselves. In that process they have constructed new physical and symbolic homes. From this perspective, emplacements are not projects that erect impermeable boundaries to separate insiders from outsiders, or even necessarily tethered to a geographic locale. Rather, they are projects that involve three simultaneous moves: location, extension, and modern subjectification.

By location, I refer to the work of fixing one's social position in a given constellation of power relations. In the case of Black Territoriality, for example, activists worked to place Black Communities in a better (economic and political) position vis-à-vis others, such as white Colombians, indigenous people, and the state. Escobar (2008) describes this process in great historical and ethnographic detail as he traces the production of the Pacific as a place. He shows that emplacement projects are necessarily entangled in intense disputes and sedimented in long histories of natural-cultural processes that range from geological formations and biotic processes to livelihood practices and resource exploitation for capitalist markets. He traces how Colombia's Pacific Region emerged as a discernible place as a result of multiple alliances—some deliberate and others makeshift—between biologists, planners, capitalists, activists, and local inhabitants with competing discourses and objectives.

Extension involves establishing linkages to other locations and relations with other people elsewhere (see Munn 1986). As scholars of globalization have shown, self-conscious struggles to make and defend a place for oneself must be played out on a game board of global dimensions (just as much they require us to keep solid footing in a specific location) (Appadurai 1990; Escobar 2001; Tsing 2000). Emplacement is therefore a statement about how one inhabits and moves through space, as well as about how one is connected to others all across the world. Additionally, as critics of modernity have shown, placemaking projects are also temporal in nature, in that they constitute historical subjects in particular ways (Trouillot 2002). In Colombia, the assertion that Black Communities are political subjects of rights locates Afro-

Colombians within modernity as citizens and fellow nationals, challenging previously dominant views of black Colombians as uncivilized (Wade 1993).

When seen in relation to the emplacement secured by the black territorial project, the aftermath of spectacular violence can appear as nothing more than the tragic destruction of that place. However, as Vergara-Figueroa reminds us, historical specificity matters when considering *destierro*. In the Americas, Afro-descendant populations have never had the luxury of being "naturally" emplaced. Rather, forced displacement must be situated within a long history of recurrent cycles of uprooting and dispossession, which begins with the original deracination of the transatlantic tragedy. This is why the notion of diaspora is more appropriate to understand this case than forced migration or displacement. While the theoretical dimensions of diaspora are multiple and scholars have dedicated much effort to outlining them in detail (Butler 2001; Goett 2016; Hall 1999, 2021; Laó-Montes 2005; Smith 2016b), I wish to focus on the experience of uprooting itself as the foundation of identity and as the bedrock of political imaginaries. In other words, on the extent to which the *destierro* becomes a group's very source of commonality and historical continuity, and functions as proof of their resolute status as modern subjects. As theorists of diaspora have shown, dislocations constitute not only losses and absences but also findings, encounters, and inventions (Clifford 1994). From this perspective, displacement can also be a creative force from which new identities are forged and with which *desplazados* carve out new places of belonging and this is not a power-innocent move. In thinking specifically about the African diaspora in the Americas, Kim Butler's (2001, 213) observation regarding the power of transnational political affiliations is relevant: "Articulations of diasporan identity by disempowered peoples suggest a quest for new alliances that might potentially confer more autonomy. The move of the 'minority' person toward alignment with an international diasporan community and ancestral homeland gives him or her an alternative basis of power that may otherwise not be available because of traditional modes of hegemony."

Further, the notion of diaspora is important to avoid reinscribing the lost homeland as a nostalgic place of origin (and implicit return) and to think expansively about how homes are built after *destierro*. Otherwise, we risk seeing *desplazados* as always and necessarily homeless and remain blind to the multiple ways in which diasporic subjects can emplace themselves—claiming new homes and forging new relations with others. To do this, we must unsettle the uncritical association of emplacement with physical permanence (Chu 2006, 2010) and instead ask which relationships are activated or disabled when subjects move or stay put. This resonates with Quiceno Toro's (2016) observation that for Black Communities on the Pacific sometimes being stagnant (*enmontado*) is tantamount to being out of place.

This move to dislodge physical mobility from displacement, and physical permanence from emplacement, casts the political projects of black IDPs in a very different light. These projects are neither the uprooted (and therefore aberrant) versions of Black Territoriality nor the nostalgic efforts of a people caught in the past. The political projects of displaced Afro-Colombians— evident in the struggle for differential reparations—seek to make and defend their emplacement. But the place that is being constructed after displacement is not the same (physical or symbolic) one that the black territorial project had carved out. In Chu's (2006) terms, this new emplacement is less a politics of return than a politics of destination. Black IDPs' demand for differential (war) reparations constitutes a technique of location, expansion, and modern subjectification. As such, it is an emplacement project and an example of the pursuit of Black Citizenship, which locates Afro-Colombians as citizens with a right to the Colombian nation and as members of an expansive African diaspora simultaneously, unequivocally, and unapologetically. Like the black territorial project of the 1990s, the political projects of displaced Afro-Colombians constitute an active and self-aware defense of their place as black citizens in diaspora.

Uprooting

Statistics on forced displacement in Colombia are staggering.[12] According to the most comprehensive data system compiled by the government, the Registro Único de Víctimas (RUV), by 2017 the total number of people who had been forcefully displaced since 1985 was 7.2 million.[13] This accounts for nearly 15 percent of the total population, making Colombia the country with the second-highest number of IDPs worldwide, after Syria.[14] Although the flow of IDPs has been relentless, the most dramatic years were between 2000 and 2008, when annual numbers ranged from 605,000 to 426,000 (RUV 2018). And although more than 450,000 returns have been documented, little is known about their success given the continued presence of *armados* vying for territorial control in the regions from which IDPs were expelled. This continues to be the case even after the 2016 signing of the peace accords with the FARC, which, contrary to hopeful projections, has not resulted in a significant abatement of armed violence.

Governmental and nongovernmental monitors of forced displacement in Colombia agree that land is the primary driver of the crisis. However, behind that single word lays a large number of actors, interests, and dynamics. Land is at the heart of territorial control for military advantage. Land is at the heart of large-scale private business ventures such as mining and oil-palm plantations. Land is at the heart of the drug war and the multiple efforts at eradication, which include fumigation and cultivation of alternative crops. And land is at the heart of Black Territoriality. This helps explain why forced displacement affects Afro-Colombians in rural areas disproportionately, and why by 2007, 79 percent of the registered members of Black Communities living in the fifty municipalities where collective land titles were granted had been uprooted (AFRODES and Global Rights 2007).

Despite this empirical evidence, systematic data on black IDPs has been slow to come by. Although black organizations and nongovernmental observers had been pointing out the ethno-racial dimension of forced displacement for some years, the state did not begin to disaggregate its data by ethnic group until 2012. The government's first comprehensive numbers on IDPs were collected in a database known as the Registro Único de Población Desplazada and processed in the Sistema de Información de Población Desplazada (SIPOD), which was created in 2000 by decree following the 1997 passage of the Ley de Desplazados (Law 387). This data was taken from the official declarations that IDPs gave at their site of arrival and included only individuals who presented their stories at state-sanctioned posts and whose cases had occurred since 1998 and were approved as legitimate. In addition to being of limited utility because of their scarce sociodemographic indicators, the numbers collected by SIPOD understated the magnitude of the crisis, given that not all IDPs present their cases to the state and that some were denied registry altogether.

Following the passage of the Victims' Law (Ley 1448) in 2011, the government corrected these errors and began collecting ethno-racial indicators and disaggregating data accordingly. Before this became the norm, several groups undertook independent efforts to approximate the magnitude of displacement among Afro-Colombians. The first of these were the National Conference of Afro-Colombian Organizations (CNOA), and AFRODES, two national black organizations based in Bogotá that collaborated on the design of an alternative data collection method. Based on the 2005 census data for ethnic minorities, they constructed a map of municipalities with significant Afro-Colombian presence. Then, they multiplied SIPOD's aggregated number of IDPs by the percentage of Afro-Colombians reported in the census.[15] Finally, they added these municipal-level data for the municipalities with the highest levels of "Afro-Colombian significance." Although these numbers suffer from the same general shortcomings as those of the Registro Único de Población Desplazada, they correct for the absence of ethnic indicators.

The second set of early independent data on black IDPs comes from the Commission for Follow up on Public Policies for the Displaced Population (Comisión de Seguimiento a la Política Pública para Población Desplazada), a group of independent observers that provides expert data and advice to the Constitutional Court in its effort to monitor the constitutionality of state programs for IDPs. The commission does not receive state funding, and although it is committed to supporting IDPs' struggles, it does not represent any given organization or population group. The commission carried out three "verification surveys" in 2007, 2008, and 2010 to determine whether IDPs had adequate access to basic rights such as health, housing, education, and employment. Following the landmark Victims' Law, the commission carried out a national-level baseline survey in 2013, intended to be used to periodically monitor changes in IDP rights to present reports to the Constitutional Court. The results of these surveys, which are based on representative population samples, provide a great deal of socioeconomic and demographic detail, which can also be disaggregated by ethnicity.

As a result of the pressure exerted by all of these actors, the Colombian government redesigned its data collection system in 2012 and created the RUV, which currently compiles the most comprehensive and detailed data not only on forced displacement but also on war victims more broadly. Even though this was not always the case, the government is now regarded as the most legitimate source of data, and as such, international watchdogs such as the Internal Displacement Monitoring Centre (IDMC) use its data in their analyses of Colombian displacement.

With this history in mind, we can ask how many Afro-Colombians have been displaced to begin to weigh the magnitude of this tragedy on Colombia's black population. While there is no simple answer to this question, table 1 includes some of the statistics collected by the various sources described here. The vast differences in the numbers should be read with the appropriate methodological caveats and considering that they were compiled in different years. More importantly, as Tate (2007) reminds us, they are evidence of the highly political and contested nature of the production of statistics on violence.

	SIPOD	AFRODES/CNOA	Comisión	RUV
Number of black IDPs	152,995	764,373	N/A	750,549
Total IDPs	6%	32%	17%	10%

Forced displacement and other forms of deterritorialization—which include confinement and armed hostility—have disproportionately affected members of Black Communities. This is evident when the perspective shifts from the national scale to the regional to ask, not what percentage of total IDPs are black, but what percentage of all Afro-Colombians have been forcefully displaced. This disproportionality becomes even starker when we examine the specific regions where Black Territories have been titled. For example, according to the IDMC (2018), one-third of all IDPs are from the Pacific Region, and according to a joint report by AFRODES, the Association of Black Organizations (ORCONE), and CNOA (2008), the number of IDPs from municipalities where ancestral territories have been recognized and collective titles granted amounts to an astonishing 93 percent of the total population in those areas.

It is important to highlight that disputes over land are at the center of this tragedy. By 2018, the Victims' Unit for Integral Aid and Reparation estimated that 4.5 million hectares of land had been violently seized from rightful owners. It should not be surprising that the consequences of the war have been more severe for those living in rural areas. Furthermore, the impact has been stronger inside of Black Communities than for the Afro-Colombian population at large, which is mostly urban. At a general level, these processes of deterritorialization have amounted to a counterreform that has concentrated effective possession of Colombia's lands in fewer hands. From the perspective of Black Communities, it amounts to an aggressive attack on territorial rights and practices.

Finally, the disproportionality of displacement among Black Communities should be read as a manifestation of ethnic and racial discrimination. While one may object to this assertion by noting that the vast majority of Colombian IDPs are not black and that black IDPs are not specifically targeted by virtue of being black, I follow the researchers at Colombia's Observatorio de Discriminación Racial who note that deliberate intention is not a prerequisite for the existence of racial discrimination, nor is it necessary to prove that a group's ethnic or racial identity is the sole or primary cause for being disadvantaged in practice. Rather, any action, omission, or social structure is deemed discriminatory if its outcomes have the effect of curtailing a given group's rights, even when its explicit purpose was not discriminatory. To be clear, forced displacement perpetuates structures of racial, ethnic, and economic inequality and disproportionately affects rural Afro-Colombians in Black Communities. As such, it is racially discriminatory (Rodríguez Garavito et al. 2009).

BUILDING WITH DEBRIS

In its textured fabric, the river is now the memory of the last destructions; its meanders are the resting places where the remains, the broken canoes, and the destroyed fishing gear seek shelter. From the riverbanks everything wants to be the road to oblivion, the faces in pain facing the great avenue, and the threatening screams, and the songs that cry for all the dead. Upstream, in the Timbiquí river, as in the Saija, the

> stampeding people forget the guazá and the drum; the people
> of the Naya only have memories of death; those in Napi hear
> frightening stories at night and ghosts accompany their sleep.
> Like a gigantic wave, the song of death arrives from far away,
> the horizon is barely a fire in Sanquianga, amid the estuaries
> death is announced, on beaches and firm ground the flags of hate
> are raised, and in Barbacoas, that place of golden histories, the
> universe is now made of shards, ruins, and debris.
> —*Villa (2001, 89)*[16]

If the balance of forced displacement is difficult to gauge in quantitative
terms, the same is not true of its qualitative consequences. Scholars have analyzed some of these outcomes in considerable detail. Restrepo (2005) sees
paramilitary violence in Tumaco as a disarticulating force that profoundly
weakened the ethno-territorial political project that had emerged and solidified in this part of the Pacific. For Oslender (2008a), the initial onslaught of
the 1990s left the landscapes of the Pacific haunted by new "geographies of
terror." That is, spaces of formerly peaceful sociality were reinscribed as sites
of bloody memories of the past or as dangerous places to inhabit and traverse
in the present. And in William Villa's (2001) sorrowful appraisal of the aftermath of this wave of violence, the Pacific's places of "golden histories" have
been reduced to "shards, ruins, and debris."

At the same time, analysts have acknowledged that these hopeless ap-
praisals of life on the Pacific Region are not entirely accurate. Restrepo (2005),
for instance, clarifies that this change has not only wrought destruction and
outlines a number of political openings that the new conjuncture has ushered
in. For example, he notes that Afro-Colombians' demands to the state are no
longer limited to the recognition of their ethnic identity but have expanded to
broader respect for human rights and the right to life. To a certain extent, Restrepo sees these changes as an opportunity for a much-needed paradigm shift
that could overcome some of the limitations of the state's ethno-territorial
project. Like Restrepo, I also see in this tragic moment an unexpected opportunity to correct multiculturalism's various points of nearsightedness and
to address some of its practical shortcomings, which I outlined in chapter 1.

Odile Hoffman, another longtime ethnographer of the Colombian Pacific, coincides. For her, the weakening of ethnic territoriality has given way to emergent forms of black identity. When referring to the settlement of black IDPs in Colombia's urban centers, Hoffman (2002, 364) describes cities as the site where "the eclectic stew of a new black ethnicity" is being produced; as a place where "in the absence of a territorial justification, other cultural and political instruments are used as the philosophical basis for 'living together.'" Wouters suggests that as a result of being put "under fire" ethnic rights may have in fact reemerged stronger than ever. For her, the crisis brought about by forced displacement "boosts the ethnic discourse once more, and this ethnic discourse in turn contributes to the creation of strategies meant to confront displacement and reconstruct new forms of peaceful cohabitation" (Wouters 2002, 370, my translation).

Despite their various approaches and somewhat divergent assessments, all these works attempt to make sense of the spectacular forms of violence that burst into Black Communities in the late 1990s, disrupting but perhaps also rearticulating newly acquired rights to ethnic territoriality. Like some of these works, this chapter unearths more than destruction to shed light on what Afro-Colombians have built in its midst. In this sense, I echo Natalia Quiceno Toro (2016, 10), who notes that "war is a situation in spite of which life goes on."[17] Quiceno Toro traces a relentless life force, which she describes as the persistent pursuit of "una vida sabrosa" inside Black Communities along the middle Atrato River.[18] My own work also traces this creative force but as it is carried along on the journeys of those who were uprooted and who gradually, despite being dispersed and arriving empty-handed in unwelcoming places, built new black communities and political projects, thereby emplacing themselves anew.

Racism and Black Subjectivity

In her relentless pursuit for economic survival in Bogotá, María Elena quickly figured out that if they registered as IDPs she and her family could be eligible to receive emergency aid. The first step in doing so was to render an official declaration of the events. Then, if the factual evidence added up and the circumstances under which they had left were deemed legitimate, she and her family would be granted the official status of *desplazados*.[19] At that time, the state's Red de Solidaridad Social (RSS) gave IDPs a small cash transfer to cover food and housing expenses during three months.[20] In her efforts to collect this money, María Elena became a regular at the local *defensoría* office, where she befriended the government officials who handled her case and her fellow *desplazados* who were also learning to navigate the system.

In 1999, two years after her arrival, one of the women with whom she had shared long conversations while waiting in line at the *defensoría* invited María Elena to participate in an organized occupation of the UN High Commissioner for Refugees office in Bogotá. María Elena was driven to the occupation site out of necessity—she wanted to add her name to the list of occupiers in case they succeeded at negotiating benefits from the state—but soon became actively involved in the event. Although she never entered the building, she and other women collected food donations at local markets to feed the occupiers. After two months of intense negotiations, the protesters secured a lump-sum grant of approximately US$1,800 for themselves and a small number of allies whose names they had added to the list of beneficiaries.

The most durable outcome of María Elena's participation was not the small business venture that she and her husband set up with the cash they received, but the relationships she cultivated in the process. During that occupation María Elena met three of the founders of AFRODES. After converging in a makeshift refugee camp in downtown Bogotá, the three *chocoanos* had decided to create a grassroots organization that attended to the specific needs of black IDPs.[21] María Elena did not know any of them from her prior life in Chocó, nor had she ever referred to herself as *afrocolombiana*, but their invitation to become involved with AFRODES was appealing. After the occupation dissolved, she stopped by the office one day, and after witnessing the precarious circumstances in which they were working to help fellow *afrocolombianos*, she decided to help out. Initially, her job consisted of making meals for the *compañeros* with the food donations that they received. But over time, after being an outspoken participant in many of their meetings and events, the organization's president encouraged her to formally join the board.

María Elena's ascent within AFRODES was as precipitous as the organization's growth. In a matter of months she learned how to successfully draft project proposals for funding and became the de facto gender expert on an otherwise all-male board. For many years she was elected secretary-general, and from 2009 to 2012, she served as the organization's national president. But the speed with which she became a leading voice for *afrocolombianos desplazados* is impressive not only because of her outstanding ability to acquire expertise in topics with which she was entirely unfamiliar but also because the steepness of her learning curve went hand in hand with a vertiginous process of political becoming. In just a few months, María Elena went from being just another *desplazada* to mobilizing a sophisticated discourse about blackness, racism, and its relationship to territory.

Why was María Elena immediately drawn to her fellow *chocoanos* at the UN High Commissioner for Refugees occupation? Why did she find the idea of organizing as *afrocolombianos desplazados* compelling, even necessary? Building on the testimonies of numerous other black IDPs, I argue that her experience of dislocation enabled her to see herself as a racialized subject in ways that had not been possible before. In other words, the particularities of her experience with racial discrimination in Bogotá precipitated a process whereby she simultaneously became *desplazada* and black, in more clearly racialized ways.

I do not mean to suggest that racism did not exist in Condoto or that María Elena had somehow managed to avoid experiencing it. In fact, I have been arguing throughout that her very uprooting is an expression of historically embedded structures of racism.[22] However, the particular type of racial discrimination that accompanied the experience of being out of place was new to her. I also am not claiming that before being uprooted she did not self-identify as black. In fact, María Elena assured me that in Condoto, "We were all convinced that we were black." But this "fact" of blackness served more to reinforce a mutual recognition of sameness among *chocoanos* than to highlight their difference (and implicit inferiority) from white-*mestizo* Colombians. Thus, she explained that, in Condoto, "there was no need to talk about that because we were all black and saw each other as black."

Being the sophisticated analyst that she is, María Elena describes these two experiences of being black as directly related to the difference between structural and interpersonal racism.[23] With this, she is making a distinction between racist acts that have a clear perpetrator and (often invisible) processes that unequally distribute benefits along racial lines. On the one hand, she explains that in her community racism was present "because of the conditions that we live in. Because there are no basic services, no drinking water, no good hospitals, because schools are not well provisioned." However, she also explains that it was not until she arrived in Bogotá—where her everyday experiences involved constant interactions with white-*mestizo* Colombians—that her blackness began to acquire different meanings: "When you're there [in Chocó] you don't even see that, you don't even talk about identity because over there we are all black, we all eat plantain, we all eat *tapado* [fish stew]. We all fish . . . and that's part of our identity. But once you arrive somewhere else . . . that's when you start to realize that you are different from everyone else." Her dislocation to a place where her skin color was coded as being out of place precipitated a different process of becoming black. In Bogotá, perhaps for the first time in her life, María Elena was not simply "convinced of her own blackness," but she was subjected to others' ascription of blackness as a sign of difference that she inevitably carried on her body.

In one of our many conversations about racism, she described how those experiences made her feel:

> I felt pain, sadness, I often cried. I also felt anger and impotence, and asked myself why black people have to endure this. When I was looking for an apartment for example, I remember once when Daniel and I were circling ads in the newspaper and scheduling appointments. So, I got my hopes up and headed over to look at an apartment. When I arrived, I saw a rental sign on the window and rang the bell but the owner stuck her head out the window and said, "Oh no, I don't rent to *negros*." I felt my heart sink and go boom! It was such a horrible thing for me, a shock. I sat on the curb and cried.

Rather than being an isolated experience, María Elena continued to have similar experiences of interpersonal racism repeatedly, "I started seeing it when I looked for a job, when they saw me they'd say the job had been filled. Or I knew that some places wouldn't even look at black women's CVs, but would interview other women."[24] And consequently, she became much more racially conscious: "That was the moment when I started seeing that they made us feel different; different but *inferior*" (emphasis added).

While María Elena's analysis draws an insightful distinction between structural and interpersonal racism, I wish to add that the difference in these experiences is also related to the different ways in which everyday and spectacular forms of violence are lived. Structural racism, as a form of everyday violence that is continuously harmful, was experienced as unremarkable and therefore more difficult to politicize. After the onset of spectacular violence that followed the entrance of *los armados* into the Pacific Region, large numbers of Afro-Colombians came into contact with virulent forms of interpersonal racism that they initially encountered as unusual and unexpected. The experience of being singled out as *negro* in traumatic interactions resonates with the Fanonian concept of racial interpellation, which explains the power of hailing individuals in producing racial identities and psychic schema (Fanon 1967). The magnitude and swiftness with which this occurred, contributed to the creation of more racially conscious black subjectivities and to the political mobilization of anti-racism.

The politicization of the racial dimension of black identity is observable on two levels. First, the aggregated experiences of black Colombians who suddenly found themselves racially interpellated in their day-to-day activities sparked the emergence of a collective identity that was forged first and foremost in racial terms and in opposition to white-*mestizo* Colombians. Whereas members of Black Communities had understood their blackness primarily in cultural terms such as tradition, ancestry, and territoriality, the category *afrocolombianos desplazados* (or "black IDPs") is a racial identity as much as an ethnic one. Note, for example, that when she lived in Condoto, María Elena identified fishing and eating *tapado* and plantains as the primary referents for black identity. Once in Bogotá, the term *negro* was no longer just a marker of cultural difference indexed by customs but a marker of biologized difference indexed by the body. In fact, I dare say that it was their coming face-to-face with overt forms of antiblack racism more than their attempt to preserve a particular set of cultural practices that attracted black IDPs to one another. It would be too easy (not to mention essentializing) to retrospectively narrate the coalescence of black IDPs into a burgeoning collective racial identity as "naturally" emerging from their blackness, as if this blackness was every-where a given. The many thousands of *afrocolombianos desplazados* who met in temporary refugee camps, at state aid agencies, or in substandard neigh-borhoods did not necessarily see themselves and one another as primarily black, nor were their notions of being black homogeneous. In relation to one another, they were women, men, *campesinos*, miners, professionals, *chocoanos*, *tumaqueños*, *guapireños*, *atrateños*. They were a very diverse set of people who due to their ethnic, geographic, and class differences might not have other-wise met. But in relation to white-*mestizo* Colombians in Bogotá, they were *negros* (black) first and *desplazados* (IDPs) second.

This was made starkly clear to me during an afternoon conversation with Rosa, a woman who had been uprooted from El Bagre, Antioquia, a mining region in a department that is largely imagined as white and that does not belong to the Pacific Region. I visited Rosa often during my fieldwork in Cazucá, an area outside Bogotá where an important number of AFRODES's constituents had resettled after being displaced. One day, Rosa confessed that before coming to Bogotá, she too held "the same [mistaken] idea that some *blancos* have about *negros*: that all *negros* are from Chocó, but over here I met some from Tumaco." A few minutes later she said, "My people, so long as they are black, are everything to me" (*mi gente desde que sea negra para mí lo es todo*). Given Colombia's deeply racialized geographies of belonging—where particular bodies are believed to belong in demarcated areas imagined as natural regions—it is not surprising that, before arriving in Bogotá, Rosa believed two things about *negros*: they were all from Chocó, and (therefore) she was not one of them. But after being displaced, her views changed sub-stantially. As a result of her interactions with people from various parts of Co-lombia, she acknowledged that blackness and geography were not isomorphic (i.e., that many *negros* were not from Chocó; some were from Tumaco, for example). And consequently, she began including herself as *negra* irrespective of the fact that she is from Antioquia.

This shift in Rosa's ideas about blackness is a result of a dual process of self-making and racial interpellation. One the one hand, although she is well aware of the regional differences between a *chocoano*, a *tumaqueño*, and an *antioqueña* (like herself), she has come to refer to all of them as *negros*, a descriptor that in this case is glossing over cultural and geographic difference to highlight their phenotypic similarities. Thus, in this case *negro* functions as a racial category. This is in part a result of her experiences with racism, instances in which *blancos* have singled out *negros* indistinctively of where they come from and what their lives were like before arriving in Bogotá. Rosa was very clear about this: "People here are very racist. Here they offend us calling us 'you black.' But I just don't pay attention because I am black [*negra*] and I am proud of it. My kids used to get picked on at school, but if you pay too much attention you just go crazy."[25] As her quote suggests, *negro* is also a racial self-adscription. Rosa has resolved to identify herself as *negra*, thus placing herself in the same identity category as her *tumaqueño* and *chocoano* friends, and this identity is as much a cause for pride as for derision.

Second, the conscious politicization of the category *afrocolombianos desplazados*, which has been spearheaded primarily by AFRODES, has rearticulated the discourse of ethnic rights in ways that deal with racism more directly. Over the years, AFRODES has crafted a discourse of blackness that interweaves the right to cultural difference with a more overtly anti-racist agenda. The very emergence and rapid growth of AFRODES is proof of the fact that the idea of organizing as *afrocolombianos* and *desplazados* resonated with many people. It made sense because it spoke to the new experiences of racialization that many IDPs were undergoing in Bogotá (and other primarily white-*mestizo* urban centers in Colombia) and because it constituted an attempt at emplacement.

When black IDPs like Rosa and María Elena converged in regions considered white-*mestizo* in Colombia's deeply racialized geographies, their numerous differences and diverse experiences of displacement were suddenly overshadowed by their commonalities as racial others who were perceived as "bodies out of place" (Cresswell 1999; McDowell 1999). In many cases, these new experiences of racialization turned into a heightened awareness of racism. As revealed by María Elena's reflections on the numerous times that she was denied a job, an apartment, or even a seat on a bus, the assignation of racial difference that she experienced in Bogotá held an implicit but widely held conviction that blacks were not only "different but inferior." I cannot count the number of times I have heard different versions of this same painful experience of interpersonal racism. For many black IDPs, these experiences constitute the social glue that holds their identities as *afrocolombianos* together. They are the foundation of a process of mutual recognition that often outweighs the claim to cultural difference, because they know that the reason a cab will not stop for them after dark has less to do with their ancestral cultural practices than with the social coding of their skin.

Becoming Afro-desplazados

Over time, a small group of black activists worked black IDPs' new experiences of being out of place into a complex analysis of racism. This process is most clearly evident in the work of AFRODES, whose organizing has gone from a near-exclusive attention to displacement to a broad struggle against racism, which is not limited to the defense of territory. The reason AFRODES has become such a prominent actor in Colombia's political landscape is in large part explained by the shifting processes of subject formation I have outlined earlier. That is, by virtue of their experiences with interpersonal racism, *afro-desplazados* became an important constituency of self-aware black subjects in Colombia; and their awareness is not merely cultural but thoroughly racialized. In this section I outline how AFRODES's work has expanded from the defense of territory to anti-racism writ large. By carefully analyzing the organization's shifts in discourses and strategies over the years, I show that forced displacement prompted black activists to rearticulate Black Territoriality in ways that openly denounced racism. At their most powerful, these emergent political projects shed light on the historical *longue durée* of racialized uprooting, thereby linking the spectacular violence of displacement with the long-standing structures of antiblack racism.

When I first became acquainted with AFRODES in 2003, its work had three main foci. First, the organization facilitated black IDPs' access to various kinds of humanitarian aid. This included everything from food donations to seed grants intended to generate more stable income. This was the oldest of its work foci, and AFRODES' role as a facilitator had evolved from simply disseminating information to applying for funding to design and implement humanitarian programs itself. The first of these projects, which it carried out in 1999, was a sociodemographic study that assessed the living conditions of black IDPs in southern Bogotá and the adjoining municipality of Soacha. By 2004, AFRODES had put those data to work on a state-funded socioeconomic stabilization project that managed income-generating activities for seventy-three families of *afro-desplazados*. They had also entered into a partnership with a religious organization, El Minuto de Dios, to build and manage a daycare center for children of displaced families in Soacha. It had an open-door policy for drop-in advising and routinely held workshops on practical skills like small-business accounting and on IDPs' rights as guaranteed by Law 387 of 1997 (known as the Law of Desplazados) and Law 70 of 1993 (known as the Blackness Law).

The emphasis on Law 70 and the cultural logic that undergirded much of this work corresponded with AFRODES's second focus: "the maintenance and promotion of the cultural values that characterize our ethnic group" (AFRODES internal documents).[26] For example, when choosing income-generating activities, members explained their preference for certain trades—such as cooking or foodstuff sales—not in terms of the population's expertise or even the racially segmented labor market, but in terms of Afro-Colombians' cultural practices. Following this culturalist logic, in 2004 AFRODES sponsored the creation of a women's handcraft collective that made and commercialized "ethnic" jewelry. And its flagship cultural project was the creation of a folkloric dance group, Palma Negra, which was housed in a handsome cultural center that AFRODES built with USAID funding in Soacha in 2003.

While this aspect of the group's work was directed internally toward its own community of black IDPs—which consisted mainly of individual affiliates in a handful of neighborhoods in southern Bogotá and Soacha—it also carried out this cultural emphasis at other scales. Specifically, AFRODES established relationships with other black organizations both within and outside Colombia, and worked to consolidate itself as legitimate interlocutor in the broader black social movement whose main political pursuit was the defense of Black Territories. There are two telling examples of this early diasporic work: AFRODES's leading role in the creation of a (now-defunct) coalition of black organizations known as the Conferencia Nacional Afro-Colombiana (CNOA) in 2002,[27] and its participation in major international events such as the United Nations' World Conference against Racism, held in Durban, South Africa, in 2001, and the first Encuentro de Afrodescendientes de las Américas, held in Honduras in 2002.

The third focus of AFRODES's work at that time consisted of "defending and protecting the human rights of the displaced Afro-Colombian population" (AFRODES internal documents). Although this work clearly overlapped with the first focus—emergency and humanitarian aid provision—it was more ambitious in scale. Here, their purpose was not simply to solve the urgent problems of their local constituency of *afro-desplazados* but rather to actively influence the creation of public policy initiatives aimed at IDPs at large. It carried this work out on two fronts. First, it inserted itself into as many political spaces concerning IDPs as possible. For example, it had a delegate in the main local political space for IDPs—Mesa de Interlocución y Gestión de Población Desplazada en Soacha y Cundinamarca—and secured a seat in one of the four working groups (*mesas*) of the National System for Comprehensive Aid for IDPs (Sistema Nacional de Atención Integral a la Población Desplazada, or SNAIPD).[28] At the same time, it began creating its own network of black IDPs by organizing periodic National Meetings of Displaced Afro-Colombians (Encuentros Nacionales de Afrocolombianos Desplazados), creating neighborhood committees of black IDPs in Bogotá, and establishing various chapters of AFRODES across the country.[29]

Over the years, AFRODES's work has undergone considerable changes in focus and scope. I focus on two main transformations that I mark as significant because they evidence the need to simultaneously organize as black and as Colombians. In other words, AFRODES's political strategies evidence its (necessary but insufficient) pursuit of Black Citizenship, which demands inclusion in the nation as both equal citizens and as ethno-racially differentiated subjects. As a scholar who is neither black nor Colombian, I navigate my critiques of AFRODES with great care. This does not mean eschewing critical appreciations, but providing analyses that engage with the political complexities at hand. In this case, I focus on how the shifts in AFRODES's political strategies have fostered a politics of emplacement, which I depict as largely positive. In the next chapter, however, I wrestle in detail with the dangers and limitations of mobilizing a victimized notion of citizenship, thereby providing a more thorough critique of some of these same choices.

From Emergency Aid to Differential Reparations

The first change in AFFRODES's political strategy is a shift from an aggregate to an intersectional analysis of black displacement. In its early work, AFRODES had to present itself as either a black organization or an IDP organization depending on the forum in which it was participating. These two options loosely corresponded with the first two foci I outlined earlier—humanitarian aid and cultural preservation. On the one hand, its emergency aid work followed existing blanket programs for IDPs, which at the time did not differentiate victims by ethnicity or race. And on the other hand, its participation in networks of black organizations had a cultural and ethnic focus, which with very few exceptions tended to elide mentions of forced displacement. The first major transformation in AFRODES's work is therefore reflected in a greater emphasis on their third line of work, which was specifically designed to advocate on behalf of displaced Afro-Colombians. In contrast to the first two foci, this third line of work was intersectional from the outset in that it maintained a simultaneous political commitment to IDPs and to fellow Afro-Colombians at large. While AFRODES could have followed an aggregate logic of doing work with *desplazados* on the one hand and with fellow *afrocolombianos* on the other, it instead honed a sophisticated analysis that tied the current condition as *desplazados* to the historical racialization as *afrocolombianos*. This was a powerful intervention that amounted to not only a refusal to conform to the mutually exclusive categories available to them but also the adoption of an open stance on antiblack racism. In a manner that is reminiscent of black feminists in the United States (Hill Collins 2008; hooks 2000; Combahee River Collective 1977), AFRODES denounced the inadequacy of the political spaces available to it—as either *desplazados* or Afro-Colombians—while carving out their own space—as black IDPs.

The height of this intervention occurred in 2009, when AFRODES played a leading role in the passage of a Constitutional Court order, Auto 005, which became known as the *Afro-Colombian auto*.[30] Auto 005 resulted from the work of a perseverant group of black organizations—PCN and AFRODES among them—that insisted on the need to design differential aid programs for Afro-Colombian IDPs. In 2004, the Constitutional Court had passed a sentence (T-025) that urged the state to design aid programs for all IDPs, irrespective of ethnicity. But in 2007, in response to the persistent pressure of these organizations, the court convened a public hearing in which activists presented a convincing argument for the urgent need to develop differential public policies for Afro-Colombian *desplazados*. AFRODES and PCN, which were the only national-level organizations that had developed an ethno-racial analysis of forced displacement and war victimization more broadly, presented the most thorough and incisive reports to the court. As the most prominent ethno-territorial organization and key actor during the drafting of Law 70, it is not surprising that PCN continued to stress the importance of protecting Black Communities' territoriality. Only this time PCN didn't just argue that territorial autonomy was central to the protection of these communities' culture; it insisted on its importance for the very preservation of life in these communities. In other words, PCN articulated the discourse of ethnic rights to that of human rights.

AFRODES mobilized a different argument from that of PCN and subtly wove anti-racism into a discussion that was initially framed around ethnic difference. AFRODES began by pointing out the deplorable socioeconomic conditions that prevail in areas where Afro-Colombians live and stated that this was the result of historical and persistent forms of structural racism that began with enslavement but continued after abolition through economic and political marginalization. Its representatives noted that these precarious conditions in turn make Afro-Colombians more vulnerable to forms of violence that result in deterritorialization—such as forced displacement and armed confinement. And because territory is the foundation for the preservation of black culture, deterritorialization makes Afro-Colombians more susceptible to cultural loss. AFRODES then sealed the argument by reminding the audience that, because culture defines Afro-Colombians as a people, deterritorialization amounts to their extermination *as black people*. This contention allowed AFRODES to explicitly tether ethnic and racial demands, and it was followed by a resolute statement that, for the state to adequately respond to Afro-Colombian displacement and other threats to Black Territoriality (e.g., the presence of *armados* in their territories), it had to work to eradicate structural racism. This argument, which was most clearly developed in the context of Auto 005, was the result of a long and concerted effort to carve out an intersectional political space for black IDPs.

Having followed AFRODES's trajectory since its early years, I can think of several preceding moments in which the organization mobilized slightly different incarnations of this argument. For example, Geiler Romaña, AFRODES's second president—who has been in exile in Washington, DC, since 2009—routinely declared that forced displacement among Afro-Colombian communities is tantamount to genocide. His logic was straightforward. According to Romaña, territorial *arraigo* (rootedness) is the foundational characteristic that makes Afro-Colombians culturally different; thus, it is what confers ethnicity.[31] In his own words, "Our culture revolves around those territories," which is to say that "without territory there is no culture," and consequently, without territory the ethnic group itself disappears. Thus, for Romaña, displacement (and other forms of deterritorialization) results in genocide. Although many black Colombians were losing and continue to lose their lives in Colombia's armed violence, Romaña was not referring to the deliberate murder of black Colombians, nor was he making a claim that Afro-Colombians were targets of violence because they were black. Instead, he was referring to the annihilation of the cultural trait that makes them black to argue that, without territory, Afro-Colombians would be no more.

This approach to black identity is not an essentialist one, but rather a nuanced and strategic argument that locates black identity in its cultural and historical differences from dominant white-*mestizo* societies and then deploys the argument as an expedient tool to protect collective territories. The question of what happens to black identity rooted in territory when black people are uprooted echoes a long-standing debate in African diaspora studies regarding cultural loss and retention after the Middle Passage and plantation slavery, and it resonates in the Colombian context.[32] I do not find this polarized debate helpful. I surmise that Geiler, like others mobilizing the language of genocide in relation to *destierro*, are making an astute political move that is neither blind nor naive but rather strategic and deeply rooted in history. His tethering of black identity to territory resonates with the concept of ancestrality furthered by community-based black scholars like Juan García and Edizon León. Based on a meticulous collection of oral testimonies that recount Afro-descendants' histories across the Pacific Region of Ecuador and Colombia,[33] García has documented how enslaved Africans carried ancestral knowledges across the Atlantic "in their heads" (i.e., in memories and oral traditions) and recultivated them in the Americas. These knowledges, which are neither "essential" nor "invented," constitute the basis of black difference. García (2017) shows that ancestrality is intimately related to *la siembra* (cultivation), and that cultivation is not only physical but also mental and spiritual, and therefore it can survive physical uprooting to be recultivated in new territories.

Also, in 2008, AFRODES participated in a project funded by the UN High Commissioner for Refugees to design ethnic-specific public policy recommendations for the state.[34] The main product of this initiative was a publication in which the authors described the nature and magnitude of Afro-Colombian forced displacement and went on to propose a practical set of public policy solutions (AFRODES, ORCONE, CNOA 2008). This document is a considerable intervention in the construction of an intersectional political space on many levels, but its main accomplishment is the authors' unequivocal stress on the structural causes of forced displacement, which are a direct reference to the historical *longue durée* of black marginalization within the Colombian nation. After lamenting the lack of ethnic-specific public policies for Afro-Colombian IDPs, the document outlines the "structural character of exclusion and discrimination" to conclude that the underlying cause of forced displacement is the historical relationship between (under) development, exclusion, and violence:

> Forced displacement and confinement are intimately related to these structural factors [discrimination and exclusion]. If we try to understand their causes by simply looking at the current conjuncture of the armed conflict over the last decade distorts the analysis because it presents them as an "unfortunate" consequence of military confrontation; and, consequently, the objectives of public policies are oriented towards the alleviation of the effects without transforming the causes of these two phenomena.
>
> Contrastingly, the recognition of *the structural character of these two realities (exclusion and displacement) and of the relation between them*, requires that we develop an ethnically-differentiated perspective that seeks to transform the structural causes that are implicit in both of them. In other words,

a public policy initiative with an ethnically-differentiated focus for Afro-Colombians that aspires to successfully halt and prevent forced displacement must first transform the structural conditions of exclusion in which Afro-Colombian people continue to live, and which have only been deepened as a consequence of the armed conflict. (AFRODES, ORCONE, and CNOA 2008, 16; emphasis added).

These two examples constitute prior iterations of AFRODES's intersectional analysis of black *destierro*, which demands rights as Colombians and as Afro-descendants. They are evidence of how forced displacement triggered the articulation of the black territorial project with a sharp analysis of structural racism. It is interesting that although some seasoned activists had long argued for the need to incorporate anti-racism to the black social movement for territorial rights, their observations regarding the relationship between ethnicity and race had not gathered traction until then, when in the midst of a discussion about forced displacement it became possible to openly speak about racism. It is also worth noting that in articulating a critique of structural racism, AFRODES presented displacement not as an isolated event or as a historical anomaly, but as the latest link in the long chain of colonialism and racism. As such, its argument—along with that of the other activists who supported the creation of differentiated reparations for black victims—is an example of how to undertake a "geohistory of displacement," which evidences the continuities of racial violence (Vergara-Figueroa 2011). In a sense, the spectacular violence of the late 1990s made more visible the everyday violence of structural racism, the constant state of "living in" violence that Black Communities were in.

These demands for ethnicity-specific aid and reparations programs for Afro-Colombians quickly became the norm within the humanitarian apparatus of the state and nongovernmental organizations. By 2011, just four years after the Constitutional Court held the hearing described above, the Colombian government passed a comprehensive law (Law 1448 of 2011) that openly charged the state with designing and implementing differential aid and reparation programs not only for Afro-Colombians but also for indigenous and Romany communities—as well as for children and women.[35] I do not want to overstate the concrete consequences of this inclusion, because in practice the implementation of these measures has been slow and ineffective, and I trace these realities with a critical eye in chapter 3. However, it is noteworthy that these activists' insistence on the unique character of black *destierro* made its way to this law and became part of the common sense regarding victim reparation.

Rerouting and Scale Making

The second major transformation in AFRODES's political strategy has to do with the routes and scales of the organization's interventions. Although it participated in international forums from the outset, over the years this participation changed both in frequency and in nature. Due to the constant need to apply to foreign donors for funding, AFRODES developed an internationalist language early on. In 2003, it entered into a partnership with an international NGO, Global Rights, which resulted in a complete overhaul of their organizational profile. In a matter of a few years, AFRODES went from being a grassroots organization with an all-volunteer executive board made up exclusively of black IDPs to being a second-degree "parent" organization with more than ninety affiliated organizations nationwide, robust (if unpredictable) funding, and three full-time paid consultants. One of the main consequences of this restructuring was that members of the national board abandoned their grassroots work in *barrios* (popular neighborhoods) to dedicate themselves almost exclusively to high-profile political activities. These included lobbying state agencies to design differential policies for aid and reparation of victims, denouncing the relentless violations of Afro-Colombians' human rights at home and abroad, and strengthening the organization's political voice within and outside of Colombia.

This shift was a scale-making project in two senses. On the one hand, it was a straightforward effort to grow. But more than being a simple matter of multiplication, growth brought about a transformation in the type of interlocutors that the organization regularly interacted with. Gone were the days when members of the board counseled IDPs on how to find housing, how to file for *desplazado* status, or how to enroll their children in public schools. Instead, the board members' regular interlocutors were now national-level politicians, governmental and NGO aid officers, and nationally renowned black activists. This shift is perhaps best captured by the words of the partner Global Rights, which after years of counseling AFRODES as a protégé organization, congratulated it as a "grown-up" human rights organization during an internal meeting in 2010.

But this change constituted a scale-making project in second sense. It was a deliberate effort to cast AFRODES into the national and international limelight as a major *black* organization, and this was accomplished not by a simple swelling in size or numbers, but by a rerouting of their political activities. AFRODES expended a considerable amount of energy developing relationships with international allies that would in turn intervene with the Colombian state on its behalf. It expanded its range of interlocutors to include international actors such as watchdog groups, human rights courts, and members of US Congress (particularly members of the Congressional Black Caucus sympathetic to the cause), and rather than continue negotiating directly with the Colombian state, it rerouted their political actions through these newly established international networks.[36] This channeling of advocacy through international routes has become so widespread in Colombia that Winifred Tate (2013) has called it "proxy citizenship." However, in the case of both AFRODES and PCN, the strategy was intended not only as a means to spur change more effectively but also as a deliberate effort to enter into global networks of African diasporic politics.

A clear example of this rerouting process is AFRODES's central participation at the Committee on the Eradication of Racial Discrimination's (CERD) 2009 session in Geneva. The CERD is an independent organ that supervises state members' compliance with the UN's International Convention on the Eradication of Racial Discrimination (1965). Although each member country is expected to send official semiannual reports, CERD also holds periodic sessions at which nongovernmental organizations are given the opportunity to present alternative "shadow reports." By examining Colombia's last two sessions (2009 and 1999) and AFRODES's participation in them, one can clearly see a shift in their analysis of racism and a significant growth in scale.

The only shadow report presented at the 1999 session had two main components: a brief description of the nature of racism in Colombia and a very

extensive compilation of specific instances of political violence against indigenous and Afro-Colombian communities. The first of these components,
which is tellingly titled "Discriminación a través de la cultura" (Discrimination through Culture), refers to the stubborn circulation of racial stereotypes
in Colombia. The examples given to illustrate this point are scant and super-
ficial: we hear of the pejorative use of the word *indio*, of the exoticization of
black women fruit vendors in Cartagena, and of the total absence of positive
representations of black people in mainstream media. But there is no in-
depth analysis of racism in Colombia, as the authors' main objective is to
provide readers with an exhaustive list of human rights violations in ethnic
communities (AFRODES 1998).

The contrast is obvious when we compare this early report to the one
presented by AFRODES at the 2009 session, which denounces displacement
(and other forms of violence) as a manifestation of the persistent, structural
racism that plagues Colombia: "Afro-Colombians' forced displacement must
be understood as the result of structural factors that go beyond the immediate causes that are related to the dynamics of the Colombian armed conflict
during recent years. Said factors are mainly related to processes of exclusion
and discrimination against this human group, which have been historically
configured and which have persisted and deepened as a result of this forced
displacement and the persistence of a development project that runs contrary
to the principle of respect for cultural diversity" (3). Unlike the preceding
report, which described racism as an inconsistent set of idiosyncratic stereotypes, this one describes it as a systematic phenomenon that is heir to the history of racial slavery and state neglect. Unlike the preceding report, in which
racism and culture are described as loosely interrelated phenomena, this one
evidences a complex intersectional analysis of ethnic difference and racism.

The main argument presented by AFRODES at CERD's 2009 session—
that ethnic difference and racial discrimination are coconstitutive—is the
same one that I have been outlining thus far, but the difference in the forum
at which it was mobilized is noteworthy for two reasons. First, CERD is not
a national space for *desplazados* or even an international forum for IDPs; it
is one of the principal global forums on racism. And second, AFRODES
participated in this forum not as a subspecialized grassroots organization, but

as a national-level independent expert on racial discrimination.[37] As such, its presence at CERD's 2009 session constitutes vivid evidence of AFRODES's consolidation as a black organization that participates in African diasporic political spaces at a global scale.

I argue that AFRODES's decisive intervention at such a high-profile event deprovincialized black displacement and rendered it a matter not of "local" or even "national" politics but an instance of global racism, and therefore worthy of immediate international attention. This recasting of black *destierro* as a global phenomenon and of AFRODES as a world-class black organization is indicative of what Tsing (2004, 58) calls the "conjuring" of the global scale. For this scale, like its "smaller" counterparts, "is not just a neutral frame for viewing the world," but a spatial dimension that must be brought into being and that renders a particular view of the world. Further, the particular views associated with different scales (the local, the national, and the global, for example) are not power innocent. For example, "ghettos" are produced as isolated, local problems by obscuring the ways they are connected to elsewhere (Gregory 1999). In other words, they are the result of deliberate processes of parochialization. Global phenomena, in contrast, are produced precisely through the inverse process, that is, hyperbolic statements about how a particular phenomenon is allegedly connected to everyone, everywhere. Overall, in its efforts to reroute political strategy and produce black displacement as an issue of global interest, AFRODES redrew its scale of intervention from the national to the global. That is, it maintained a place-based stance while refusing parochialization, and as a result of this dual strategy, it projected Afro-Colombians' defense of territory onto a global scale.

A PLACE ON THE MAP

The political projects of displaced Afro-Colombians opened up various possibilities to rethink blackness and ethnic rights in ways that had previously been impossible. When mobilized politically, Afro-Colombian IDPs' experiences with interpersonal racism at their sites of arrival enabled the articulation of ethnic identity with an analysis of structural racism. By looking at the emergence and solidification of AFRODES, its pursuit of differential aid and reparations, and its entry into a transnational field of African diasporic politics, I argued that its politics is one of emplacement that projects outward while staying grounded. *Afro-desplazados* have carved out a new place for themselves, one that is ironically founded on being out of place and that unequivocally denounces the historical continuities of racialized violence. Black IDPs inhabited their experience of dislocation and converted it into a standpoint from which to launch a demand for rights as *black citizens* who are due ethnicity-specific forms of reparation from violence. Their discourse, which tethers ethnic difference to antiblack racism, sees the disproportionate effects of war violence on black Colombians as a continuation—not an anomaly or rupture—with the past, as an echo of the enduring forms of racialized dispossession to which their ancestors were subjected. As such, the logic that supports the demand for differential reparations carries within it an embedded historical analysis of black Colombians' deracination that lays bare the colonial origins of today's allegedly anomalous war violence (Vergara-Figueroa 2018). It exposes Afro-Colombians' encounters with spectacular forms of violence as a modality of the centuries-long experience of living in violence.

Since the passage of Auto 005 the situation of displaced Afro-Colombians has not improved significantly. And yet I have repeatedly heard top-level activists identify Auto 005 as a landmark achievement in Afro-Colombian struggles for justice. For example, the former president of AFRODES, Geiler Romaña, routinely mentioned it as the third major milestone in the history of Afro-Colombians' liberation, after the abolition of slavery and the passage of Law 70. In a country with a clear tendency to overlegislate and an embarrassingly large number of ineffectual laws, why did Auto 005 capture the interest and hopes of seasoned black activists like himself? At an immediate level, Auto 005 was an effective, if unexpected, route to continue the fight for Black Territoriality precisely at a moment when its pursuit seemed doomed. Just when the spread of violence on the Pacific had undermined Black Territoriality—both in its effective exercise and as a viable political discourse—Auto 005 facilitated the reintroduction of Afro-Colombian issues into national-level government agendas. But it also broke with the multicultural logic of ethnic rights in important ways. On the one hand, it interrupted Colombia's geographies of blackness in the common sense. By evidencing the growing numbers of black people living in Colombia's major cities (Cali, Cartagena, Bogotá, and Medellín, in that order), Auto 005 redrafted Colombia's blackness maps and expanded the possible ways of being black beyond the rural, riverine subject on the Pacific Basin. And on the other hand, by articulating the defense of the right to cultural difference to an explicit anti-racist politics, it expanded the terms of the multicultural conversation beyond cultural and territorial rights and toward differential war reparations.

These two simultaneous moves—regrounding the defense of Black Territories and expanding the terms of its central demands—constitute a place-making project in line with the pursuit of Black Citizenship. By this, I mean that being displaced became a vantage point—sometimes a fairly advantageous one because of its hypervisibility—from which to launch political projects for rights as black and as Colombian. This was made starkly clear to me in the testimony of an Afro-Colombian woman who had been displaced from her hometown of Calima that was collected by the Colombian anthropologist Enrique Jaramillo Buenaventura. When asked about the consequences of forced displacement, she commented on the contradictory nature of the outcome: "there have been beneficial and harmful consequences, because Calima was a town whose name was never uttered; it was as if it didn't exist on the map and after the mass displacement that took place there it became nationally and internationally known, and that's an advantage" (Jaramillo Buenaventura 2009, 72). In a sense, then, forced displacement has been a long and painful route through which *afro-desplazados* carved out a place not only for themselves but for Afro-Colombians at large on the global landscape of ethnic and racial politics.

CHAPTER 3

BEYOND VICTIMIZED CITIZENSHIP

From Misfortune to Historical Redress

One Sunday morning in 2009, like so many others before, I stopped by María Elena's apartment just south of downtown Bogotá so we could ride the bus up to Cazucá together. María Elena, who was secretary-general of the AFRODES board at the time, had scheduled a meeting for *Afro* women in the cultural center that AFRODES had built in Cazucá, the conglomerate of shantytown neighborhoods outside of Bogotá where the organization's local work was concentrated.[1] As the only woman on the board she was in charge of women's and children's issues and was responsible for disseminating information that affected these two subgroups of IDPs (internally displaced people). María Elena started the meeting by getting a show of hands to determine how many people had received the government cash transfer for underage IDPs that had recently gone into effect. There was substantial confusion because the majority of the attendees' names were not on the list compiled by AFRODES. Some of the attendees suggested that her lists might be from another *barrio* or organization, but María Elena disregarded this explanation and later told me that she thought the discrepancy was suspicious.

Next on her agenda was to inform attendees, composed primarily of black women with young children, of an upcoming deadline to request a subsidy to purchase an urban lot. María Elena framed it as an opportunity to "maintain *our* ancestral traditions and historical rural-urban relations" and encouraged them to claim their plot of land to grow crops, keep an herb garden, and raise chickens. The rest of the meeting was dedicated to bringing members up to date on current sources of humanitarian aid. Specifically, she counseled them on how to apply for the national housing subsidy for IDPs and to remain alert for an upcoming call for a supplementary subsidy earmarked specifically for Afro-Colombian women.

Every single person at that meeting, except for myself, self-identified as a *desplazada*. Independently of whether they had acquired the state-issued ID for displaced persons, their very attendance at the meeting indicated their intent to be regarded as such.[2] Furthermore, the mix-up with the lists of beneficiaries was indicative of the overabundance of people whose basic human right to shelter, food, and health services had been denied by the state and for whom aid for *desplazados* had become a critical means for survival. It also bears noting that, although there were a handful of non-black attendees, the meeting was explicitly directed toward black people. This was clearly evident when María Elena made reference to Afro-Colombians as a community of people with particular relations to land—"our ancestral traditions"—a statement clearly in line with Colombian multiculturalism.

While attaining IDP (*desplazado*) status is often the only way for people in Cazucá to survive in their place of resettlement, being an *afro-desplazado* entitles some people to apply for additional sources of humanitarian aid that target black victims specifically. This is because the state and international aid organizations have earmarked monies for Afro-Colombian victims and because humanitarian NGOs have followed suit by developing "ethnicity-specific" programs. However, despite the plethora of state and nongovernmental humanitarian aid programs and organizations, actual relief for *desplazados* is insufficient and difficult to access. Thus, local residents continue to live in abject poverty, many *barrios* remain without public services, and violence—both indiscriminate and political—is rampant. In the absence of other sustainable and effective ways to make a living in their new urban settings, it is not surprising that many people make do with the precarious assistance they can secure.

This became painfully evident to me when I conducted a survey documenting income levels and sources for two hundred households with people who self-identified as *afro* and as *desplazados* in 2009. When I and the other survey takers asked respondents about their sources of income, they repeatedly mentioned *el rebusque*.[3] In Colombia, the term *rebusque* refers to any resourceful means to generate income and includes activities that would normally be included under the rubric of informal economy, such as street sales and nonregistered services. But when we asked respondents to be more specific in describing what these activities included, we noticed that they routinely mentioned the search for *ayudas* (aid) alongside activities such as selling fruit and trash bags on the streets, braiding their neighbors' hair, or providing neighbors with childcare. Thus, it became clear to me that the time invested in accessing humanitarian aid benefits can be considered on par with the time spent on informal economic activities. In other words, getting *ayudas* has become another strategy of *rebusque*, an occupation that requires a significant investment of energy and time.

I recount this story to illustrate several things. First, the overabundance of people seeking out sources of humanitarian aid speaks to both the sheer magnitude of forced displacement in Colombia and the dearth of stable means of subsistence for IDPs. Second, the rush to find *ayudas* stands as evidence of the state's general inability (or unwillingness?) to protect its citizens' basic rights, a matter that has become more pronounced with the entrenchment of neoliberal policies in Colombia over the past thirty years. And finally, both the eagerness with which the women in Cazucá wished to be included in AFRODES's lists of beneficiaries and the mere fact that these programs for *afro-desplazados* exist, suggest that forced displacement has disproportionately affected Afro-Colombians.[4] In other words, the state's inability to fulfill the promise of citizenship—which is broad and endemic—is particularly acute for black people in Colombia. For many of them, claiming status as an *afro-desplazado* is the most viable route to access basic citizenship rights. Even though not all individuals who have been uprooted choose to identify this way and there is significant stigma associated with being a *desplazado*, the numbers of people who do so are staggering.[5] Over the past two decades, I cannot count the number of people I have encountered whose life trajectory follows a similar pattern of entrenched social and economic vulnerability and who have at one moment or another registered as *desplazados* in an effort to make do. Significantly, as the previous story suggests, for many individuals the decision to register as IDPs is often supported by black organizations, for whom the broad demand for ethnicity-specific war reparations has become an expedient political strategy as well.[6]

In this chapter, I delve into another face of the articulation of multiculturalism and Colombia's war politics, which I refer to as victimized citizenship. First, I recount the emergence of victimized citizenship as a recognizable strategy of black individuals and organizations by tracing the convergence of two discursive formations over the past two decades: war victimization and state multiculturalism. Most important, I offer a critical assessment of its political risks and promises. What is gained and lost when citizenship rights for Afro-Colombians are tethered to their victimization? While recognizing that the pursuit of differential war reparations for Afro-Colombians has been a valuable tool for the expedient redress of harm, my objective in this chapter is to imagine deeper and broader avenues to repair black suffering, which are based on conversations with black activists themselves. For this reason, in the final section of the chapter I contrast the pursuit of victimized citizenship with the diasporic movement for historical reparations. By doing this, I explore the possibilities of moving from the narrow recognition of the contextual victimization of black people (as a result of the war) to a more expansive demand for historical redress. While relatively small and not yet very visible, the movement for historical reparations has gained some ground in Colombia in recent years, adding to the historical pursuit of citizenship—from which black Colombians have so systematically been excluded—a more diasporic focus on the necessary redress of humanity's historical debt to Afro-descendants.[7]

CONVERGENCE: FROM MURK TO SYSTEMATIZATION

> If terror thrives on the production of epistemic murk and
> metamorphosis, it nevertheless requires the hermeneutic violence
> that creates feeble fictions in the guise of realism, objectivity, and
> the like, flattening contradiction and systematizing chaos.
> —*Taussig (1987, 132)*

Isaías

As a cop in the mid-1980s, Isaías patrolled banana plantations in the Urabá region of northwestern Colombia. He evicted squatters who settled in private plantations and "neutralized" union activists who stirred rebellion in the area. Located in a high-traffic trade area, he made additional income by cooperating in contraband circles that imported arms and exported the usual illicit merchandise from Colombia. After a few years of enjoying success, however, one of his commanding officers demanded a portion of his contraband profits, and when Isaías refused to comply, the commander retaliated by accusing him of murder. At that time, Isaías abandoned the police force and went back to his hometown of Urrao in northwestern Colombia to start a new life.

With a high school degree, Isaías quickly secured a job as a teacher in a village distant from Urrao's municipal center. For four years he taught first to fifth graders in the mornings and tended to his farm and cattle in the afternoons. He went into town occasionally to buy household items and collect his pay. After some months, he befriended some *guerrilleros* who began stopping by his place periodically to stock up on food items, but this closeness soon proved troublesome.

Because of his travel patterns—from his farm to the municipal center and back—his background as a cop, and his constant communication with *guerrilleros*, it was not long before he was accused of being an army informant and once again had to flee. To escape, he walked through the wilderness for two days, eventually reaching Medellín. But after a year there, he couldn't shake the feeling of being constantly hounded, so he moved to Bogotá, where he could better hide from his enemies. By the time I met him in 2006, Isaías had settled in Bogotá and was serving as president of the local chapter of the

Association for Displaced Afro-Colombians, AFRODES, the first organization of black IDPs in Colombia.

Wilson

When he was in his late teens, Wilson moved in with a young woman and began to work to sustain his new household. His father-in-law gave him and his common-law wife a small plot of land, and her uncles taught him how to grow coca. At first, he earned a steady income selling unprocessed leaves in bulk, but after a few years, his plot was aerially fumigated by the government and he lost his harvest. Although he swore never to cultivate coca again, economic hardship soon compelled him to replant. By that time, paramilitary groups were routinely present in his hometown of Cajapí, in the southwestern department of Nariño. In this area, local *campesinos* were often intimidated into entering into risky economic relationships with paramilitary groups. At first, paramilitary groups taught *campesinos* how to process coca paste and sold them the necessary chemicals at low cost. Over time, however, they would establish a monopoly over a given area by both controlling prices and using violence to prevent other buyers from entering. Thus, although *campesinos* might initially see an increase in their marginal profit, they would soon find themselves entangled in dangerous and coercive arrangements that they couldn't get out of. For Wilson, as for many others *campesinos* who participated in the coca economy, the bonanza was short-lived and very costly in the end. Soon after Wilson extended his plots and began cultivating his father-in-law's farm with coca as well, President Uribe implemented his drug eradication program. The area was repeatedly fumigated, and Wilson was again left empty-handed.

When she heard of his dire situation, Wilson's oldest sister, who had worked as a domestic worker in Bogotá for nearly twenty years, offered to pay for his bus fare to the city. Aided by his sister, who was deeply knowledgeable of the humanitarian aid system, Wilson managed to navigate the bureaucratic nightmare of acquiring official IDP status, which entitled him to a three-month stipend to pay for food and rent and a small lump-sum transfer to set up a small business in Bogotá.[8]

Florinda

Although she was born in Munguidó, Chocó, Florinda lived there only until she was thirteen years old, when one of her uncles took her away to work as a domestic servant in Medellín. At that point she embarked on what she described as a thirty-year-long odyssey of working and traveling all over the country. After two decades of cleaning homes and supporting three children, she got tired of the low pay and indignant conditions of domestic work. So when Beatriz, a distant relative of hers, offered to lend her the money to get to Bogotá, she didn't hesitate to leave.

Upon her arrival in Bogotá, Florinda stayed with Beatriz for a few months while she found her way around. She tried to make a living selling trash bags at traffic lights in the wealthy parts of the city, but she had a difficult time staying afloat. Although she knew that there was a mechanism to apply for IDP status to receive humanitarian aid, she didn't immediately do so. After some time trying to make ends meet, she reconsidered:

> Ever since I first arrived Beatriz started telling me that I should testify [as an IDP], but she wouldn't tell me how to do it and I was afraid that I wouldn't sound convincing. People had told me that you had to tell the same story four times in four different places to four different people and I was afraid I'd get caught, so I wouldn't go. But then one day I resolved to do it.
>
> There were four of us [who testified together]. I was given one hundred thousand pesos [at the time, roughly US$50] in coupons to shop for groceries. I said that I came from Chocó and that I had arrived on March 24. I testified two years after I arrived. And I told them that it was because of the war.

The life stories of these three people have very little in common. But although the trajectories that they have followed before arriving in Bogotá are profoundly dissimilar, all of them have officially become *afro-desplazados*. In addition to physically converging in Cazucá, they have all adopted identities as black IDPs vis-à-vis the Colombian state and aid organizations. This category, simultaneously suggesting racialization and victimization as a result of Colombia's civil war, flattens the complexity of their experiences. It is, in Taussig's (1987) words, "a feeble fiction" that attempts to systematize chaos by eliding the murky contradictions produced by the terror of war. And yet these fictions are highly productive. In the interactions between the state and nongovernmental agencies that promote them, and the aid recipients who adopt them, categories such as *afro-desplazado* actively reorganize the very reality they appear to describe.

My intent in this section is to analyze the discursive convergence that has made the *afro-desplazado* and other racialized victims visible. I examine the process through which disparate experiences such as those of Isaías, Wilson, and Florinda are flattened and circulated as analogous stories of racialized war victimization. In doing so, I identify two discursive apparatuses that have recently become entangled in unexpected ways in Colombia: the politics of war victimization and state multiculturalism. The former produces "victimized or "at risk" subjects with rights to special protection, whereas the latter bestows special rights upon those who successfully make claims to cultural difference. This convergence is heir to an older articulation, which Stavenhagen (2009) remarked on when writing about indigenous populations across Latin America. In the context of the early 2000s, Stavenhagen noted that the language of human rights had become the avenue par excellence for ethnic and racial redress. In writing about the Wayuu indigenous population in Colombia, Pablo Jaramillo (2014) builds on Stavenhagen's observation to note a very similar convergence of human and ethnic rights discourses. But because in Colombia the language of human rights has become inextricably linked to the war, this phenomenon has its particularities. Namely, the magnitude of the war and the centrality of multicultural reforms have created a situation in which claims to war victimization become the primary route for many indigenous people and Afro-Colombians to attain citizenship rights.

This convergence has had two contradictory effects. On the one hand, as I show in chapter 2, it has helped strengthen black consciousness and political organization by creating links of racial solidarity among people who may not have otherwise seen their lives as different expressions of the same mechanisms of exclusion and discrimination. In other words, had it not been for the very category *afro-desplazado*, Isaías, Wilson, and Florinda may have never identified as part of a collective and collaborated as allies in the same cause.[9] At the same time, this convergence carries with it a danger of creating a narrow association between black suffering and the armed conflict rather than with the pervasive structures of systematic racism in Colombia. This danger is particularly present within state institutions, which create and disseminate flat categories to implement quick responses to crisis. In the end, the notion of *afro-desplazado*, as utilized by state and international humanitarian aid institutions, may hide more than it elucidates. It hides multiple forms of black suffering that precede and perhaps converge with the armed conflict but are not exclusively tied to it. Thus, it makes a continuous and structural situation of discrimination and exclusion appear as a temporary anomaly, which will necessarily be resolved with the end of the war. In addition, it establishes a perverse hierarchy that makes visible and legitimates some forms of black suffering—that of war victims—as worthy of immediate redress, while continuing to minimize or entirely silence the seemingly unremarkable suffering of those who are systematically denied their rights by virtue of being black.

State Multiculturalism

In the 1990s, Colombia passed one of the most comprehensive sets of multicultural reforms in Latin America. This resulted from the convergence of two major and seemingly unrelated processes. On the one hand, a global wave of struggles by indigenous people was winning recognition of a variety of rights that were redefining homogeneous notions of culture and citizenship. On the other hand, the Colombian state was undergoing a process of reform to restore its legitimacy in the eyes of its citizenry. The 1980s had seen the state's ability to maintain order eclipsed by the insurgencies of leftist guerrilla groups and the growing power of armed drug cartels. By the 1990s, a full-scale, open counterinsurgency war by Colombia's armed forces, along with a "dirty war" of extrajudicial killings and disappearances by paramilitary groups, had not only failed to restore order but also further alienated large sections of the population. It was then that Colombia's ruling circles, while continuing their war, also turned to reform to try to restore order. In response to this crisis of governance, a student-led group of liberal reform seekers called for a constituent assembly in the hopes that a new Magna Carta would breathe democratic life into Colombia. What followed was a process in which members of traditional and new political parties as well as representatives from previously marginalized sectors of civil society—including indigenous and Afro-Colombian populations—were invited to participate in the writing of the 1991 constitution.

The debates and negotiations surrounding the inclusion of multicultural rights for indigenous and Afro-descendant people in the new constitution have been well documented (Agudelo 2005; Bocarejo 2008; Gros 2000; Van Cott 2000b), and I do not intend to reproduce them here. The proposition that black people were members of a culturally distinct collective—hence the term *Black Communities*—was fiercely debated both within the constituent assembly and among groups of Afro-Colombian activists. In the end, the notion of black ethnic difference gained sufficient traction to be written into law—Law 70—and over the past thirty years it has become profoundly entrenched within the state apparatus and as a definition in the common sense of blackness among Colombians—both black and nonblack (Paschel 2010). This process, which Restrepo (2013) refers to as the ethnicization of blackness, was basically modeled on the indigenous movement's precedents of mobilization, whose claims to special rights were premised on possessing a culture distinct from the dominant Euro-*mestizo* one.

Unlike indigenous people, however, Afro-descendants could not make a claim to autochthony, nor did they possess some of the characteristics that unequivocally signal a group as a *pueblo* or nation (e.g., language). Instead, the basis of their claim to ethnic difference hinged on the documentation of Black Communities' "traditional production practices" in the predominantly rural region of the Pacific Basin. Within the law, traditional production practices were defined as "the techniques and activities of agriculture, mining, forest extraction, cattle farming, hunting, fishing, and natural product gathering in general that black communities have customarily used for the conservation of life and sustainable development" (Congreso de Colombia 1993). As a result of this process, blackness as ethnic difference became territorialized (Ng'weno 2007).

A lot can be said about the political risks and opportunities of tethering blackness to territoriality (Cárdenas 2012a, 2012c). But for now, I simply emphasize that the ethnicization of blackness resulted in the further entrenchment of Colombia's racialized geographies of difference. For those unfamiliar with Colombia, it bears noting that dominant imaginaries of the nation (re) produce the idea that Colombia is a nation of regions, which are profoundly distinct from one another geographically, culturally, historically, and racially (Appelbaum 2003; Arias Vanegas 2005). Although the taxonomy of regions has changed over time and is certainly contested and unstable, the Pacific has generally been constructed as Colombia's paradigmatic black region (Restrepo 2013; Wade 2000). Law 70, its multicultural recognition, and attendant discourses and institutions thus solidified an already-prevalent idea that blackness and black people in Colombia originate and belong in certain places—and not others.

It is important to note that multiculturalism isn't confined to the state apparatus and that we could certainly speak of "multiculturalisms from below" (Wade 2005). For example, much of the organizing by Black Communities against logging companies, shrimping farms, and other threats to their territorial autonomy in the 1980s started as grassroots initiatives (Asher 2009; Escobar 2008). And yet as I've shown elsewhere, when ethnic recognition became official, the convergence of state multiculturalism with "green capitalism" often ended up putting Black Communities in a bind (Cárdenas 2012c). On the one hand, ethnic subjects had to prove their worthiness as recipients of multicultural rights by exhibiting "green" values and behaviors. On the other hand, because the fundamental structures of capital remained unchanged, they continued to be subordinate to the interests of big industries, which simply greenwashed their exploitative practices to make them dovetail with the state's new multicultural rules. In the end, this "green multiculturalism" put natural resources in the hands of multicultural subjects while charging them with global environmental responsibility and continuing to place them in disadvantageous relationships with others.[10] Today, black people in the Pacific and beyond both utilize and challenge the borders of multicultural rights to wage numerous battles, including urban organizing against violence and resistance to new waves of extractivism. Despite this diversity of multiculturalisms, in this chapter, my focus is on state multiculturalism—its agents, institutions, devices, and effects.

Politics of War Victimization

Colombia's politics of war victimization are made manifest in a whole set of representations, institutions, and practices that define who is a victim and therefore a legitimate recipient of special rights such as state reparations, protection, and humanitarian aid. This discursive formation saturates nearly every level of Colombian politics, and it has intensified in the context of the peace accords signed in 2016 that require that the government establish and carry out clear mechanisms for victims' reparations. Although the politics of war victimization are a product of the national conjuncture, their emergence has been enabled by a complex set of circumstances and actors that exceed the Colombian nation-state. This discursive formation spans the realm of international human rights and involves governmental and civil society organizations from both within and outside of Colombia.

The politics of victimization are an attempt by government institutions and NGOs to rationalize the epistemic murk created by the extreme violence of war. The seemingly transparent definition of IDPs as "individuals who have been forced to abandon their homes, or habitual economic activities because their lives, security, or freedom has been threatened by violence" (Aparicio 2010, 25) is a construct that is employed to make sense of a nearly senseless scenario. As such, the essential separation of who is a victim (and by extension, who is a victimizer) is superimposed on a complex landscape of violent encounters in which such clear-cut distinctions are not always possible. This is evidenced by the diversity of "displacement stories" that I opened with in this section. In the end, what these displacement stories have in common is the fact that they have been actively constructed—both by their protagonists and by others—as narratives of *afro-desplazados*.

The categories of war victim, in general, and IDP, in particular, are fairly recent constructs that are used to describe a very unruly set of circumstances. More to the point, the designation of particular events as "violence" and therefore officially recognized as "legitimate" causes of "forced displacement" is complicated by at least two factors. On the one hand, no hard lines exist between the different reasons that motivate people to move. Take Wilson and his story of coca cultivation, fumigation, and involvement with armed actors. Is his an economic migration, or is he a victim of paramilitary violence? Should the legitimacy of his IDP status be called into question because he was involved in illicit activity? Clearly, the lines that separate forced migration from chosen migration, and victim of violence from perpetrator of violence, can be quite blurry.

On the other hand, there is the issue of historical continuity. In Colombia, the forced movement of people as a result of armed combat, intimidation, and other threats can be traced at least as far back as the period known as La Violencia, which historians date to 1948. Of course, the broader history of internal migration in Colombia stretches far before that and includes causes that would today be classified as both violent and nonviolent. As I outline in detail in chapter 1, the very people who became members of "Black Communities" in the 1990s and *afro-desplazados* soon after, had been involved in long-standing practices of mobility both within the Pacific and to other regions in Colombia and beyond (Hoffmann 2007; Almario 2002). But before the 1990s, these itinerant groups of people had never been referred to as IDPs, nor had they been folded into the broader category of victims. The IDP is therefore a product of a discursive shift, which I trace here. It is meant to separate those who fled the armed conflict from other itinerants (e.g., economic migrants) and to signal the emergence of an allegedly new problem in the historical and geographic continuum of human mobility.

The International Context of Humanitarianism

Juan Ricardo Aparicio's (2010) analysis of the emergence of the IDP is a useful point of departure to understand the production of racialized victims in Colombia. Following a Foucauldian approach, Aparicio historicizes the figure of the IDP to highlight both its continuities with prior discursive formations (e.g., that of the refugee) and its emergence as a new disciplinary regime that produces particular truth effects. He traces its conditions of possibility to the Enlightenment and the Declaration of the Rights of Man, which were enshrined in numerous treaties and declarations that designated the state as the guardian and guarantor of these rights. Following Hannah Arendt (1951) and Lippert (1999), he then identifies the period after World War I and the "impressive movement of people between states" (Aparicio 2010, 19, my translation) that was spurred by the war as the critical point of inflection at which refugees became thinkable as people who were experiencing a distinctive type of victimization. At this time, a whole "series of programs, technologies and apparatuses emerged . . . to respond to this new problem" (Aparicio 2010, 19). Aparicio notes that the postwar period brought about a significant reorganization of the Enlightenment ideas that produced the configuration of nation-state, sovereignty, citizenship. Namely, at this time states were deemed necessary but insufficient guarantors of human rights, a deficiency that justified the creation of a robust international apparatus of human rights institutions such as the League of Nations, which later became the United Nations.

Aparicio identifies the convergence of international discourses of development and humanitarianism as the final turning point that enabled the emergence of the IDP as we know it. He shows that in the midst of the Cold War, there was a "growing consensus that supported the intervention of Western countries in the internal affairs of the developing world" (Aparicio 2010, 23), which laid the groundwork for a new kind of humanitarianism that combined aid to victims and at-risk populations with the promotion of development projects. Two logics guided this convergence, which he terms *interventionist humanitarianism*. First, that emergency aid was an insufficient strategy to improve the conditions of victims in the long run. And second, that states often acted against their citizens' best interests. This last argument went hand in hand with a reconfiguration of Westphalian notions of sovereignty that depicted (mostly) Third World states as "failed" and represented violence in the Global South as if it were disarticulated from global inequalities and ongoing processes of colonialism.

The Stabilization of the Colombian Victim

In Colombia, the Social Solidarity Network (Red de Solidaridad Social, or RSS) was launched in 1994 as an initiative of the Office of the President with the announced aim of attending to the needs of the poorest and most vulnerable populations in Colombia and overseeing their inclusion in state-run programs meant to alleviate poverty.[11] The RSS's creation coincided with a critical turning point in the war that was marked by the institutionalization of a nationwide paramilitary force—the Autodefensas Unidas de Colombia (AUC)—that became infamous for its brutal displays of violence, which remain mostly unpunished to date. At that time, the number of people who were caught in the crossfire between guerrillas, the army, and the AUC skyrocketed, generating alarming waves of mass rural-urban exoduses. In Bogotá, which quickly became the largest recipient of *desplazados*, the city government managed the situation in an ad hoc manner that made use of the institutions that had been designed to deal with other emergency situations such as natural disasters. Thus, the large numbers of people who were fleeing the escalated violence of their rural homes were incorporated, by default, into the institutional framework that served "vulnerable population groups" under the RSS.

By 1997, this situation, which had remained unnamed, was gaining greater visibility worldwide. Following two international conferences that were held in Norway and Guatemala in the late 1980s to discuss the plight of refugees, returnees, and displaced persons in southern Africa and Central America respectively, the United Nations' Human Rights Council urged the secretary-general to examine whether these populations' rights were being protected. In response, in 1991 the United Nations undertook the first world-wide evaluation of the situation and produced a comprehensive report on displaced persons. With this report, the United Nations began to draw the contours of a new global subject: the IDP (Aparicio 2010, 25).

Particularly noteworthy is the fact that the "IDP" category emerged simultaneously as a global and national phenomenon in Colombia. On one hand, the United Nations needed evidence from around the world to effectively claim that a "new" humanitarian crisis was underway, while the Colombian government needed the United Nations' new category to label the problem at home to garner the international funds necessary to address it. The two most obvious manifestations of this coconstitutive process were the passage of Law 387 in 1997, which became known as the Ley de Desplazados (Displaced Persons' Law), and the establishment of the first office of the UN High Commissioner for Refugees (UNHCR) in Colombia in 1998.[12] The law defined the IDP as an object of special state protection and mandated the creation of a centralized information system that collected data on IDPs nationwide (Sistema de Información de Población Desplazada, or SIPOD) and a system of government agencies to oversee the implementation of aid programs for IDPs (Sistema Nacional de Atención Integral a la Población Desplazada, or SNAIPD) (Almario 2004). The establishment of the UNHCR office in Bogotá, on the other hand, marked Colombia's recognition as a legitimate recipient of international aid monies to remedy forced displacement. Although by this point a legislative framework that dealt directly with IDPs had been established, there was a significant gap in implementation, and meanwhile, IDPs were still in need of urgent solutions. So in 2000, the RSS was designated by presidential decree as the default government agency responsible for IDPs. Thus, over the following five years, the problem of "vulnerable populations" and "IDPs" were managed together with the resources and institutional frameworks that were originally established to alleviate poverty.

By 2005, all the makeshift information systems and programs that had sprouted over time and were scattered across the state apparatus were consolidated under a single government agency, Acción Social. The creation of Acción Social is noteworthy for two reasons. First, because it was a gigantic government agency that sat directly under the Office of the Vice President, it enjoyed a great deal of discretionary decision-making power. And second, because it brought two seemingly unrelated government agencies together: the RSS, and the agency in charge of receiving and disbursing international aid moneys, the Colombian Agency for International Cooperation (Agencia Colombiana de Cooperación Internacional). As such, it is a clear example of what Aparicio identifies as a new kind of humanitarianism, which merged the discourses of human rights and development into a single interventionist apparatus. Together, these developments signal the emergence of the IDP as a distinct and recognizable subject of special rights in Colombia.

Once these systems were in place, the judiciary played a key role in further cementing the *desplazado* as a new political subject. Specifically, in 2004, the Constitutional Court issued a groundbreaking ruling that affirmed that the state of affairs for IDPs in Colombia was unconstitutional and urged all the newly formed government institutions to improve their information and service provision systems for *desplazados*.[13] The Constitutional Court was also amenable to a perseverant group of Afro-Colombian organizations—among them AFRODES and PCN—who had been insisting for some time that programs for IDPs were in dire need of an ethnicity-specific focus. Thus, at the activists' behest, the court held a public hearing in 2007 in which representatives from twenty-two black organizations presented a convincing argument about the urgent need to develop differential public policies for displaced Afro-Colombians. The result of this hearing was the court's 2009 passage of a decree (Auto 005), which mandated specific government offices to design and implement ethnicity-specific actions for displaced Afro-Colombians, as described in chapter 2.

Another major milestone in the legal apparatus surrounding war victims was the passage of Law 1448 in 2011, which became known as the Victims' Law. Following the law, the government established a new office to centralize services for victims, which is known as La Unidad de Víctimas.[14] This office coordinates information systems as well as state-led initiatives to identify war victims and provide them with aid and reparations. The office sits within the Departamento de Prosperidad Social, which was formerly Acción Social. Then, after the signing of the peace accords in 2016, a whole new set of institutions emerged to manage the so-called transition to peace. The main transformation in the management of victims following the peace accords was the shift toward a wholistic system (*sistema integral*), which attempted to coordinate a number of initiatives and institutions that dealt with different aspects of victims' experiences. This included new state apparatuses such as a truth commission, a special justice system, and an office dedicated to finding the disappeared, which were added to the existing initiatives to oversee land restitution and victims' reparations.

This is by no means an exhaustive description of all the laws, institutions, and programs that have mushroomed in the past twenty-five years to deal with the problem of IDPs. But it is a sketch that illustrates the overall processes and allows me to draw some conclusions. First, it is evident that the politics of war victimization stand at a point of convergence between development projects and human rights discourses. Second, more than a transition that began with aid programs for vulnerable population groups and was transformed into assistance and development projects for victims, the interplay of the two categories has amounted to a de facto conflation. This conflation is evident in the fact that in Colombia there is a significant overlap in the institutions that serve the two and imagine them as similar objects of special protection.[15] The third observation is the central object of analysis in this chapter. Namely, that the international regime of human rights, which parses out victims of Colombia's war, has become entangled with the logic of state multiculturalism, which extends differential citizenship rights to ethnic populations in Colombia. When they converge—in defining the figure of the *afro-desplazado*, for example—they amount to a process that I describe as the victimization of blackness.

VICTIMIZATION OF BLACKNESS

The process of making oneself and others into *afro-desplazados* involves a give-and-take on many registers. At some moments, *afro-desplazados* like other IDPs are called on to embody vulnerability and present themselves as suitable recipients of aid, while at others they are called on to perform acceptable forms of cultural difference. But in all these cases, there is a simultaneous process of victimization and ethno-racial othering taking place. That is, in a single breath *afro-desplazados* are presented as black and as victims, and this confluence is what makes them visible, sometimes hypervisible, as political subjects. The great attention that the politics of victimization receives in Colombia has magnified war victims in the national imaginary, and this attention has been deepened by the work of Colombia's best-known black organizations, who have increasingly shifted their attention to human rights law as a strategy to claim differential war reparations for Afro-Colombians (see chapter 2). Although it is true that the attention to victimization does not exhaust all political manifestations of blackness, its strength and ubiquity in Colombia today merit attention. In what follows, I offer an analysis of the possibilities and limitations of pursuing a black politics anchored in the recognition of victimization.

Victimized Citizenship

> Resign yourself to your color the way I got used to my stump;
> we're both victims.
> —Home of the Brave *(1949 film directed by Mark Robson)*

The most obvious consequence of the victimization of blackness is that it has provided some of the most disenfranchised members of Colombian society with an effective avenue for accessing some of the basic rights of citizenship that they should have enjoyed all along. But this is a very particular kind of citizenship—victimized ethno-racial citizenship. Under this logic, as the anthropologist Pablo Jaramillo (2014, 156) notes in his work with the indigenous Wayuu in northeastern Colombia, "to outline a given [indigenous] population or person as a subject of rights, they must be conceived as a collection of vulnerabilities that makes them the object of the state's politics of care and development".

According to Jaramillo, victimized citizenship has several consequences. First, because victims have to produce themselves as defenseless creatures in dire need of state intervention, that is, as objects of care, they exercise an ambiguous kind of agency that only partly constitutes them as subjects. They are subjects only insofar as they can constitute themselves as objects. Second, at those critical moments when victimized citizenship is exercised—for example, when IDPs claim state benefits—humanitarian care and war reparations tend to be conflated with full enfranchisement and political inclusion. For example, as an IDP receives aid for emergency medical treatment at their point of arrival, these services may stand in lieu of their more consistent access to health services, which are guaranteed by the state to all citizens. Jaramillo argues that this conflation muddles the difference between being a victim and being a citizen more broadly. Third, Jaramillo notes that the articulation of multiculturalism with victimized citizenship in Colombia has deepened the tendency for the state to monopolize the implementation of multicultural politics (see also Van Cott, 2000). This has meant that victims, particularly those who belong to the ethnic groups recognized by official multiculturalism, have been further folded into the state apparatus through the numerous points of contact they have with government institutions. In fact, Jaramillo finds that victimization has become the most common means whereby indigenous Wayuus are included as citizens, and that this citizenship is always-already ethnicized and racialized.

Although Jaramillo's fieldwork took place in a different context than mine—among indigenous populations in the northeastern Guajira region—his findings resonate with my own. However, the differences between the indigenous and black cases merit discussion. Most important, the historical construction of indigenous and black people as victims in Latin America has profound differences. Whereas indigenous peoples have been recognized as victims since colonial times (see de Las Casas 1552), the descendants of slaves did not and have not yet received an analogous official recognition.[16] This means not that Afro-descendants have not sought out this recognition for centuries, but that the nation-states of which Afro-descendants became citizens, have not been amenable to these claims[17].

A brief clarification of my usage of the term *victimization* is warranted here. Most concretely, victimization refers to acts of violence that produce death, destruction, and wounds, but it can also be used to refer to the process of attributing or appropriating the category of victim. Clearly, both indigenous and black people in Latin America have been victimized in the first sense of the word and I am not interested in comparing their wounds. Rather, my interest is in the comparative recognition of the two population groups as historically victimized. That is, in the second meaning of the term. In this sense, it is clear that blackness in Colombia has not been defined in victimized terms from a *longue durée* historical perspective.[18]

As the logics of multiculturalism became conjoined to those of victimization politics, a new kind of Afro-Colombian subject—the *afro-desplazado* or *afro-víctima* more broadly—emerged. The discourses and technologies employed in state programs for war victims (namely IDPs)—such as emergency aid, psychosocial therapy, and socioeconomic stabilization, to name a few—created a seemingly inherent link between blackness and vulnerability. I argue that if these programs are not designed and put in practice in such a way that makes their contextual character clear, stressing the contingency of Afro-Colombians' vulnerability, the link between blackness and vulnerability can become dehistoricized and naturalized.

This dehistoricization can shift the logic of multicultural recognition and rights in dangerous ways. Instead of recognizing Afro-Colombians' cultural difference as the foundation for their claim to special rights, Afro-Colombians would be deemed deserving beneficiaries of the state's largesse by virtue of their *current* misfortune as victims of the war. This shift has a worrying temporality effect. Unlike the claim to cultural difference, which has a self-reproducing logic, the denunciation of misfortune has a cross-sectional temporality. On the one hand, because it focuses on current victimization and the need to eradicate it, this victimized brand of multicultural recognition employs a self-annihilating logic that is similar to that of affirmative action. In other words, it doesn't project into the future; it is designed to have a finite life. But unlike affirmative action, it does not make explicit links between contemporary vulnerability and historical victimization; therefore, it doesn't project back to the historical past either. Although it creates a link between vulnerability and blackness, the relationship between the two is seen more as an unexplainable calamity than a historical continuity.

Overall, the intersection of the politics of victimization and state multiculturalism has narrowed the political field within which Afro-Colombians can claim differential rights. It has prioritized the claims of "victimized" or "at risk" Afro-Colombians to such an extreme that ethnic claims that do not clearly intersect with victimization politics can become secondary or inaudible to the state. Although this has favored a good number of people in truly dire conditions, the heightened preoccupation with "victimized" or "at risk" Afro-Colombians often comes at the expense of attending to other, more structural demands. The result has been that while the terms of recognition expand on one end, they contract on the other in a zero-sum game that pits Afro-Colombians against one another or compels them to do everything possible to construe themselves as "victimized" or "at risk," in an effort to make visible injustices that are more historical than conjunctural.

While the armed conflict has framed the current articulation of black victimization within a narrow historical period, a broader pursuit of reparations for slavery and the transatlantic slave trade is not entirely impossible. Unsurprisingly, the former has been wholeheartedly embraced by the state and humanitarian aid organizations, whereas the latter has been met with resistance or indifference. Nonetheless, a persistent and visionary group of black activists continues to make slow, steady progress in this pursuit by moving outside the Colombian state and into more diasporic networks of influence. In the rest of this chapter, I outline the difficulties and promises of mobilizing a more comprehensive recognition of black victimization into a global movement for historical reparations.

TOWARD HISTORICAL REPARATIONS

In 2005, the Uribe administration passed Law 975, known as the Peace and Justice Law. Although its primary objective was the demobilization of armed groups (mainly paramilitaries), the law also appointed a committee (the Comisión Nacional de Reparación y Reconciliación, or CNRR) that was charged with managing reparations for victims of the war. Soon after the CNRR was formed, an Afro-Colombian working group was established within it. Its purpose, as stated by one of its coordinators, was to draft a document with general guidelines on how to adequately administer reparations for ethnic groups, which under Colombia's multicultural constitution are considered collective subjects of rights. The working group was organized by a young anthropologist and called on well-known Afro-Colombian activists and academics as well as state officials to participate. The group convened on several occasions and held a few workshops with civil society organizations, but within a matter of three months it completely disbanded.

When I interviewed some of its members a few years later, they expressed disappointment at what they saw as a missed opportunity to engage in a discussion about historical reparations for Afro-descendants. The working group, situated at the intersection of victimization politics and multicultural rights, attempted to raise the issue of historical reparations for Afro-descendants by resorting to two arguments. The more radical members of the group argued that the transatlantic slave trade was a crime against humanity commensurate with those committed by contemporary armed groups and recognized by international law. As such, the descendants of its victims deserved reparations. Their suggestion that the notion of war crime should be expanded to include slavery, however, was easily overturned by referring strictly to the law, which circumscribed the CNRR's mission to victims of the armed conflict. The officials' response was that the law applied only to victims of current crimes, and a recognition of the compounded victimization of descendants of slaves simply had no place in it. The second and more conservative approach was to make the continuities between present and past victimizations of Afro-descendants explicit. The working group's coordinator described this more indirect strategy in the following way:

> When one begins to discuss the issue and understands that the fact that black people on the Pacific have been disproportionately affected by the war is in part due to state negligence, to living in a marginalized region with very low socioeconomic indicators . . . one can say that this is a result of history. It is because of the place that black people have occupied, and continue to occupy, in the formation of the nation, and that this is a result of their enslavement. . . . Then we understand that the current victimization of Afro-Colombians derives from past victimizations and that the two cannot be separated.

When I spoke to the members of the working group four years after the group's dissolution, all that remained of their efforts was a file with meeting reports. Tellingly, one of the disgruntled academics who participated in it said that the CNRR's director had referred to their attempt to expand the notion of victim as a point of "epistemic rupture," simply too radical to contemplate.

Although the CNRR was a potential site for the productive articulation of diasporic anti-racism and victimization politics, the attempt to expand the political scope within which the victimization of blackness could be mobilized utterly failed. The limits of the notion of victim established by the Peace and Justice Law simply did not allow for a notion of black victimization with historical depth to fully crystallize. Although it was possible to contemplate victims who happened to be black (or indigenous), the idea that Afro-Colombians were victimized by virtue of being black was unintelligible to the Colombian state. Clearly, the working group had hoped to make explicit the links between contemporary vulnerability and historical victimization to elicit conversations about historical reparations, but its efforts didn't get off the ground. In the end, the CNRR's attempts did in fact create a link between victimization and blackness, but the grid of intelligibility under which it operated made it impossible to see this connection as anything more than an unfortunate calamity.

While the struggle for wartime reparations has been an expedient political strategy in many ways, the claims to redress that they are capable of mobilizing are simply insufficient. When successfully executed, wartime reparations are capable only of restituting the prewar status quo. In fact, that is precisely what they are designed to do. For Afro-Colombians, however, the prewar status quo is still an unfavorable position that does not take stock of the accumulated disadvantage generated by centuries of enslavement and racialized dispossession. As some Afro-Colombian activists fully recognize, only historical reparations can create the conditions for full citizenship and equity.

The Power of Reparations

The arguments supporting historical reparations for the descendants of enslaved people in the Americas are long-standing and powerful (Coates 2014; Walters 2008; Reiter 2018; Franke 2019; Robinson 2001). As Walters (2008) reminds us in his analysis of historical reparations in the United States, the process of arriving at reparations could generate a public discussion of Afro-descendants' rights that is based on the memory of black suffering and its relevance to the present. This would be an important step toward rewriting the dominant historical narratives that have made Afro-descendants invisible and advanced the notion that abolition constituted a sharp break with slavery, allegedly making it entirely a thing of the past. Initiating a conversation around reparations would entail an unearthing of historical memory that would necessitate a rewriting of national histories.

From a more pragmatic perspective, the demand for historical reparations could open up new political avenues for Afro-descendants everywhere. In Colombia, it presents several promising possibilities. Because discussions and initiatives to address historical reparations are mostly taking place in an international political field, their participation in these diasporic networks could offer Afro-Colombian activists an avenue to circumvent the Colombian state and its entrenched deafness on this topic. Second, by shining light on European colonialism and its living legacies in the Americas, the pursuit for historical reparations could significantly interrupt the global narrative that blames entrenched inequality in postcolonial countries solely on their "failed states" and "internal corruption." And finally, in addition to providing a strong moral ground for redress, Afro-Colombian activists may be able to move beyond the symbolic and into a serious discussion about material reparations. In a sense, this confluence of victimization politics and multiculturalism might usher in an unexpected set of political openings.

Historical Precedents

In recent years, the demands for historical reparations for descendants of enslaved Africans have gained greater visibility worldwide. While the demands
themselves are not new, several historical events have reinvigorated their potential to be seriously considered a concrete political project, moving them
from being perceived as fringe items espoused by radicals to being seriously
discussed in mainstream political spaces.[19] This was the case in the 2020 US
presidential election debates and most remarkably, they were brought into the
mainstream political field by Francia Márquez when she was the vice presidential candidate for Pacto Histórico during the 2022 elections in Colombia.

The end of World War II and the reckoning with the aftermath of the
Holocaust spurred many initiatives for reparations for wartime survivors.
From the French government's public recognition of its collaboration with
the Nazi regime to the financial settlements provided by the German government to the State of Israel and to Holocaust survivors in the United States
and funds created by European banks and insurance companies that participated in that genocide, the examples of successful reparations programs are
numerous. In the United States, the 1988 approval of reparations for Japanese
Americans who were held in internment camps during World War II is an
additional example of reparations made successfully to a group victimized
during wartime. Together, these cases stand as important precedents in Afro-
descendants' own unfulfilled pursuit of historical reparations.[20]

In addition to these historical precedents, the global political climate
today presents some openings to further the struggle for historical reparations. In Latin America, the end of the Cold War and the attendant fall of
repressive dictatorships across the region initiated a period of an effervescent
civil society in the 1990s that favored black mobilization at large. Scholars
of this wave of "new social movements" were quick to identify the recognition of multicultural rights as the major political accomplishment for Afro-
descendants during this period (Escobar and Álvarez 1992). While this was an
important success, some scholars have also observed that in Latin America,
Afro-descendants' focus on the pursuit of citizenship rights and national inclusion has derailed them from building a movement for reparations (Araujo
2017). I argue instead that the struggles for differential rights and ethnic

citizenship that have unfolded in Colombia over the past thirty years have incorporated the foundational arguments that can sustain the burgeoning movement for historical reparations today and into the future. While overt demands for historical reparations were not built into the agenda of black organizations in the 1990s and 2000s, Afro-Colombian leaders routinely highlighted the link between contemporary inequalities and the historical legacies of slavery in their pursuit of full citizenship rights. In this sense, they echoed what civil rights activists in the United States had done to lay the groundwork for future movements for symbolic and material redress (Araujo 2017). Thus, rather than seeing struggles for full citizenship as necessarily interfering with claims to historical reparations, I see them as the seeds sown for a future movement.

Parallel to the flourishing of multicultural rights struggles across Latin America, during the late 1990s and 2000s there was a wave of public acknowledgments of the global debt accrued to descendants of slaves. At this time, activists across Europe, Africa, and the Americas called for the construction of monuments, memorials, and museums to honor previously enslaved men and women. These public sites initiated the work of rewriting the dominant historical narrative that had erased or undermined the memory of enslaved people's lives. As Araujo (2017, 157) notes in her transnational history of reparations for slavery, local communities and governments rescued heritage sites and built new monuments to recover these histories in a number of countries, including Senegal, Ghana, Republic of Benin, Brazil, Cuba, Colombia, Venezuela, Jamaica, and the United States. While momentous, it is important to note that these initiatives remained purely symbolic and did not turn into material restitutions like those for survivors of the Holocaust or of American internment of Japanese and Japanese Americans.

Diasporic Dialogues

The United Nations' 2001 Conference against Racism in Durban was a critical event in the ongoing struggle for historical reparations. During preparatory meetings, numerous organizations from across the Americas and Africa discussed reparations for slavery as an important item to address at the conference. In the end, the declaration from Durban did not directly refer to historical reparations. However, the conference provided an opportunity for black activists who had been stressing the historical legacies of slavery to meet and see the connections between their struggles. For the next decade, black activists across Latin America went back to furthering their agendas for full citizenship in their respective countries. In Brazil, the black movement made unprecedented gains during President Lula's two terms. In Ecuador, Bolivia, and several Central American countries, black activists secured a range of multicultural rights for Afro-descendants (Hooker 2005b). And in Colombia, the struggle for collective land titles and cultural rights deepened. While none of these movements made explicit demands for historical reparations during this time, the groundwork for an international movement that articulated smaller, local struggles was being laid.

In 2013, the Caribbean Community (CARICOM), the fifteen-member organization for Caribbean integration, created a reparations commission led by the renowned scholar Sir Hilary Beckles, himself the descendant of enslaved people in Barbados. Following the commission's recommendations, in 2014 a caucus of all CARICOM presidents adopted a ten-point plan that outlined both symbolic and financial reparations for slavery, the slave trade, and the genocide of indigenous populations (CARICOM 2014).[21] A few days after its release, other nations in the Americas publicly endorsed CARICOM's plan, thereby reinvigorating local movements for historical reparations and inaugurating a period of concerted international organizing.[22] For example, less than a month after the plan's release, the Institute of the Black World held a forum in Chicago titled "Revitalizing the Reparations Movement Program." With Sir Hilary Beckles as keynote speaker, the event brought together activists from a number of (mostly US-based) organizations that had been pushing for reparations. Then in 2015, CARICOM's Reparations Commission and the National African American Reparations Commission organized a summit at which delegates of more than twenty countries committed to consolidating a global movement for reparations.[23]

Perhaps the most visible consolidation of this burgeoning global movement can be seen in the United Nations' public recognitions of the need for historical reparations. This was first evident in the 2016 annual report of the UN Working Group of Experts on People of African Descent, where the authors endorsed CARICOM's ten-point plan and emphasized the importance of reparatory justice as a means to challenge structural and institutional racism and Afrophobia today.[24] Then, in a 2019 report to the UN Human Rights Office of the High Commissioner, Tendayi Achiume, UN special rapporteur on racism, stated that "the historic racial injustices of slavery and colonialism . . . remain largely unaccounted for today . . . [and] require restitution, compensation, satisfaction, rehabilitation and guarantees of non-repetition" (Achiume 2019, 4). Sparking conservative backlash, Achiume's report revived the call for more than symbolic redress by stating that "the urgent project of providing reparations for slavery and colonialism requires States not only to fulfil remedial obligations resulting from specific historical wrongful acts, but also to transform contemporary structures of racial injustice, inequality, discrimination and subordination that are the product of centuries of racial machinery built through slavery and colonialism" (Achiume 2019, 4).

Most recently, at an urgent UN debate on racism, which was called in response to the murder of George Floyd at the hands of Minneapolis police officers in June 2020, the UN's human rights chief and former president of Chile, Michelle Bachelet, stated that "behind today's racial violence, systemic racism and discriminatory policing lies the failure to acknowledge and confront the legacy of the slave trade and colonialism." To address this legacy, Bachelet stressed the need to move beyond symbolic recognition by stressing the urgent need to make amends through "formal apologies, truth-telling processes, and reparations in various forms" (AFP 2020). Bachelet's statements are proof that the demands for historical reparations for descendants of enslaved people have acquired significant international visibility in recent years, and that there has been a shift from relatively isolated cases demanding redress from specific governments or corporations to a well-articulated global movement that is legitimated by one of the most respected international arbiters of human rights today, the United Nations. The movement has thus moved from the margins to the center of the global movement for black lives and holds large promise for deep political change in the near future.

From "Epistemic Rupture" to Emergent Possibility

In Colombia, the route to articulate a broader politics of historical reparations has been somewhat circuitous. While black activists at the frontlines of
the struggle for citizenship rights have been highlighting Afro-descendants'
historical disadvantage for decades, they had not articulated clear arguments
for historical reparations until the past fifteen years, in tandem with the war's
intensification. As I have been showing throughout this chapter, the entanglement of victimization politics and multiculturalism narrowed the political
scope of the struggle in many ways. At the same time, the struggle for war
victims' reparations has also broadened over the years, moving from exclusive denunciation of contemporary suffering to the gradual denuding of the
deep historical debt owed to Afro-descendants. While still emergent, this
shift has the potential of expanding the scope of redress, in both temporal
and geographic terms. In contrast with struggles for differentiated citizenship under multiculturalism, which make demands exclusively to the Colombian state, historical reparations expand the onus of reparations to all
those who benefited from the enslavement and forced labor of Africans and
their descendants. Thus, for the proponents of historical reparations, former
European colonizers and their descendants must also assume this responsibility. The global scope of reparations also shifts the role of multilateral
actors (e.g., the United Nations) from protectors of state sovereignty to overseers of accountability—not only from states to their citizens but also from
former colonial powers to current postcolonial states. In the case of Latin
American (and other postcolonial) states, this shift opens up the possibility
of interrupting the deep-seated narrative that explains away violence in the
so-called Third World as a pathology. In Colombia, this could mean that,
rather than understanding political and social violence as a result of a "failed
state" (McLean 2002) or an entrenched "culture of violence" (Waldmann
2007), there can finally be a serious and sustained reckoning with the enduring effects of colonialism. Colonialism and its deep-seated structures—
what Aníbal Quijano has termed "the coloniality of power"—rather than
the misnamed "internal conflict" could then be more clearly identified as
the origin of the contemporary systems of inequality that continue to reap
violence today. Most important, this framing makes clear that an adequate

response to this injustice requires a recognition of the *longue durée* of black victimization and its diasporic dimension.

Mobilizing Diasporic Suffering

Although the experience within Colombia's CNRR in the early 2000s was undoubtedly frustrating for the Afro-Colombian activists who participated in it, the Colombian state's unwillingness or inability to deepen the historical scope of the conversation is unsurprising. The expansion of this scope would provide irrefutable grounds for historical reparations and thereby place a considerable moral and financial burden on a state that is undoubtedly eager to avoid such responsibilities. The visionary activists who have been pushing for historical reparations know this all too well. And while they continue to hold the Colombian state accountable, they are also aware that the state is not the only relevant interlocutor in the pursuit of reparations. In fact, they know that when it comes to mobilizing black victimization for political action, the transnational field of African diasporic politics has proved a much more fruitful ground than the state has.

As I mentioned in the previous section, the most notable instance of this kind of transnational political mobilization was the 2001 Conference against Racial Discrimination in Durban. Durban was a watershed moment in that it made black Colombians visible to others as African diasporic subjects, and in this sense, it facilitated a process of mutual diasporic recognition—between black Colombians and Afro-descendants elsewhere.[25] When they returned to Colombia, conference participants brought back the lessons gathered from their diasporic dialogues abroad. At home, they faced a deep political and humanitarian crisis. In the midst of the bloodiest years of the war, some activists had started to speak out against the armed conflict's disproportionate impact on Black Communities. Organizations that had been focused on multicultural recognition from the state—like PCN—shifted their focus from ethnic and territorial rights to human rights. New organizations—like AFRODES—were also created to attend to the humanitarian crisis that was hitting Afro-Colombians particularly acutely. For the most part, their strategies and claims for redress were directed at the Colombian state, and activists limited their historical scope to the war itself. But for some visionaries, it was clear that the war was not itself the origin of Afro-Colombians' victimization but had exacerbated their vulnerabilities, which were in turn a result of centuries of accumulated disadvantage and marginalization. They understood and clearly articulated that the disproportionately acute violence that Black Communities were facing—forced displacements, disappearances, targeted death threats, community massacres, and armed combat—was the result of long-standing structural conditions. While still few, they pointed to the continuities between Afro-Colombians' contemporary victimization in the war and their historical experiences of racial violence over the course of five hundred years. Thus, in their response to the humanitarian crisis, these activists paved the way for the future pursuit of historical reparations.

In addition to outlining a historical perspective, the activists also understood that in seeking an effective response to Afro-Colombians' heightened victimization they had to expand the discursive field in which they operated. To this end, they substituted the language of ethnic rights with that of international human rights, and they expanded their range of interlocutors to include international actors such as watchdog groups, human rights courts, and US Congress members. This amounted to a significant change in political strategy, where rather than continue negotiating directly with the Colombian state, they rerouted their demands for victims' redress through their newly established international networks. These activists knew that the Colombian government was more likely to respond to their denunciations of human rights violations when the pressure came from abroad, in particular from the United States, which had provided gargantuan sums of direct aid to the Colombian armed forces during the war in the form of Plan Colombia.

While weaving their international networks, Afro-Colombian activists knew that cultivating solidarity across the African diaspora was key. Because they shared a common historical experience of uprooting, enslavement, and disenfranchisement, other Afro-descendants across the diaspora could be critical allies in the burgeoning pursuit for reparations. To do this, it was important not only to sustain diasporic dialogues but also to visibilize the continuing victimization of Afro-descendants in Colombia. One of the clearest examples I have seen of this mobilization of diasporic suffering was in 2010, when Angela Davis first visited Bogotá as the keynote speaker for the

National University's inauguration of its graduate program in gender studies. The idea of inviting such a prominent international representative of global blackness to Colombia was something that Carlos Rosero, founding member of PCN, had contemplated as a concrete possibility ever since I mentioned that she was a faculty member at the university I was attending.[26] When PCN learned that the National University would be covering her international travel costs, they jumped at the opportunity to extend her stay in Colombia so that she could visit key communities in the southern Pacific region.[27] Thus, I worked with PCN to coordinate that visit and was Davis's full-time interpreter during the trip.

Davis's 2010 visit to Colombia came at the height of the armed conflict, and Rosero aptly thought that she could be a key witness and global spokesperson for the ongoing dispossession and victimization of black people in Colombia. For Rosero and other members of PCN's national coordination team, establishing a working relationship with Davis was an opportunity to draw international attention to the heightened victimization of black Colombians, and therefore an expedient way to spur effective political intervention on their behalf. Davis was thought to be an ideal candidate for this work of African diasporic solidarity because she was both well known in Colombia and, in his view, well-positioned to influence political decisions in the United States that would have direct bearing on Black Communities in Colombia.[28]

The news of Davis's presence in Colombia quickly spread, and tensions between PCN and other black organizations immediately surfaced regarding the purpose of her visit and the concrete events she was invited to attend. In Cali, the black student organization Afro-Colombian Collective for Human Rights, Benkos Lives (CADHUBEV), at the local public university UniValle welcomed her with the Black Panther salute and granted her the highest honors given to a visitor by handing her the keys to their institution. They also convened a lunch with the region's black mayors, organized a press conference, and scheduled a public question-and-answer session that was attended by hundreds of people who showed up on campus early on a Sunday morning. But all these events were secondary to PCN's main political objective.

For PCN, the main purpose of Davis's visit to Cali was to hold a closed-door witnessing session in which representatives from various regions in the southern Pacific would describe the horrific victimizations that their people were currently undergoing. For this purpose, PCN summoned more than a dozen community representatives to give firsthand testimonies on the forced displacement, disproportional imprisonment, extreme poverty, political persecution, and various forms of territorial encroachment suffered by black people in Colombia. The session, for which I provided live interpretation, was closely moderated by a member of PCN who had coached each of the community representatives on how to effectively communicate the particular cases of racialized victimization that PCN wanted to evidence. In this way, PCN succeeded in giving Davis a broad sense of the systematic ways in which black people's human rights were being violated in Colombia.

A particularly poignant intervention by a man who had recently been displaced from López de Micay stood out. He introduced himself as a traditional healer and a local leader in his community. After describing the political persecution of which he was a target, his voice broke and he declared: "We live the worst lives of all human beings on Earth. This government fumigated us people, not crops. We, the leaders of López de Micay, are not being persecuted by the *guerrilla*, but by the government. I have been displaced twice. If you could see where I'm sleeping now, you would surely weep. *Nobody cares for me, nobody protects me*, and I can't give public declarations." Davis listened attentively and diligently took note of the details that each of the testifiers relayed. Then the meeting ended abruptly, and she was escorted next door for the public question-and-answer session organized by CADHUBEV.

If ever I have witnessed a call to transnational racial solidarity based on the recognition of ongoing (and implicitly historical) victimization, this was it. Although there was no explicit mention of racial sameness between Davis and the testifiers, everything about the meeting suggested that this was implicitly understood by everyone.[29] In addition, the tone of confidentiality in which the meeting was held to guarantee anonymity and enable open denunciations of the Colombian state made it clear that PCN's intent was to establish international solidarity networks that bypassed national governments. The line of sameness that PCN was tapping into and that it hoped Davis would in turn recognize was based on the common objective to denounce black victimization—but one framed not by the particularities of the Colombian state and its violent history of civil war but rather by a mutual awareness of a diasporic legacy of suffering.

Shortly after Davis's departure, I and other international collaborators worked with PCN on an agenda for further solidarity actions that she could help steer in the United States. These included items such as "denouncing the militarization and violation of human rights taking place on black ancestral territories" and "writing to the President of Colombia, the US Congress and US embassy in Bogotá to denounce the systematic violation of Black Communities' rights." To be fair, Davis did not continue to play a central role in any of these actions going forward. However, her trip solidified a burgeoning friendship with Francia Márquez, the environmental activist who was elected vice president in 2022, and over the years, Davis made several key interventions in her support. This was the case in 2014, when she sent a video supporting the black women's march that Francia led from her community to the capital to demand the government's response to illegal encroachment on their territories. Davis also issued a statement condemning the armed attack that Francia and her *compañeros* from PCN suffered in May 2019. And most recently, Davis held an open dialogue with Francia during her precampaign for the presidency in 2021. Thus, while still a clear relationship of diasporic solidarity, the focus shifted from an emphasis on victimization to a cultivation of joint struggle.

AN EMERGENT MOVEMENT

Because they are couched in an awareness of the deep historical debt that is owed to the descendants of enslaved Africans, many of the struggles advanced by major Afro-Colombian organizations like PCN and AFRODES carry with them an implicit demand for historical reparations. For these organizations, everything from the right to ethnic difference and collective territories to the pursuit of differential reparations for the war is couched in a vision of justice that is deep and structural. While attending to the urgency of the moment, some of the organizations and activists that participate in these struggles have also sought more structural measures intended to undo historical patterns of violence against Afro-descendants. In this sense, the main items on the political agendas of these major black organizations have deep resonances with the principles of historical reparations. However, until very recently, these connections remained implicit. It is only in the past twenty years, and in great part due to the articulation of multiculturalism and victimization discourses that I have outlined throughout this chapter, that these demands have gradually become explicit.

In an unexpected historical turn, the intensification of the armed conflict in the late 1990s and early 2000s gave black activists in Colombia a particularly insightful analysis of their political situation writ large. As the fallout from the war, which came hand in hand with the Colombian state's deepening of its neoliberal economic project, fell disproportionally on the backs of indigenous and black Colombians, the ethnic and racial dimensions of Colombia's intractable violence became appallingly clear. In some ways, the war itself also helped establish and strengthen racial solidarities among Afro-Colombians. For example, as I outline in chapter 2, as Afro-Colombians forcefully displaced from various parts of the country organized together as black IDPs, their racial analysis deepened, and they incorporated a more deliberate denunciation of racism into their discourses. In the midst of all this, some black activists developed a particularly acute analysis of the contemporary violence in their communities and began incorporating the explicit language of historical reparations into their agendas. PCN specifically began including discussions of historical reparations in its national assemblies in 2007 and has consistently continued to do so since.

Over the years, PCN has not only maintained discussions of historical reparations firmly on its agenda but has also increased their visibility nationally. The concept of a historical debt to Black Communities has entered mainstream political spaces to a degree that was unimaginable when the CNRR's director dubbed it a point of "epistemic rupture." For example, during his first commemoration of National Afro-Colombian Day in 2011, President Juan Manuel Santos publicly recognized that Colombia "has a debt with its Afro-Colombian population" and he stated that he was committed to "making all efforts to generate change" (WRadio 2011). More than the promise of change, which is an unsurprising instance of pandering, what is salient about his statement is the public recognition of a debt owed to all black people. This isolated statement doesn't amount to much of a political victory, but over the years, the principles and language of reparations have begun to enter mainstream institutional discourses in Colombia, slowly creating more space for a direct articulation of demands for historical reparations. By 2019, for example, PCN spearheaded an open call to create a national reparations commission. Once again, during a commemoration on National Afro-Colombian Day, the Colombian congress held an open hearing with black civil society organizations that reported on the state of Afro-Colombian rights writ large. As Esther Ojulari, who presented PCN's report during the hearing recounted to me, this was an important step toward building a more formalized political process, which PCN followed up with a virtual forum a year later.[30]

During an informal interview with me in early 2021, Ojulari observed that the political opening for the pursuit of reparations had recently cracked open as a result of the changing international context and the mainstreaming of racial justice more broadly, which she described as "suddenly fashionable." Ojulari was referring specifically to the worldwide mobilizations that followed the murder of George Floyd by the Minneapolis police in the summer of 2020. Following the massive street protests, a group of more than six hundred organizations worldwide called for an urgent investigation into police violence, and fifty-four African countries presented a petition to the UNHCR to hold an urgent debate on racism. It was at this forum that the UN human rights chief, Michelle Bachelet, not only acknowledged "the legacy of the slave trade and colonialism" but also stressed the need to "make amends for centuries of violence and discrimination, including through formal apologies, truth-telling processes, and reparations in various forms" (AFP 2020).

While the global context is undoubtedly an important factor in this slow mainstreaming of reparations, Ojulari also emphasized a particularity of the Colombian case. Following from her work as both an activist and a researcher, Ojulari (2021) observed that Afro-Colombian activists' participation in the transitional justice process that followed the peace negotiations and formal end of the war in Colombia gave them new language particularly well-suited to speak about historical reparations.[31] According to Ojulari, "the context of transitional justice created a new political opportunity [for reparations] because when [Afro-Colombian] organizations began pushing for the inclusion of an ethno-racial lens in the mechanisms of transitional justice, the questions 'What is justice?' 'What is truth?' 'What is reparation?' 'And what are guarantees of non-recurrence?' became part of the conversation."[32] Due to their experience with wartime reparations and their participation in a formal transitional justice process, Ojulari noted, Afro-Colombian activists have a lot to contribute to the global movement for reparations. More specifically, she observed that because they have anchored their political demands in collective forms of redress—such as collective land titles and collective war reparations—and have incorporated the language of transitional justice, Afro-Colombian activists working at the juncture of ethno-racial rights and victims' reparations have a deeply structural vision of justice:

> The principle of truth [which is embedded] in transitional justice is fundamental, as is the principle of reparations, obviously. This [principle] offers some clues—as does the concept of guarantees of non-recurrence—because if we understand that we have a right to stop this [injustice] from continuing, we have to understand why it is ongoing and how to end it. That's where I see that Colombia contributes a lot to the [international] conversation on historical reparations. [Colombia contributes] a more structural view—to the discussions taking place in the US, for example—by understanding that this crime took place in the context of an economic model (neoliberalism) and that the reason why we are where we are today is because the model remains and has deepened. So, it isn't simply about getting a check, I don't just want inclusion, I want my right to difference, my right to live according to my view of the world.

I concur with Ojulari's observations about the unexpected and productive confluence of ethnic, racial, and wartime demands and the analytical clarity that this experience brings to the pursuit of historical reparations. I also want to note that Afro-Colombians' engagement in diasporic dialogues has added a critical element in the development of an emergent movement in Colombia. In the case of reparations, specifically, CARICOM's leadership catalyzed the push to create commissions across the continent. In addition to learning from the Caribbean case, Afro-Colombian activists have initiated and sustained exchanges with African American activists to establish relationships and learn from one another as they each develop their own plans. For example, in 2017 PCN hosted an international forum on historical reparations in Cali, where representatives from the United States, Jamaica, Guadeloupe, and Saint Lucia were present.[33] Later that year, Afro-Colombian representatives were invited to attend the National African American Reparations Commission's meeting in New Orleans. In these exchanges, Ojulari herself has been a key network builder, linking international spaces; translating cultural, linguistic, and historical contexts; and insisting on maintaining the focus on historical reparations both at the grassroots level and within the agendas of the highest echelons of international politics, such as the United Nations.

The challenges to the solidification and growth of a movement for historical reparations in Colombia are formidable. Despite the formal end of the war—as I show in the following chapter—the humanitarian crisis in Colombia has not abetted. In a context of relentless violence and uninterrupted material precariousness, it is difficult to convince people of the urgency and importance of historical reparations. As Ojulari attested, while PCN continues to include the item in its agendas, the pressing needs of the contemporary moment keep pushing it down and postponing its discussion. Perhaps the first task at hand, then, is internal to the Afro-Colombian social movement itself, and as Ojulari identified, it involves doing the work to clarify that historical reparations are about not only the past but also the present.

THE WINDING PATH TO REPARATIONS

A difference of kind, not degree.
—*Coates (2014)*

I began this chapter by describing the convergence of multiculturalism and Colombia's politics of victimization in the early 2000s. There, I lingered on the dangers of this articulation by outlining the political shortcomings of mobilizing around the pursuit of victimized citizenship. And yet Afro-Colombian activists working at the intersection of multicultural rights and reparations programs for war victims have catalyzed profound changes in the landscape of Afro-Colombian politics. First, and very importantly, the war has crystalized a racial analysis of Afro-Colombians' current situation, and an attendant set of anti-racist demands that are now routinely mobilized as such. While the logic of multiculturalism—posed narrowly as a set of cultural demands—has not been entirely replaced by an attention to racism, the two have been unequivocally articulated and are routinely invoked together. A second important shift involves an expansion of the political field in which Afro-Colombian activists and organizations are working from the national to the global. As Paschel (2016) notes in her analysis of the black social movement in Colombia, since the early 2000s, Colombia has shifted both from what she terms a "multicultural alignment" to a "racial equality alignment," and from operating within a domestic political field to working more within a global one.

Over the years, Afro-Colombian activists engaged in diasporic dialogues have also begun to incorporate more explicit demands for historical reparations in their agendas. While the numbers of people and organizations doing this is quite small, the potential impact of their insight is not. Moving from a pursuit of victimized citizenship to a demand for historical reparations means shifting from a political analysis of the conjuncture to a reckoning with the *longue durée* of racialized violence. It means righteously and altogether shifting the terms of the conversation, because as Ta-Nehisi Coates (2014) notes in his description of the accumulated disadvantages of African Americans in Chicago, the magnitude of black poverty and disenfranchisement is so staggering that it can be understood only as "a difference of kind, not degree." Of course, Coates is not writing about Colombia, but one can hardly sustain an argument that would identify the Colombian case as an exception to the centuries of plunder and violence faced by Africans and their descendants all over the Americas. The theft of black land, labor, and life is a hemispheric reality that, if anything, has been made more acutely clear in Colombia as a result of the war. And there, for that same reason, Afro-Colombians can provide considerable leadership in pushing the struggle forward.

Harm of a different order calls for redress of a different order. Historical reparations are not simply commensurate with Afro-descendants' full inclusion as citizens. They are a precondition for full citizenship. Full citizenship with an unfulfilled debt is an illusion at best, if not entirely a farse. Historical reparations will do much more than extend equal protection of the state to black Colombians; they will pay the accumulated and delinquent debt of all those people and institutions that have profited from enslaved labor. Their potential import is as deep as the intractability of the responsible parties in recognizing our debt.[34] Because if the struggle for citizenship and inclusion has proved difficult, the struggle for reparations may appear nearly impossible. And clarifying—both for Afro-Colombians themselves and for the population at large—the current relevance of a struggle for historical redress is perhaps the most formidable challenge that black activists face in this regard. In a country wrought by decades of armed violence, a national conversation about the distant past may seem out of order. But as Coates reminds us, we—all of us implicated in the long history of colonialism and enslavement in the Americas—cannot afford to continue seeing antiblack racism as a fact of the inert past, or as "a delinquent debt that can be made to disappear if only we don't look" (Coates 2014).

CHAPTER 4

BLACK VISIONS
OF PEACE
Against the Genocidal Spectrum

"THEY ARE KILLING US"

Emilsen

After watching a movie together on a lazy Saturday morning in early 2017, Emilsen kissed her young son goodbye and left with her partner, Joe Javier, in a taxi. Three days later their two bodies were found stabbed and bound in a rural area of Buenaventura. Emilsen, who was only thirty-one years old, had organized local residents in her neighborhood of Playita to create a space of resistance against armed actors who had turned the area into a hotbed of drug trafficking and gruesome assassinations. Ironically, Emilsen had also been working for the national Truth Commission documenting murders and disappearances to contribute to Colombia's so-called transition to peace (Hernández 2017; La Paz en el Terreno n.d.).

Bernardo

Death hounded Bernardo for seventeen years. He left his native Tumaco in 2000 after two assassination attempts on him, only to learn that a year later, Sister Yolanda Cerón, a nun with whom he worked at the local archdioceses, had been shot down at the Merced Church's doorstop for defending black and indigenous communities' right to collective lands. The attempts against Bernardo's life continued for several years in the small Caribbean town where he sought refuge. And though he continued to do political work with AFRODES for nearly two decades more there, in 2017 he was shot to death in front of his wife inside their home. Less than a year after his murder, his two grown sons, Silvio and Javier, who had remained in Tumaco after their father's departure, were mysteriously shot and killed. Death hounded Bernardo even after he was murdered (*La Silla Vacía* 2017; *Semana* 2018b).

The Angulos

For the Angulo family, no means of protection was sufficient to shield four of their members from untimely death in early 2017. On April 17, two of the Angulo brothers—Héctor and Obudulio—and their cousin Simón were kidnapped by an unknown illegal armed group. In his search for his family members, Iver—the third brother—contacted the local ombudsman's office for protection. He had been searching for two weeks when on May 5, the boat where he was being escorted to safety was stopped by fifteen men with long-range rifles and grenade launchers who took him away. That was the last time Iver was seen alive. His body was found two months later in an advanced state of decay. His brothers and cousin too were last seen alive on a small boat floating down the Naya River, but unlike Iver's their bodies never surfaced (*El Espectador* 2018; *TeleSur* 2018).

Contrary to the hopes of millions of Colombians and international observers, since the signing of the peace accords with the FARC in November 2016, violence on some fronts has dramatically escalated rather than abated. As of March 2022, 1,327 social leaders and human rights defenders had been assassinated in Colombia, making it one of the most dangerous places in the world to be a human rights defender (infobae 2022).[1] As activists have vehemently exclaimed with the grim phrase "they are killing us," social leaders have become highly vulnerable in postconflict Colombia because they prioritize their own communities' definitions of peace and demand direct participation in decision-making processes that affect them.[2] They are quickly targeted for elimination when their demands go against the interests of the numerous groups that still operate through violence. And while it might be tempting to think that this heightened state of violence is a product of a society reeling in the aftermath of armed conflict, these assassinations are more systematic than aberrant. They are less indicative of a peace process gone awry than of an ongoing dispute surrounding the very meaning of peace.

The human cost behind these numbers is tremendous and impossible to adequately convey. Although it might appear like a futile exercise in counting, I wish to pause long enough to name some of those who have been murdered and disappeared:

1. Juan Mosquera Rodríguez (January 7, 2017), Riosucio, Chocó; community leader, community council of Salaquí. Murdered with his son Moisés Mosquera.

2. Emilsen Manyoma (January 17, 2017), Bajo Calima, Valle del Cauca; member of CONPAZ. Murdered with her partner Joe Javier Rodallega

3. Álvaro Arturo Tenorio Cabezas (May 18, 2017), Magüí Payán, Nariño; member of the Ethnic and Popular Movement of the Pacific (COCCAM, by its Spanish acronym), Marcha Patriótica, and Magüí Humana.

4. Bernardo Cuero (June 7, 2017), Malambo, Atlántico; member of AFRODES. His two adult sons Javier Bernardo Cuero Ortiz and Silvio Duban Ortiz Ortiz were murdered the following year in Tumaco.

5. Eugenio Rentería Martínez (July 3, 2017), Quibdó, Chocó; leader of the civic strike of Chocó.

6. Héctor William Mina (July 14, 2017), Guachené, Cauca; Afro-Colombian leader, member of Marcha Patriótica.

7. Fernando Asprilla (August 9, 2017), Piamonte, Cauca; coordinator of Marcha Patriótica for the village of La Tigra, Cauca.

8. Manuel Ramírez Mosquera (August 17, 2017), Riosucio, Chocó; ex-president of the community council of Truandó, Chocó.

9. José Luis García Berrío (October 5, 2017), Cartagena, Bolívar; member of the local neighborhood council of Barrio Henequén.

10. José Jair Cortés (October 5, 2017), Tumaco, Nariño; member of the community council of Alto Mira y Frontera, Nariño.

11. Luz Yeni Montaño (November 12, 2017), Tumaco, Nariño; community member and religious leader in Barrio Viento Libre.

12. Juan Camilo Sevillano (November 22, 2017), Tumaco, Nariño; rapper and teacher, member of PCN.

13. Edison Marcial Ortiz Bolaños (November 30, 2017), Magüí Payán, Nariño; representative of the community council Manos Amigas. He died in cross fire between the ELN and the criminal group Resistencia Campesina.

14. José Olmedo Obando (January 22, 2018), Ipiales, Nariño; leader of the community council Nueva Esperanza, and member of Coordinación Nacional de Pueblos, Organizaciones y Comunidades Afrocolombianas (CONAFRO) and Marcha Patriótica.

15. Fares Carabalí (January 23, 2018), Santander de Quilichao, Norte del Cauca; manager of the miners' cooperative of Buenos Aires, Cauca.

16. José Fernando Castillo (January 23, 2018), Buenos Aires, Cauca; member of the community council Cerro Teta, PCN, Guapi.

17. Temístocles Machado (January 27, 2018), Buenaventura, Valle del Cauca; leader of the civic strike in Buenaventura.

18. Nicomedes Payán (January 29, 2018), López de Micay, Cauca; community leader of Taparal, Río Micay.

19. Jesús Orlando Grueso (February 9, 2018), Guapi, Cauca; member of the community council of Río Guapi, Cauca

20. Jhonatan Cundumí Anchino (February 9, 2018), Guapi, Cauca; member of the community council of Río Guapi, Cauca.

21. Tomás Barreto Moreno (March 7, 2018), San José de Uré, Córdoba; member of the community council of San José de Uré.

22. Silvio Duban Ortiz (March 19, 2018), Tumaco, Nariño; son of Bernardo Cuero, member of AFRODES's national board who was murdered the previous year.

23. Javier Bernardo Cuero Ortiz (March 19, 2018), Tumaco, Nariño; son of Bernardo Cuero, member of AFRODES's national board who was murdered the previous year.

24. Obdulio Angulo Zamora (April 17, 2018), Buenaventura, Valle del Cauca; member of the community council Río Naya and Marcha Patriótica.

25. Hermes Angulo Zamora (April 17, 2018), Buenaventura, Valle del Cauca; member of the community council Río Naya and Marcha Patriótica.

26. Simeón Olaye Angulo (April 17, 2018), Buenaventura, Valle del Cauca; member of the community council Río Naya and Marcha Patriótica.

27. Iver Angulo Zamora (kidnapped May 5 and found July 19, 2018). Río Naya, Valle del Cauca; member of the community council Río Naya.

28. Carlos Jimmy Prado Gallardo (June 2, 2018), Satinga, Nariño; national representative for Asocoetnar, member of Satinga Joven.

29. Adrián Perez (June 23, 2018), Curvaradó, Chocó; son of a land claimant.

30. Santa Felicinda Santamaría (July 3, 2018), Quibdó, Chocó; president of the local neighborhood council for Barrio Vigía del Carmen.

31. Ana María Cortés Mena (July 4, 2018), Cáceres, Antioquia; campaign coordinator for presidential candidate Gustavo Petro.

32. Ibes Trujillo Contreras (July 10, 2018), Suárez, Cauca; member of CONAFRO.

33. Libardo Moreno (July 23, 2018), Jamundí, Valle del Cauca; president of his neighborhood council.

34. Valentín Rúa Tezada (August 1, 2018), Suárez, Cauca; radio host and community leader.

35. Luis Alberto Rivas Gómez (August 18, 2018), Turbo, Antioquia; member of Autoridad Nacional Afrocolombiana (ANAFRO) and PCN.

36. James Celedonio Escobar Montenegro (August 29, 2018), Tumaco, Nariño; member of the community council of Alto Mira y Frontera.

37. Alexander Rentería Palomino (October 28, 2018), Vigía del Fuerte, Antioquia; survivor of the Bojayá massacre.

38. Yesica Viviana Carabalí (November 4, 2018), Buenos Aires, Cauca; member of the community council of Cerro Teta.

39. Esteban Romero Núñez (December 15, 2018), Tumaco, Nariño; member of the community council and of the village council of La Chorrera.

40. Gilberto Valencia Agrono (January 1, 2019), Suárez, Cauca; social entrepreneur, peace builder, and cultural worker.

41. Maritza Isabel Quiroz Leiva (January 5, 2019), Santa Marta, Magdalena; social leader for women, war victims, and specifically displaced Afro-descendants.

42. Víctor Manuel Trujillo (January 15, 2019), Monte Cristo, Bolívar; leader of the farmworkers' strike in 2013 and urban artist.

43. Maritza Ramírez Chaverra (January 24, 2019), Pasto, Nariño; president of the neighborhood council of Aguas Claras, Tumaco.

44. María del Pilar Hurtado Montaño (June 21, 2019), Tierra Alta, Córdoba; leader of victims groups and land restitution.

45. José Arlet Muñoz (June 26, 2019), Tuluá, Valle del Cauca; member of the grassroots organization Afro Unidos del Pacífico.

46. Ariel López Romero (August 1, 2019), Soledad, Atlántico; teacher and LGBTI activist.

47. Jeferson Preciado Ovando (August 6, 2019), Olaya Herrera, Nariño; supporter of local youth cultural programs.

48. Wilson Charley Tenorio Quiñones (August 15, 2019), Magüí Payán, Nariño; mayoral candidate for Magüí Payán.

49. Víctor Campaz (September 3, 2019), Guapi, Cauca; local ethnic authority and member of the community council of Chanzará.

50. José Cortez Sevillano (September 5, 2019), Tumaco, Nariño; leader of program for substitutions for illicit crops.

51. Yunier Moreno (September 9, 2019), Cartagena del Chaira, Caquetá; community organizer and social activist who worked with victims of forced displacement.

52. Ferney Vélez Valencia (October 6, 2019), Caloto, Cauca; member of the community council of Quita Calzón.

53. Robinson Romaña (November 11, 2019), Carmen del Darién, Chocó; bodyguard affiliated with the workers' union SIMPROSEG.

54. José Ardel Muñoz (December 14, 2019), Tuluá, Valle del Cauca; member of the local council Villa Colombia of Tuluá—Afro Unidos del Pacífico.

55. Richard Nilson Caicedo (December 22, 2019), Mocoa, Putumayo; member of the Community Council for the Development of Black Communities of the Highland, Nariño.

56. Lucy Villarreal (December 23, 2019); cultural activist and human rights defender.

57. José Antonio Riascos (January 25, 2020), El Tambo, Cauca.

58. Segundo Martín Girón Zambrano (February 1, 2020), Tumaco, Nariño.

59. Luis Mario Talaga Wallis (February 20, 2020), Puerto Tejada, Cauca.

60. Teodomiro Sotelo Anacona (April 17, 2020), El Tambo, Cauca.

61. Andrés Cansimance Burbano (April 18, 2020), El Tambo, Cauca.

62. Jesús Albeiro Riascos (April 22, 2020), El Tambo, Cauca.

63. Sabino Angulo (April 22, 2020), El Tambo, Cauca.

64. Gracelio Micolta Mancilla (June 17, 2020), Guapi, Cauca.

65. Pola del Carmen Mena (July 5, 2020), El Tambo, Cauca.

66. Armando Suarez Rodríguez (July 7, 2020), El Tambo Cauca.

67. Patrocinio Bonilla (August 11, 2020), Alto Baudó, Chocó.

68. Nathalia Andrea Perlaza (August 21, 2020), Palmira, Valle del Cauca.

69. Edis Manuel Care Pérez (August 25, 2020), Riosucio, Chocó.

70. Audberto Riascos (November 1, 2020), López de Micay, Cauca.

71. Rocío Alomía Mantilla (November 1, 2020), López de Micay, Cauca.

72. Guildón Solís Ambuila (December 4, 2020), Buenos Aires, Cauca.

73. Joaquín Antonio Ramírez (December 6, 2020), Buenaventura, Valle del Cauca.

74. María Adriana Díaz (December 16, 2020), Buenos Aires, Cauca.

75. Luis Alberto Anai Ruiz (December 27, 2020), Tumaco, Nariño.

76. Fredman Herazo Padilla (January 15, 2021), La Apartada, Córdoba.

77. José Riascos (April 8, 2021), Nuquí, Chocó.

78. Margarito Salas (April 8, 2021), Nuquí, Chocó.

79. Harold Angulo (June 13, 2021), Cali, Valle del Cauca.

80. Gustavo Solís Ramos (June 18, 2021), Buenaventura, Valle del Cauca.

81. Danilo Torres (June 26, 2021), Roberto Payán, Nariño.

82. Yeisi Campo (July 14, 2021), Morales, Cauca.

83. Henry Perea Montaño (September 30, 2021), Puerto Leguízamo, Putumayo.

84. Omar Cárdenas Lozano (October 16, 2021), Litoral San Juan, Chocó.

85. Edinson Valenzuela Cuama (October 30, 2021), Buenaventura, Valle del Cauca.

86. Libardo Castillo Ortiz (January 20, 2022), Barbacoas, Nariño.

87. Julio Victoria Cárdenas (February 24, 2022), Litoral San Juan, Chocó.

88. Hery Olivero (May 1, 2022), Olaya Herrera, Nariño.

89. Jesusita Moreno (June 7, 2022), Cali, Valle del Cauca.

This list I've compiled identifies Afro-Colombians among the missing and assassinated to highlight the specificity of black death in postconflict Colombia.[3] It is an attempt at doing the accounting that is necessary for a proper reckoning with antiblackness, the kind of reckoning that can move us closer to a reparation of harm and therefore to justice. In doing this, I follow black scholars working in Latin America—such as Jaime Alves, Luciane Rocha, Christen Smith, and João Costa Vargas—who see the systematic and enduring nature of untimely black death as genocide and as a foundational aspect of modern polities. (Alves 2018, 2020; Rocha 2012; Smith 2016b; Vargas 2008). I begin this chapter with a discussion of genocide and its relation to black life and premature death to better understand its flip side, peace. I pause to first lay out a theory of genocide as a multidimensional spectrum to underscore that antiblackness is a continuum of different forms of violence. This allows me to move into a full consideration of peace as the absence of all forms violence and to examine the ways in which Afro-Colombian activists are mobilizing this notion. The ethnographic focus of the chapter is on the various strategies used by prominent black organizations and activists to further their visions of peace. In doing this, I pay particular attention to their differing forms of engagement with the state, because I believe that their choices in selectively engaging with and moving beyond the state are evidence of the pursuit of Black Citizenship.

Following Vargas, Smith, Alves, and others, I begin with the assertion that genocide is a multidimensional spectrum. It is multidimensional because it involves a number of seemingly distinct mechanisms that include institutional discrimination, psychological terror, economic exploitation, political marginalization, and physical violence. I also find it helpful to understand it as a spectrum to see these multiple forms of violence in all their gradients of severity, from the subtlest and nearly imperceptible to the most dramatic and hypervisible. As Vargas (2008) reminds us, these seemingly disparate practices are sutured together by the common thread of symbolic violence, which renders black life either anomalous or incomprehensible.[4] And while genocide cannot be subsumed into symbolic violence, Vargas's observation highlights the connections between these different dimensions and gradients of violence—from microaggressions to black death—which together form a genocidal spectrum.

The people on the list above were at the far end of the genocidal spectrum: physical death. The harrowing violence inflicted on them prematurely ended their lives. And along that genocidal spectrum are multiple forms of violence that make black lives precarious: lives lived in poor health resulting from state neglect; lives lived under the constant physical strain of poverty; lives worn down by the daily aggressions—big and small—of interpersonal and institutional racism. In addition to being facilitated and legitimized by symbolic violence, these conditions—like the gruesome assassinations suffered by those named here—are also expressions of structural violence (Dest 2019, 44). That is, they are the result of historical forces that have made inequality so entrenched that it has become naturalized, like the idea that poverty and poor health for black people are "normal" and therefore inevitable. The structural nature of several forms of violence—like racism and sexism—also make it difficult to identify culprits, because the mechanisms of reproducing injustice are so deeply embedded in our institutions and in the forms of organization of our societies that they have become common sense. This helps explain not only the systematic and enduring nature of black premature death and precarious life but also the appalling degree to which it has become acceptable.[5] Because they seem so ordinary and ubiquitous, the social structures that make black lives precarious—political exclusion, social marginalization, and economic exploitation—may appear unremarkable, but by placing them squarely on a continuum of violence that includes the horrific deaths of the men and women remembered here, I hope to contribute to making the harm they cause visible. Perhaps when placed alongside the undeniably and repulsively violent, these social structures can be perceived in their full insidiousness.

Most important, if the multiple dimensions of violence that constitute genocide are part of a totalizing phenomenon, its flip side—the absence of violence, or peace—must also be understood comprehensively. The search for a comprehensive notion of peace, as the absence of *all* forms of violence, is the subject of this chapter. In what follows, I show how Afro-Colombian activists are mobilizing various views of peace—many of which are not neatly aligned with or contained by the Colombian state's project for national development and reconciliation. Although some are indeed fighting for inclusion in this major project of national renewal, others are working to further a comprehensive view of peace that precedes and exceeds the 2016 peace accords. The vision of peace articulated by these latter Afro-Colombian activists is defined as care for all life—both human and nonhuman. Informed by their *longue durée* experiences of violence—lived as both direct attacks on their physical existence and the long-standing deterioration of the social conditions in which they live—these Afro-Colombian activists do not reduce peace to the immediate elimination of premature death; they seek to dismantle the various structures that produce precarious lives. They seek not simply to eradicate the most extreme forms of antiblack violence but to completely undo the genocidal spectrum itself.

While this powerful black affirmation of life is taking place in many places, in Colombia it is unfolding in the midst of a sixty-year war and its official aftermath, that is, in a political field where differently positioned actors are waging competing meanings of peace.[6] Despite the multiplicity of actors, this scenario that has been dominated by the Colombian government, whose ultimate purpose is to renew rather than dismantle the nation-state. In seeking national reconciliation, the government has established its priorities and pursued a clear agenda, which includes a reaffirmation of Colombia's existent economic and political model. Thus, it is not surprising that from the beginning of the talks in 2012, the government unequivocally stated that Colombia's commitment to neoliberal capitalism was not up for negotiation.[7] Thus, the breadth of official discussions of peace have been framed by these narrow limits. In a perverse dynamic, the government invites members of civil society to contribute their visions of peace, if and only if those visions do not conflict with the dominant national project of renewal, which reaffirms the very source of violence. Evidently, an expansive and fully transformative vision of peace is not possible within the confines of a capitalist nation-state, and yet Afro-Colombian activists are compelled to work within this field to further their definitions of peace.

This chapter analyzes the multiple ways that black activists and organizations navigate this restricted terrain to imagine and produce more liberating futures. As the anthropologist Anthony Dest (2019) notes in his ethnography of the postconflict period in the Northern Cauca region of Colombia, the question of whether and how to participate in the peace process is not a simple one. For Afro-Colombians it involves entering a difficult and contradictory terrain where they attempt to simultaneously engage with and defy a model—neoliberal capitalism—that is ready to destroy them when they pose a challenge to its reproduction (Dest 2019). In the end, they are engaging with an institution that, like most postcolonial nation-states with a history of enslavement, was founded on the exploitation and devaluation of nonwhite lives.[8] I concur with Dest's observation that in doing this, black and indigenous people in Colombia have not followed a straight line from working "in and against the state" to moving "against and beyond it."[9] Rather, many people "continue to struggle to transform the nation-state through official avenues in order to attempt to build a better life for themselves" (Dest 2019, 44). This both-and stance in the construction of peace is yet another manifestation of Afro-Colombians' struggles for Black Citizenship. It is an affirmation of their right to participate in the reconstruction of the nation of which they are rightful citizens and an exercise in more expansive and black-centered pursuits of justice.

A CONTENTIOUS PEACE

After four years of intense negotiations, in November 2016 the Colombian government and the FARC, Colombia's largest left-wing guerrilla group, signed a peace agreement that was internationally celebrated for finally putting an end to the longest and deadliest war in modern Latin American history. Even as myriad reports of six decades of violence are still being compiled, we know already that the balance of Colombia's war is chilling. According to the Observatorio de Memoria y Conflicto, the war left a toll of more than 260,000 dead and more than 80,000 disappeared (Caracol Radio 2018), which amounts to nearly five people disappeared and sixteen murdered every day for forty-five years.[10] Colombia's war has also left the largest accumulated number of internally displaced people in the world—7.8 million according to the UNHCR's 2018 numbers (*Noticias ONU* 2019). The conflict has earned Colombia some other ignominious "first places," such as the largest mass grave in Latin America, which despite the government's conflicting reports, international observers have confirmed at roughly two thousand unmarked bodies (*TeleSur* 2017). To make this even more appalling, many of these bodies add to the more than four thousand documented cases of so-called *falsos positivos* (false positives), in which members of the military kidnapped and murdered poor and mentally impaired civilians and presented them as *guerrilleros* killed in combat. It is now well known that they inflated the number of enemy casualties with innocent civilians' lives to receive promotions and monetary compensation, as well as to bolster support from US foreign military aid (Izagirre 2014).

The road to end this horrifying violence has been long and tortuous. When President Juan Manuel Santos began peace talks with the FARC in late 2012, he faced intense opposition from his former ally, Álvaro Uribe, the two-time president infamous for his excessive use of military might, staunch refusal to negotiate with *guerrilla* groups, and documented links to illegal extreme-right paramilitary groups. When the FARC and the government finally signed the first agreement in Havana in September 2016, Uribe's new party, the misnamed Centro Democrático (Democratic Center), launched a disinformation campaign whose strategy, in the words of the campaign director himself, focused on "exacerbating voters' fears and indignation" rather than on explaining the actual content of the accords (*El Espectador* 2016; *Semana* 2016b). To achieve this, Uribe's campaign perversely tethered the accords to highly polarizing issues such as LGBTQI and abortion rights, claiming that supporters of the accords wanted to erode good, Catholic, family values (*Semana* 2016a). In this way, Uribe's campaign generated a moral panic around the alleged "gender ideology" of the accords, which his party affirmed threatened the hetero-normative basis of the nation. This was so successful at generating opposition that on October 2, when a popular referendum was held to ratify the peace accords, a majority voted against them.

But the margin of Uribe's success was very slim—the no vote won with less than 1 percent difference—and the 6.3 million Colombians who voted yes to support the accords did not capitulate. Immediately after the referendum's results were announced, university students nationwide called for a mass protest—La Marcha del Silencio—which in Bogotá alone convened more than thirty thousand people to demand that the peace process proceed despite the no vote (*CNN en Español* 2016). Following the march, more than one hundred people from all over the country set up a permanent encampment in front of the presidential palace to demand the maintenance of the cease-fire and the immediate definition of a concrete route to revise and implement the accords. The campaigns and marches were organized by a broad sector of the population that included *campesinos*, indigenous and Afro-Colombian activists, members of the left-wing coalition Marcha Patriótica, university students, and emergent interest groups from all over the political spectrum. Despite their political and sociodemographic differences, they all converged around a refusal to align with any political party or figure. Their call, aptly captured in the students' hashtag #EstamosListos (We are ready) sought to move forward with the implementation of the accords despite the polarization manufactured by the political machine. The message was clear: Colombians were ready for peace.

Fueled by the unwavering determination of the Colombian people, Santos's government quickly established an impressive institutional apparatus charged with designing plans for each of the six points of the accords: developing a comprehensive agrarian reform; creating more opportunities for political participation; reaching an agreement on a final cease-fire and disarmament; solving the problem of illicit drug production; guaranteeing the rights of victims; and defining a process for the implementation, verification, and public endorsement of the accords.[11] To expedite the actual implementation process, the Constitutional Court approved a mechanism known as "fast track," intended to halve the duration of regular legislative processes. But despite the herculean efforts of common citizens and the manifest political will of the Santos administration, the accords have failed to produce the single most important outcome for most Colombians: an effective reduction in violence. Furthermore, less than one year after the peace accords were signed, the presidential elections put power in the hands of the *uribista* machine, which has staunchly opposed a negotiated end to the war. In 2018, President Iván Duque—a pupil of Uribe and member of the Centro Democrático—assumed power and has since launched numerous initiatives to dismantle the structures that had just been designed to implement the peace accords.[12]

The peace accords are the most recent and still-unfolding conjuncture at which Afro-Colombians are actively renegotiating the terms of their citizenship and their insertion in the Colombian nation. Beyond the question of violence, the accords are important because, like the 1991 constitution discussed in chapter 3, they are a formal call for citizen participation in a major project of national renewal. In the words of Marino Córdoba (2015), president of AFRODES, the negotiations in Havana were a critical historical event that would define the country's future. In his view, if they were not included in the negotiations, Afro-Colombians would be effectively erased from that future (*borrados del mapa*). The accords are also important because the definition of peace constitutes the most contentious field of Colombian politics today, both at large and among different contingents of Afro-Colombian political groups. As I show, for some Afro-Colombian activists, the peace process is an opportunity to insert themselves in the existing projects of governance and development defined by the state. They see the peace process as a point of entry into the political system in order to redefine it. These activists insist that peace is possible only after there has been adequate reparation for victims of violence and after the structural conditions that created this violence have been fundamentally changed. In this sense, they echo the popular African American protest slogan "No justice, no peace." For others, the peace process is an opportunity to challenge and redefine national projects of governance and development. For this latter group of activists, peace is less about seizing opportunities for participation in the existing political system than about re-imagining politics in a way that centers Afro-Colombians' lived experiences. This vision is most eloquently articulated by activists who define their struggle as the care of life itself—*el cuidado de la vida*. And while the terminology is different, the vision itself resonates with the fundamental insight of Black Lives Matter, which highlights that when the most vulnerable lives are attended to, all lives can flourish. Thus, the stakes are high. As the numbers of human rights defenders murdered in their efforts to implement their visions of peace shows, this is a matter of life and death.

IN AND AGAINST THE STATE
#SinNegrosNoHayPaz

If we assume that the object of Colombia's peace process is to bring an effective end to the war, it is only logical that Afro-Colombians—who have been particularly hard hit by it—would be deeply invested in it. One of the major mechanisms by which Afro-Colombians have participated in crafting the contours of this peace is by actively demanding a seat at the negotiating table—a task that has been very demanding and highly unrewarding. As I have shown in previous chapters, this struggle precedes the peace negotiations by at least a decade, when Afro-Colombians began to demand differentiated approaches to humanitarian aid and victims' reparations. But perhaps the most iconic example of the demand for inclusion in the definition of peace was the creation of the National Afro-Colombian Peace Council, or CONPA, in 2015.

Initially, the peace negotiation process, which began in Havana in November 2012, was set up to include only the government and the FARC. The inclusion of members of civil society was to be delayed until the implementation phase. However, in response to pressure from civil society organizations, this procedure was revised early on to include a mechanism for citizen participation throughout the negotiating process.[13] Members of Afro-Colombian organizations responded to this opening with a demand for a seat at the table, claiming that as Colombian citizens who had been disproportionately affected by the war's violence, they had a right to participate in defining the nation's future.[14] Anticipating an invitation to Havana, a group of black activists created a coalition with representatives from various organizations, which was charged with bringing Afro-Colombians' concerns to the negotiating table. Thus, CONPA was officially created in early 2015, and by March 2016, it had formed an alliance with the largest indigenous organization in Colombia, ONIC, to create the Ethnic Commission for Peace and Territorial Rights. Together, black and indigenous activists hoped to exert greater pressure for inclusion in the negotiations through the commission. But the government's invitation to Havana never came. According to confidential sources, in mid 2016, when the signing of the accords appeared imminent, a group of Afro-Colombian and indigenous activists decided to take matters into their own hands and organized a self-designated delegation that traveled to Havana uninvited to demand a hearing. In response to this direct action, the negotiating table finally invited the Ethnic Commission to a hearing in June, where Afro-Colombian and indigenous delegates urged the government and the FARC to include an intersectional ethnic lens in the accords.

Following the June hearing, the Ethnic Commission drafted an "ethnic chapter" of the peace accords that included a shared set of principles, guarantees, and safeguards to protect the rights of Afro-Colombian and indigenous populations. At the core of these principles was the protection of collective territorial rights, the differential reparation of black and indigenous victims of the war, and the government's continued observance of all previously signed international agreements on ethnic peoples' rights. However, the document that contained this robust list of demands never saw the light of day. Instead, the chapter was a condensed four-page version that the commission, the FARC, and the government agreed on during the last few weeks before the public signing of the accords.

Like most coalitions, CONPA is politically diverse and has its own internal tensions. Yet it is noteworthy that, despite its personal and political differences, a significant number of activists within CONPA (and other Afro-Colombian organizations) continue to devote a great deal of their time and effort to engaging with the state and to actively demand participation in the terms and implementation of the accords. In fact, CONPA members celebrated the inclusion of an ethnic chapter in the final text of the peace accords as a triumph. This in spite of the tremendous difficulties of being included in the first place and the glaring disrespect that consistently marginalized Afro-Colombian voices. The activists working on the ethnic chapter saw it as a key mechanism to reassert Afro-Colombian people's citizenship by claiming inclusion in the nation and ensuring participation in the process that would renew it.

Despite what I initially interpreted as the failure to include a more robust text, Helmer Quiñones, an Afro-Colombian activist who participated in the negotiations to include the ethnic chapter in the accords, explained that the opposite was true. For Helmer, the ethnic chapter was "an enormous gain" precisely because the drafters had managed to include language that could be broadly interpreted to protect Afro-Colombians in a number of unforeseen situations. He explained that rather than providing a list of specific demands (which could never be exhaustive), the chapter identified principles, protections, and guarantees, such as the inclusion of an ethnic lens that cuts across all six negotiated points of the accords and a commitment to *no regresividad* (no regression), which guarantees the maintenance of all previous laws, treaties, and commitments made by the government.

On the one hand, then, Afro-Colombian activists saw the peace process as an opportunity to reassert their right to *difference*: to differential rights (cultural and territorial) and to differential reparations warranted by their particular histories of being subjected to colonialism and racism. They utilized the ethnic chapter (and the peace process more broadly) to continue to further the agenda of multicultural rights that they had been pursuing since the 1990s—as an expedient means to right the wrongs of the past, not only those of the war. As Marino Córdoba, president of AFRODES explained to me in 2015 shortly after CONPA's creation, their primary motivation was activists' continued search for ways to address: "a number of things that haven't been resolved in this country, that have been there for decades and have not created the conditions for Afro-Colombians to move forward and have a quality of life that is equivalent to the rest of country."

History had taught Afro-Colombians that a blanket negotiation process that did not consider their people's particular histories would simply not put an end to the violence that afflicts them. As such, they identified the peace process as an important historical event—for some, commensurate with the abolition of slavery and the passage of Law 70—and understood that their presence within it would help prevent their erasure from the nation's history and geography yet again.

However, while CONPA and the ethnic chapter are important mechanisms to protect Afro-Colombians' rights to citizenship and difference, they are an attempt to integrate Afro-Colombians into the national project rather than a fundamental questioning of the national project itself. For example, one of the main preoccupations with the implementation of the accords (and the ethnic chapter, by extension) was to make sure that black communities be contemplated in the drafting of the National Development Plan for 2018–2022 (Plan Nacional de Desarrollo, or PND). In these plans, which are drafted every four years, the government outlines public policy priorities and allocates budgets that reflect those priorities. The first plan following the peace accords was built following a participatory process of consultation with members of civil society. Thus, it was a space—albeit one with limits designed and overseen by the government—in which Afro-Colombian activists could demand that their communities' interests be included. Many of the activists with whom I spoke in 2018, when the plan was being finalized, mentioned the

importance of having a separate ethnic chapter included within it. Through
the PND, they sought basic citizenship rights, such as improved access to
health services, education, housing, and water. But they also reaffirmed their
differentiated status as ethnic subjects. In this capacity, they demanded better
statistical tools to count black and indigenous people, continued defense of
their territorial rights, and more power to decide the terms on which these
territories articulate with government entities. For Helmer, for example, the
PND was the main concrete mechanism through which the ethnic chapter
would be implemented following the signing of the peace accords. It was concrete because it designated resources—in the end, a total of 19 billion pesos
earmarked for Afro-Colombians—but it was also constrained in that it could
not stray from the overall national economic model.[15]

In essence, then, the negotiations were about how to reform the nation
without fundamentally altering its social, political, and economic structures,
which are grounded in colonialism and capitalism and therefore perpetuate
racism and other forms of structural violence. In this sense, efforts that seek
inclusion in the official (and state-led) terms of Colombia's peace process have
by definition been incapable of bringing about a comprehensive vision of
peace as anti-genocide. Although they seek to denounce the historical structures that have produced disproportionate violence on black bodies and territories, and even make demands to repair the damage, struggles for inclusion
in state-defined projects of peace are ultimately couched in terms that perpetuate the precarity of life for Afro-Colombians.

Reckoning and Reparations

Although the elimination of all forms of violence is a sine qua non for black
activists mobilizing around the peace process, many have also stressed that
national reconciliation and renewal necessarily require a restorative approach
to justice, one that accounts for the harm done to victims of violence and
defines clear paths for reparation of that harm. As mentioned in chapter 3,
in Colombia, the national conversation surrounding reparations for victims
of the war emerged in the early 2000s and culminated with the passage of
Law 1448 in 2011, widely known as the Victims' Law. Since then, discussions
about victims have saturated government offices, nongovernmental organiza-

tions, and the mainstream media. Despite their ubiquity, programs for victims did not initially consider the disproportionate effect that the war had on Afro-Colombians, nor did it contemplate the specificities of their victimization. While this struggle began more than a decade before the final round of peace talks, the peace process breathed new life into it. The peace process was an opportunity to revisit and continue to expand the terms under which reparations for war victims were defined and implemented.

Two things become immediately evident in reviewing the struggle that Afro-Colombian activists have waged on this front. First, the Colombian government is constantly attempting to limit or backpedal the gains that Afro-Colombians have made in regard to differentiated rights. The government's recurrent response has been to ignore the existence of legal mechanisms—both domestic and international—that currently protect Afro-Colombians' differential rights. When pressed to uphold them, the government resorts to the most limiting definitions of these rights, as granted by the initial multicultural logic that was inscribed in the 1991 constitution and Law 70. This is the case, for example with the application of prior and informed consent, which shows that even the rights that are legally guaranteed must be continuously defended (Cárdenas et al. 2020). Second, the difficulties of making their rights effective are compounded when Afro-Colombians try to expand the rigidly culturalist logic of rights that sustains them, for example, by making ethnic demands that are also informed by gender or race.

The government's backtracking becomes apparent when we recall that the Victims' Law itself failed to include a differential mechanism for reparations for black and indigenous people. Despite having ample evidence that economic exploitation, political marginalization, and racism exacerbated Afro-Colombian and indigenous people's victimization in war, the government did not include specific mechanisms for their reparation within the body of the law. Instead of a comprehensive inclusion of Afro-Colombian and indigenous demands, the law mandated the creation of two subsequent decrees that would address these populations separately—and it did so only in response to activists' pressure. For Afro-Colombian activists and organizations such as AFRODES and PCN, which had been working on related issues for many years, the task at hand was again to demand inclusion in the writing of the ensuing decree (Decree 4635) and to ensure that a proper process of consultation be followed.

Even though these organizations, which were working in a coalitional space called the Mesa de Organizaciones Afrocolombianas, prepared a draft of the decree with a comprehensive definition of reparations, the government drafted its own document and sanctioned it with the approval of the official body of Afro-Colombian representation rather than through a legitimate process of prior and informed consent with the population at large.[16] Despite this questionable process, many identified the passage of the decree as a victory against yet another attempt to exclude Afro-Colombians. For Helmer Quiñones, for example, the fact that the decree included an article on racism and discrimination was a small victory. The bigger challenge, as is often the case with Colombian legislation, would be in its application. This was made clear to me when Luz Marina Becerra, the secretary-general of AFRODES, described the difficult journey of making the decree applicable to a collective of displaced black women that she had been organizing with for more than a decade. In her work with this group, the government's unwillingness to expand the most narrow interpretation of cultural rights was made evident.

Ironically, when the work of designing and implementing reparations for war victims began, the government did not recognize people who had been displaced to the cities as collective subjects of reparations. According to the law, collective subjects of reparations could be recognized only when they belonged to previously existent collective bodies such as community councils (which had been defined by Law 70). But after more than fifteen years working with displaced black women across the country, Luz Marina is adamant that this population deserves to be recognized as a collective subject of reparations because of the specific horrors that they have faced in light of the war. Luz Marina created the Coordinación de Mujeres Afrocolombianas Desplazadas en Resistencia (COMADRE) in 2016 to highlight the gendered and racialized specificity of their victimization in the war.[17] The struggle has been long, and to finally gain the state's recognition in 2017, she began organizing grassroots women's groups first in Bogotá and then across the country to document displaced black women's affectations. Although eventually the women from COMADRE won and were included in the Unidad de Víctimas register of collective subjects of reparations, I find their struggle indicative of the government's resistance to recognize gendered and racial demands that break out of the strict multicultural logic of rights to cultural difference. At every turn, activists seeking a broader interpretation of rights for black people face pushback and retrenchment. And even when there is a victory, it is important to note yet again that the recognition of victimization is limited to affectations by the war—and even when it is implicit, as it is in this case, that these affectations are disproportionate because of racial and gendered structures that exceed the war, the compensation that is issued is not commensurate with those historical inequalities.

"El Palo en la Rueda"

Many of the activists who have participated in various initiatives related to the peace process are quite aware of its limitations. As Astolfo Aramburo, a member of PCN, told me during an interview in 2018: "Really, the point is this, is this [the peace process] an opportunity for us black people to solve our problems? Truthfully, is it? We are invested in it because we do think it is an opportunity. We are victims of this process and we see an opportunity for it to benefit us, as black people. But since we are not present in the implementation process, since they don't want us to be there, they don't want to recognize us, well, *that's the wrench in the works*."[18] Afro-Colombian activists continue to participate in the peace process led by the government knowing full well that it will not bring an end to the multiple forms of violence that afflict Black Communities. Even as they work in and against the state's limits they are disillusioned by the lack of support from the broader population and by the government's lack of political will to truly include Afro-Colombians as full citizens while respecting their right to difference.

For these reasons, they also move outside of the state to pursue projects that affirm black life and, in this way, pursue broader visions of peace. Astolfo, for example, told me that he had abandoned his work with the Planes de Desarrollo con Enfoque Territorial (PDETs), a mechanism created by the Colombian government to design and implement regional plans for integral rural reform as part of the implementation stage of the peace accords, to work with a university-based observatory to title more than two hundred collective territories that have not yet been allocated to Black Communities. Somewhat cynically, he noted that the government's promises were circular: "You know what the government's agenda is? To promise that they'll honor their previous agreements. They propose nothing new." These black activists, as well as their collaborators, understand that a more substantive peace depends on the elimination of the structures that reproduce precarious lives for Afro-Colombians. In the end, many of these activists have lost faith in the possibility that a state-run process can fully bring about justice. They recognize that a black vision of peace must stretch back in history far beyond the beginning of the current war. As Astolfo put it:

> Our peace is not circumscribed by a mere negotiation. It is not born from this situation. Our people's aspirations were not born on occasion of the war [*conflicto*], right? We have a different history that goes back farther and the future will not be solved with more investment for rural areas [*campo*], with a new political party, with political participation in congress, with policies against illicit crops . . . if maybe the accords included the structural issue of racism and historical reparations maybe we'd say 'well, this is interesting!" . . . but we participate because we are involuntarily part of this process, because it is about our dead and our territories, we contribute to the solution, but this doesn't solve black people's situation.

The wrench, as Astolfo put it, is a structural one. It has to do with the structural impossibility of addressing a historical debt with a form of redress designed for the current conjuncture. This does not mean that we should throw our hands up and lament the impossibility of ever being able to adequately attend to that pending debt. Rather, we must get creative and bold in designing new avenues for redress.

AGAINST AND BEYOND THE STATE
Although the government may be satisfied with a definition of peace that formally eliminates armed dissidence to carry on with business as usual, for many Colombians the peace accords are an opportunity to revise their social contract with the state and to reimagine the contours and very substance of their nation. For Afro-Colombians in particular, a satisfactory definition of

peace—as the elimination of all violence—necessarily precedes the current implementation process and exceeds the contours of the capitalist nation-state. For this reason, some activists are moving beyond the state by working in diasporic networks to strengthen autonomy in their communities even as they continue to work in and against the state. This broad vision of peace is also evident in the tireless work that ordinary people do to defend life—not only for their own lives but also for those of their neighbors and their communities, not only human life but also what scientists call biodiversity and what economists call natural resources—that is, the life in the rivers and oceans, the forests and mangroves, and above and below the earth's surface. This is not an easy task: there are formidable forces that seek to destroy life in all its magnificent manifestations, and the struggle involves tensions and contradictions within Black Communities themselves. For example, as black activists who make demands to the government are selectively invited to participate in decision-making spaces, the risk of co-optation by capital and the state is ever present. But there is a fundamental difference between pursuing a better life for oneself and caring for all life, and in the latter lies the power to interrupt the genocidal spectrum.

Given the high stakes involved, it is critical to ask how this work to defend life can disrupt the structures that reproduce black death and antiblackness more broadly. In doing this, I find the debate surrounding Afro-pessimism and black optimism useful for two reasons. First, this debate is fundamentally concerned with life (and death), and thus echoes the main concerns of the activists and communities whose lives and work I describe here. Second, many of the theorists who are outlining the nature and expanse of antiblackness today centrally consider the role of the state as an apparatus of violence and thus as key in the perpetuation of black death (Alexander 2012; Mbembe 2019; Vargas 2008).

Unfortunately, there has not been much formal recognition of the resonances and linkages between activists and scholars theorizing antiblackness in the Global North and those in the Global South (particularly in Latin America, which has the largest population of African descent outside of Africa), so I want to do the work of tying these two diasporic threads together.[19] Undoubtedly, since the emergence of the Black Lives Matter movement in the United States, the connections and exchanges between organized black groups all over the Americas have multiplied and become more deliberately articulated, but the connections are deeper and older. The preoccupation with black life and the experience of creating mechanisms to protect it are at least as old as Afro-descendants' presence in the Americas and that history's entanglements with the history of capitalism (Bledsoe and Wright 2019; McKittrick 2011). In Colombia, one of the responses to the forces of black death has been to nurture the care for life, what some activists themselves call *el cuidado de la vida*, a practice and epistemology that articulates with what in the United States is currently articulated as the preoccupation with black lives (and the concomitant denouncing of untimely black death). The coincidences and resonances between the two are not accidental.

While much has been written on the seeming disagreements between Afro-pessimists and black optimists, I briefly lay out the two positions to argue that in Colombia those pursuing *el cuidado de la vida*—like Black Lives Matter and other movements centered on the defense of black life—move in a middle ground between these two currents. I begin with Linscott's (2017) assertion that the difference between the two is more a matter of emphasis than substance, as they both wrestle with the inevitable structures of black death while recognizing some form of black life. Afro-pessimists, on the one hand, point to the black "death-world" (Mbembe 2019) as an undeniable and inescapable structure of modern societies (Linscott 2017). Insofar as black social death is necessary for white sovereignty to flourish, the state is always-already implicated in conditioning black life. Afro-pessimists understand black life as "the afterlife of slavery" (Hartman 2008), which exists as black social death (Sexton 2011). For Sexton (2012), "Black life is not lived in the world that the world lives in, but it is lived underground, in outer space." Afro-pessimists are also categorical about the state's central role in perpetuating black death, not only through its most conspicuous apparatuses of violence—such as the police and the prison system (Alexander 2012; Alves 2018; Gilmore 2007; Vargas 2008)—but also through myriad mechanisms that together regulate the totality of modern life.[20] It is precisely this emphasis on totality that makes the Afro-pessimist approach distinct.

Black optimists, like Fred Moten (2013), refuse the totalizing logic of structural antiblackness. Although they do not deny the power and reach of slavery's afterlife, they insist on finding space for black optimism in the interstices, in the underground. They see and celebrate a fabric of black life that is made up of everyday, joyful expressions capable of escaping the reach of white sovereignty. Harney and Moten (2013) also propose the concept of the undercommons as the space in which there is room for struggle, where building on the black radical tradition enables ways of living otherwise and animates the promise of escape. Moten's refusal of collective social death sees a possibility for a stolen life, but a life nonetheless. Black optimists, however, are not misled by the mirage of a panacea, of an everlasting joyful existence lived in the interstices. They recognize that a number of forces work to undermine the undercommons at every turn and that black optimism is necessarily "a runaway optimism."

When crafting strategies to care for life, some black activists and communities in Colombia operate in the space between these two poles. They denounce death, working in the fissures of structural antiblackness to find black optimism while on the run. In doing this, Afro-Colombians do not (cannot?) entirely escape the structures that reintroduce repressive actions of antiblackness at every turn, but they persist; they *remain*. Further, I argue that a key tactic they use in this is learning how to simultaneously operate within, against, and beyond the state. They engage with it, push its limits, and sometimes simply disregard it. This is an additional manifestation of what I have been calling the pursuit of Black Citizenship, as the both-and position that demands inclusion while vindicating difference. In doing so, Afro-Colombians necessarily wrestle with the structural forces that reproduce antiblackness within the state, both challenging them and breathing life along the margins.

El cuidado de la vida

In the more than twenty years that I have been traveling to and living in Colombia, I have witnessed the care for life in many places and in myriad manifestations, but the life of Francia Márquez is perhaps the most steadfast expression that I have had the privilege to witness of the tireless work to defend all life.[21] I met Francia in Suárez, Cauca, in 2009, when she was centrally involved in her community's struggle against a title that had been granted to an individual from outside the community to carry out large-scale, open-pit gold mining on their lands. While this struggle eventually threw her into the global limelight as a world renown environmental activist and anti-racist warrior, I start this story much earlier to center Francia's lived experience as a black woman who grew up in a rural community constantly hounded by capital's appetite.[22] I do this to highlight her lived experience as the foundation of her political commitment to the defense of life. This is not an essentialist reading of her biography as a fixed or teleological condition but a recognition that the *longue durée* experiences of black people—and black women in particular—with intersecting forms of violence that produce precarious lives and premature deaths is a powerful source from which to learn how best to care for all life. In this, I am reminded of Farah Griffin's (2003) insistence on measuring the success of any social movement by the status of black and brown girls. Griffin follows other black women before her, like Toni Cade Bambara, in ethically assessing adults "by the extent to which they work for a world free of sexism as well as white supremacy and poverty, a world where . . . little girls [of color] are able to grow up as free women" (77). The resonances of this position with the central lesson of the Black Lives Matter movement in the United States are also worth noting here. For those whose own lives are systematically and intentionally targeted for demise, life in all its expressions is extremely precious; and we *all* stand to learn a great deal from their relentless efforts to care for it. For generations, Francia and the members of her community have worked to create the conditions that can afford all of us peace—that is, the absence of violence; the flourishing of all life. This work is dangerous and incomplete, but there is also great joy in doing it. As Francia described in an interview in 2019, the people of her community "fight to survive in order not to die, to die of sadness, to die of disease, or because they declare us military targets" (*Revista Diners* 2019).[23] The fight against all of these forces of death—what she herself calls *el cuidado de la vida*—is what can interrupt the genocidal spectrum; and that is a comprehensive view of peace.

Francia was born in the village of Yolombó, a small community of mostly Afro-descendant people whose ancestors have been living at the skirts of the

mountains since 1635. There they were first enslaved, and after the final abolition of slavery in 1851, they remained in the area doing artisanal gold mining,
farming, and raising animals for self-subsistence, while also doing occasional
paid labor in neighboring towns and cities. Unsurprisingly, land titles and
mining concessions remained mostly in the hands of white elites and landowners, who preserved their economic control of newly freed people by regu-
lating their labor and limiting their autonomy (Jaramillo Buenaventura 2018;
Rojas 2014). Even though I have known Francia for many years and have
interviewed her on several occasions, she hadn't systematically recounted her
life story to me until 2018, when, after being awarded the Goldman Environmental Prize, she visited my home in New York. When I asked her to tell me
the story of her political trajectory, she began by identifying the key moments
of her life that had marked her political consciousness. Somewhat surprisingly, she did not begin with a story of attending meetings or participating
in organized politics. Instead, Francia began by recalling the birth of her first
child, Andrés, when she was only sixteen years old, as the first significant
moment in her process of political becoming.[24] In her small mining town,
it was common for men from other parts of Colombia to come for work,
impregnate young women, and never be heard from again. Andrés's father
was a *paisa*[25]—a white man—who disappeared before he was born. Francia
noted that most of the women in her family—including her mother who
raised six children on her own—were heads of households. And in her case,
history repeated itself, first with Andrés and later after the birth of her second
child, Alex, whose father denied his paternity. This and other gendered forms
of violence, which were common in her childhood and young adulthood,
marked Francia's life as important experiences against which she forged a political stance. As she herself remarked when remembering how her stepfather
beat her mother and siblings, and the absence of her own father and her two
children's fathers, "I had to live through a lot of violence."

When he was still an infant, Francia left her oldest son, Andrés, behind
to work in Cali as a domestic worker. After living through innumerable hu-
miliations and constant exploitation for a couple of years, she vowed never
to do that kind of work again. So, by the time she was eighteen years old,
she returned to the gold mines and fields of her native Yolombó and joined a

community group that did theater, dance, and musical activities organized by the cultural center at the municipal town of Suárez. These were her first experiences attending gatherings where people talked about politics and where she first heard that the government had plans to change the course of the Río Ovejas to further increase the size of the Salvajina Dam. In these meetings she also learned about the dam's history, whose construction was completed in 1985 to provide electricity for Cali and for the benefit of large-scale agricultural development in the region—of which sugarcane monoculture is a major part. She noticed that although the harmful environmental and social effects of the dam were palpable, water service in her own community was still nonexistent, and the promises of regional development had never materialized for them. This was in the early 1990s, when members of PCN were very active socializing the content of Law 70 across the Pacific, and it wasn't long before she became involved with the organization.[26] As she did so, she started traveling as a spokesperson for PCN, and in those journeys she learned black history from elders across the Pacific and heard about the emergent demands for multicultural rights and collective land titles from seasoned activists.

The early 2000s were times of spectacular violence across the Pacific Region, and Francia's region of Northern Cauca was not exempt from its viciousness. Not far from her community there was a bloody massacre perpetrated by paramilitary groups in the Naya River in 2001.[27] Meanwhile the struggle against diverting (*desviar*) the Río Ovejas intensified and news of multinational companies that intended to do mining exploitation in Northern Cauca spread across the region. The area was quickly flooded with paramilitaries (then members of the AUC) who terrorized the population with lists of alleged "drug addicts, prostitutes, and delinquents" whom they targeted for assassination. Soon, the lists included community leaders as well. In the area surrounding Cerro Teta, where Afro-descendant communities have lived from gold mining since 1536 in the neighboring municipality of Suárez, a paramilitary battalion of over two hundred men took over the entire town of Munchique in preparation for the Naya massacre (*Verdad Abierta* 2012). Even after the most intense violence subsided, paramilitaries settled by force through multiple means, including weapons, coerced unions with local women, and questionable acquisitions of land titles.

In Francia's community of Yolombó and neighboring villages a formidable enemy was beginning to unfurl a strategy that was paving the road for large-scale extractivism. The world's third-largest gold-mining multinational, the South African corporation AngloGold Ashanti,[28] began to draft corporate social responsibility projects that created jobs for locals to court their favor. Those who were suspicious of the company's intent—a small group of no more than ten people that included a twentysomething Francia—were accused of being *guerrilleros* and irrational opponents of national development and were targeted by paramilitaries for elimination through intimidation. But Francia's suspicions of the multinational company were confirmed when businessman Héctor Sarria received a title to carry out open-pit gold mining in the area, ignoring the community's historical presence on those lands, its constitutional right to collective land titles, and its internationally recognized right to prior and informed consent.[29] In August 2009, Francia's community received an eviction notice, and the military began heavily surveilling the area. Locals suspected that Sarria had privately entered into business agreements with AngloGold Ashanti.

PCN became centrally involved in the struggle against the alliance of Sarria and AngloGold Ashanti and began to unfold an international strategy to make the case visible—the story circulated under the name of the neighboring town of La Toma.[30] In the span of a few of years, Francia was involved in a number of high-visibility actions organized by PCN in its campaign to protect La Toma. At the time, I was living in Colombia and collaborated with several of these initiatives. In early 2010, PCN sent Francia on a US speaking tour to community centers and universities and to meet with activists and congress members including Angela Davis and Barbara Lee. Later that year, PCN coordinated a visit by Angela Davis to Francia's community, where she witnessed their struggle firsthand and returned to the United States to speak publicly about the stakes.[31] These actions catapulted the case's visibility, bringing it into the limelight of international human rights. In the next year a number of media outlets produced pieces on La Toma, denouncing the violations and further garnering international support for the community's right to remain (Hollman Morris 2013; Mendoza 2010). After an intense legal battle, in December 2010, the Constitutional Court ruled in favor of La Toma and revoked Sarria's title.

Unfortunately, this was not the end of Francia's community's struggle against extractivism. Once the legal mechanisms for dispossession were exhausted, the aspiring miners—mostly *paisas*—turned to illegal mechanisms to achieve the same ends. By 2013, bulldozers flooded the area to set up illegal mining points. Mostly owned by outsider *paisas*, these makeshift points did also provide locals with an opportunity to make a quick dollar by scraping small amounts of gold left behind by the bulldozers—a practice known as *barequeo*, which has been taking place since colonial times. And while the government carried out symbolic actions to seize the illegal bulldozers and appease public complaints, the illegal mining points kept mysteriously multiplying. Then, in May 2014, there was a tragic accident in the neighboring municipality of Santander de Quilichao, in which scores of people were buried under an avalanche from a negligently built, illegal mine (*El Tiempo* 2014).[32] After the tragedy, tensions in the area reached a boiling point. A group of local women wielding machetes approached the mining points demanding that the *paisas* and their bulldozers leave immediately. The local *barequeros* in turn threatened the women with violence for not letting them work. All the while the government continued to turn a blind eye to the situation. After a tense meeting with government officials following the accident, local activists demanded that the government implement income-generating projects to provide *barequeros* with alternative ways to make a living. At night, the bulldozers, which the government was supposed to confiscate, quietly left Santander, only to appear later in the neighboring municipalities of Buenos Aires and Caloto. And later that year, Francia, who had been recently elected as the legal representative for her village's community council, left her home in Yolombó under the intensifying pressure of anonymous death threats. Initially, she moved to Aguablanca—an impoverished district of Cali—with hundreds of thousands of other *desplazados* from across the Pacific Region. Francia has been displaced ever since.[33]

When recalling this story in 2015, during a speaking tour that brought her to the university consortium where I work, Francia was very clear in describing the violent efforts to dispossess her community as an expression of structural racism. In fact, she was then working on a thesis for her law degree, in which she argued that the Colombian government's systematic violation of prior and informed consent was racist. When I asked her about the process through which she had come to recognize it as racism, she said: "I learned that by being close to many black people, activists from different places—like Angela Davis herself—and at different events, but also by reading texts that speak of racism. I read a book by Malcom X . . . and there I saw [and thought] 'that's everything *I* have lived through!' And it's important to call things by their name." Heir to a diasporic genealogy of political action and thought, Francia seamlessly placed both the racism lived by herself and her community and their struggles to resist on a continuum with those of African Americans. For her, Doña Paula, the most respected *mayora* (elder) of Yolombó stands shoulder to shoulder with figures like Malcolm X and Angela Davis.

In May 2019, the relentless forces of death that Francia confronts on a daily basis became crudely apparent when two heavily armed men attacked a meeting of black organizers that she was attending in Santander de Quilichao. It is impossible to know what her fate would have been had the two bodyguards that the state provides her with (since she started receiving death threats) not been there. What is certain, however, is the temperance and determination with which she carries on with her work in spite of the forces of death that constantly hound her (Cárdenas 2019). Francia knows that staying alive and doing political work is a daily triumph. Reflecting on the vicissitudes of her political trajectory during an interview with *Semana Rural* a few days after the attack on her life she was asked what had been her greatest victory and without skipping a beat she responded "staying alive" (Ramírez Baquero 2019). Just staying alive. And still, in the midst of this relentless struggle to stay alive, there is joy, because that is precisely what the defense of life is about. This came to life in a visit I made to Yolombó a few months after the attack with a solidarity delegation of women of color.[34] As part of our itinerary, we spent a day with Francia and the women of the Association of Afro-Descendant Women of Yolombó, or ASOMUAFROYO, a local women's organization.[35] There, we listened to stories of resistance against mining and land usurpation, we learned about local flora and healing traditions, we exchanged cooking tips, and we danced and ate together. And for a day, we shared in their daily practice of caring for life.

Francia's political trajectory is intersected by numerous forces, which are grounded in her encounter with multiple forms of violence as a black woman from a rural area in Colombia. But these life experiences have also included travels through numerous spaces of black affirmation and empowerment—that include conversations with local elders, participation in regional and national gatherings, and exchanges with activists in the African diaspora. She has been marked both by the relentless efforts to target her and her community's lives for demise and also by the resilient and joyful life-affirming work of black people across Colombia and the diaspora. In these fires she has welded her uncompromising commitment to care for all life. Hers has been a lifelong practice of protecting, cultivating, and celebrating life, and as such, she is engaged in a practice that interrupts the genocidal spectrum; she is enacting a black vision of peace.

A Dual Strategy: "Playing the Game" and Building Community

In her years of political work against extractivism and in defense of life, Francia has witnessed the myriad ways the government generates, reproduces, and endorses violence. She is acutely aware of the Colombian government's dealings and silent complicity with many forces of death, ranging from paramilitary death squads to multinational corporations and other agents of so-called national development. Even as she is deeply engaged in multiple battles to defend her community through the recourse of the law, she realizes that the terms of these battles are framed by the state itself and she questions its legitimacy. Recounting the numerous times in which she heard racist arguments from government representatives, she stated: "But who manages the state? It's the same white people from the elite who inherited the Spanish colony. It's the same families who define what is done in our national territory. If it were really the state, *we* are part of the state and *we* would have a right to decide what *we* do with the territory. But we don't."

Francia identifies the corrupt structures that engender vicious cycles of privilege and destitution without hesitation. The government, as arbiter of Black Communities' right to collective land titles, decides who is and is not a worthy recipient of those rights. Recalling her community's ongoing battle to be granted a land title, she asked rhetorically, "But who grants that collective title? It's the white person who decides whether they give it to me or not. It's the same state, which is administered by a racist white elite with a colonial inheritance." In saying this, Francia was identifying the Colombian state as a direct product of European colonialism and, in a sense, as inherently incapable of bringing about justice for black people.

Francia has also witnessed the selective traps of inclusion that the government routinely lays out to co-opt activists like herself. She recounted the pain of seeing how "for those so-called leaders, the state gets them a room in a five-star hotel and then they don't want to go back to their community, because they want that life even if that means selling off their people's rights." Using language carefully chosen to signal the continuities from a colonial past, she added, "The master gives you food of the best quality, and those people today are lost, they don't care anymore, they just want their own little business." She is aware that this strategy of tokenism and co-optation has obstructed black solidarity because it engenders mistrust and conflict among black people: "We [black people] don't believe in each other and we are fighting among ourselves instead of creating a strategy to confront the government. And for all these reasons . . . we don't have legitimate spaces of representation; we don't have spokespeople who are willing to take on the fight against the government, and against the world if that is necessary to defend the community's rights—people who refuse to favor the interests of the government who is our enemy today because they themselves are obstructing the rights that they themselves have granted."

And still, Francia continues to engage with the state in her fights to defend life. In 2012 she started law school, in 2013 she became her community council's legal representative, in 2018 she launched a grassroots campaign for a seat in congress alongside the former M-19 *guerrillero* candidate Gustavo Petro, and in 2020 she announced her intent to run for president in the 2022 elections. I find it remarkable that even Francia, who has such a lucid and vocal critique of the structural impossibility of attaining true peace under the current nation-state (which she describes as racist and colonial), continues to wage battles that are grounded in the law and state-sanctioned rights. When I asked her why she had decided to run for office in 2018, after seeing the corruption, co-optation, and false promises of the government time after time, she explained to me that she understood that the state is a game: "The state is a game with some rules, some playing chips and some players. It's a game that was not designed by us [black people], but we are invited to play and sometimes we accept the invitation. When we go and we play . . . sometimes we are very astute and even try to beat them, or at least come out even, but *bam* every time we try that they change the rules of the game on us. I think that today we have to play to change the game and think about a game that is ours [*un juego desde nosotros*]."

Later she referred to this *juego desde nosotros* as *gobierno propio* (self-government) and explained that she believed that if she could get inside that game that we call the state—by having a seat in congress for instance—she would be in a better position to rally her people and to amplify their voice. Continuing with the metaphor of a game, she added, "I think that we now have to think about what kind of players we are and we have to create rules that favor us, because we have been on the sidelines cheering the players on, but now, we have to be playing the game and making new rules that benefit us."

This game was more than evident in Francia's and her community's struggle against large-scale gold-mining companies. The rules first dictated that the subsoil belonged to the state, then they were modified with the ILO's Indigenous and Tribal People's Convention (No. 169) in 1989 and the 1991 constitution—under much pressure from grassroots movements—to extend to black and indigenous communities the right to prior and informed consent.[36] But Francia's community was excluded from the right to collective land titling because they did not conform to the dominant definition of Black Communities enshrined in the law (see Cárdenas et al. 2020). Thus, they had to prove their very existence as an ancestral black community before their right to prior and informed consent was recognized. And when the burden of proof showed that an ancestral black community had lived there for centuries, their right to prior and informed consent was patently violated.[37] Thus, it became clear to everyone that the government selectively applied its own rules. On the one hand, it turned a blind eye to the illegal miners violating the official rules of the game. When it came to removing bulldozers, the state was mostly absent. On the other hand, the government unfurled the violent rigor of the law against the local residents, citing the very rules it overlooked systematically itself. In the uneven confrontation between local residents and outside miners (both legal and illegal), the government designated Francia's community as "occupants in bad faith."

When this happened, Francia mobilized a small group of women from her community to a march to Bogotá. After months trying to push the government to remove the illegal miners, Francia suggested during a community meeting that the only thing left to do was to walk to Bogotá in an act of protest. Her *compañeras* from the local women's association ASOMUAFROYO were initially fearful and her fellow activists from the national leadership of PCN reprimanded her for what they saw as an impulsive and insufficiently planned action. But for Francia and the eighteen or so women who began the march with her, this was a matter of life and death. Frustrated with the government's inaction and unwilling to wait for a nationally coordinated protest, she told her fellow PCN activists that the women of her community couldn't wait any longer: "Go tell those women that they have to wait and plan . . . Those bulldozers are everywhere along Northern Cauca today and you are telling me that I have to continue planning [an action]? When the stakes here are the lives of those women and the people here? Go tell them that, because they are saying that they would rather die [walking] on the streets." And so they quickly organized and started walking. Some left their children with family and neighbors, others brought them along, and by the time they arrived in Bogotá, the group had grown to roughly eighty women and youth.[38]

Once in Bogotá, more people joined the protesters and their numbers grew to roughly 130. They camped outside the Ministry of Interior, waiting in the bitter Andean cold for days while government officials tried to silence their protests by offering a select number of them rooms in a hotel. In the end, a small delegation of the protesters was invited inside the building to a hearing with government representatives. Their message, *Permaneceremos*, was simple and forceful: we will remain. The single Spanish word signaled their intent to remain: to remain outside the building until the illegal occupiers were removed from their territory, to remain on their territory resisting violence and eviction attempts by both the state and outsiders, to remain alive. When her turn came to address the government officials inside the ministry's building, Francia delivered a powerful speech that reasserted the marchers'

determination to remain and repeatedly questioned who the rightful and unlawful occupiers of the territory were:

> We are not willing to let the government come and tell us if we are or are not
> a black community; we *are* a black community and you all have recognized
> a set of rights, *so now abide by them*, that is our demand.
>
> . . . The Colombian Constitutional Court issued a sentence, T-1045A in
> 2010, and in it, the court established:
>
> First: To suspend the mining titles that had been granted without prior
> consent. We have to say that this was negligent on the part of the National
> Mining Agency because we know that they have interests behind the titles
> they granted.
>
> We saw the National Mining Agency (when it was Ingeominas) arrive
> in our territories accompanied by multinationals. We saw how the public
> forces—the national army who is supposed to exist to defend us—confronted
> the community and escorted the multinationals to take samples from the
> mines inside our territories, protecting private interests over public.
>
> We saw how in meetings, government officials declared us "disturbers
> of bad faith."
>
> "Disturbers of bad faith?" I ask, Four hundred years contributing to the
> construction of this country . . . And we are "disturbers of bad faith"? Four
> hundred years bleeding our people dry . . . And we are "disturbers of bad
> faith"? Four hundred years enriching the pockets of others while impover-
> ishing us . . . And we are "disturbers of bad faith"?
>
> We need you to respond very clearly. Because we are not "disturbers of
> bad faith"! *What we have done is construct peace in this country! Real peace! Not
> the peace of empty speeches! Not the peace by way of arms! It's the peace of creating
> and giving birth to men and women of good will! And that is what we've done as
> Black Communities, as black women!*
>
> How many of our women have been displaced from their territories so
> that they can raise your children while you are in these offices? Instilling
> your children with values . . . And we are "disturbers of bad faith"?
>
> How many of us have had to go to your homes to wash your panties?
> And we are "disturbers of bad faith"?

What we want, as the *compañera* stated, is for you *let us live in peace*!
(Márquez 2014)

Pressured by the women's mobilization and the visibility it quickly garnered
(Kane 2014; Las2Orillas 2014b), the government once again committed to
remove the unlawful occupiers and agreed to respect the community's rights,
but unsurprisingly failed to uphold their promises. To this day, the Community Council of La Toma does not yet have a land title, illegal mining has not
been completely removed, and the threat to community organizers is higher
than ever before. Dest (2020) documents this disenchantment with the state
in his own work with indigenous and black organizers in Northern Cauca as
well. In a very similar vein to what I have outlined in this chapter, he notes
that social movements and political organizations in Northern Cauca follow
what he terms an inclusion-autonomy dialectic. That is, even though they
are increasingly frustrated with the government's unfulfilled promises, they
continue to participate in a game that is ultimately defined by the state. But
as Dest notes, this is not a paralyzing position. Instead, the disenchantment
also "creates space for imagining possibilities and enacting alternatives that
move beyond the trappings of the nation-state's discourse of multicultural
rights" (Dest 2020, 18).

Unsurprised by the government's lack of response, the women who led
the protest have continued their daily work of caring for life, even amid the
heightened violence of the so-called post-conflict. This work involves their
everyday activities in their communities—raising their families, mining gold,
and tending to their farms—as well as organizing work that links them to
other black women across the diaspora. In December 2015, for example, they
hosted an international meeting at which black women across the diaspora
gathered to exchange knowledges and experiences to care for life and ancestral territories. The guests included black women organizers from Honduras, Brazil, the United States, and several regions of Colombia. Planned
and carried out entirely autonomously, during the gathering, women learned
about others' struggles, shared strategies for organizing both locally and dias-
porically, and publicly recognized their elders' legacies. When recalling this
encuentro, intended to commemorate the first anniversary of the Women's

March, Francia explained that the funding had been entirely collected from grassroots organizing and that the government had not had any participation in the event. "That was ours," she said proudly. Seeing how fondly she remembered that event and how frustrated she was at the government's broken promises, I asked her why she continued to play "the game," referring specifically to her decision to run for a seat in Congress in 2018, to which she responded: "Because only doing community work has not worked. Even though we do community work, there are laws that get used against us . . . so I decided to become a candidate, although initially I didn't want to do it because I also know that's not the most ideal space to seek transformation, because of the corruption there, because it's a system that is difficult to navigate." In the end, it was clear from both her words and her actions that Francia was opting to both play "the game" and build a world outside of that game. In her political vision to care for life, the two events—the Women's March and the Meeting of Afro-Diasporic Women—were critically linked in their efforts to hold the government accountable and to autonomously build community: "I think it's two strategies that we have to carry out. On the one hand we have to make demands so that the government won't hurt us, so that it will fulfill its constitutional duties, but on the other hand people have to build [on their own] and that's what we wanted to do. We wanted to think about how we, from within our own communities, can make self-government. What does it look like when women care for the territory as space for life? We wanted to have a dialogue about that and to put it in practice." In Francia's vision and practice the care for life is facilitated by a pursuit of Black Citizenship, that is, by adopting a both-and position that makes demands from the state while cultivating a black political community beyond and against the state.

PEACE AS ANTI-GENOCIDE

In this chapter, I have traced several of the responses that Afro-Colombian activists have crafted in the ongoing discussion about peace in Colombia. Some have responded by occupying the spaces opened up within the state and demanding the insertion of various forms of racial and ethnic redress into national (and often color-blind) visions of peace. Such is the case of the CONPA and its work to have an ethnic chapter included in the final draft of the accords. Others have been more selective in choosing which of these state-warranted spaces to occupy. But more important, they have been more expansive in their definition of peace, not as an end to armed conflict but as anti-genocide. This vision of peace, which seeks to eliminate all forces of death, is grounded in Black Communities' ancestral cultivation of the care for life. As Francia Márquez eloquently describes this political project, the challenge "is to transform the politics of death into politics for life" (Zuluaga 2018).

The diasporic debate around Afro-pessimism and black optimism illuminates the continuities in the historical experiences and contemporary political practices of black people across the diaspora, but it does so in a way that does not reproduce the common north–south inequalities that have tended to invisibilize the radical legacies of those in the Global South. The politics of care for life articulated by black women like Francia Márquez in Colombia, certainly resonate with the Black Lives Matter movement in the United States, but they are not derivative of it. Rather, the two have emerged in tandem. I note this not only to rehabilitate the status of black movements of the Global South but also to strengthen the articulation of a black radical politics that binds together the Global North and the Global South.

Thinking with Afro-pessimists and black optimists is also effective in identifying and denouncing structural racism in Colombia as part of the global phenomenon of antiblackness—while remaining attentive to its national particularities. In Colombia, as in the rest of the Americas, the black experience has been irrevocably marked by colonialism and the transatlantic slave trade, or what Saidiya Hartman (2007) calls the "afterlife of slavery." Thus, in Colombia—as in the United States, the United Kingdom, Brazil, and Nicaragua—black people have been deeply preoccupied with the preservation of life for centuries. In response to the relentless attacks on their lives, they have cultivated knowledges and practices to confront and prevail over the genocidal spectrum. As such, it is unsurprising that the affirmation of life is a common thread that weaves many of these black politics together.

In Colombia, however, the preoccupation with untimely death has acquired a new resonance in light of the peace accords. As a national conversation to define the terms of Colombia's "peace" unfolded over the past few years, some black activists quickly moved to contribute their visions of peace to the ongoing process. In doing so, they have sought to broaden the historical depth of the analysis, arguing through different mechanisms that racism (rooted in the nation's colonial origins) is a key force of precarious life and premature death that makes peace impossible. As such, they have sought to shift the discussion from a conjunctural analysis of the war to a structural wrestling with racism. In pursuing this black vision of peace, they have made recourse to strategies of Black Citizenship, which simultaneously hold the state accountable for their rights as Colombians and craft political communities of belonging outside of the state's purview. This is best exemplified by Francia Márquez's political trajectory, which weaves together a deep involvement in national politics with an ongoing investment in and cultivation of black autonomous life.

Most important, the debate around Afro-pessimism and black optimism is useful for gauging how disruptive black movements can be to the structures that reproduce black death and antiblackness more broadly. The point of engaging with the debate is not to arrive at a definitive answer about who is right but to explore concretely what are the spaces for a black undercommons. The purpose is to build movements that do not end up being mere scaffolding in antiblack structures that continue to condemn black bodies to (social) death. Only then will a comprehensive vision of peace be attained.

EPILOGUE
The Promise of Vivir sabroso

Sueñan las pulgas con comprarse un perro y sueñan los nadies con
salir de pobres, que algún mágico día llueva de pronto la buena
suerte, que llueva a cántaros la buena suerte; pero la buena suerte
no llueve ayer, ni hoy, ni mañana, ni nunca, ni en lloviznita cae del
cielo la buena suerte, por mucho que los nadies la llamen y aunque
les pique la mano izquierda, o se levanten con el pie derecho, o
empiecen el año cambiando de escoba. Los nadies: los hijos de nadie,
los dueños de nada. Los nadies: los ningunos, los ninguneados,
corriendo la liebre, muriendo la vida, jodidos, rejodidos.
Que no son, aunque sean.
Que no hablan idiomas, sino dialectos.
Que no hacen arte, sino artesanía.
Que no practican cultura, sino folklore.
Que no son seres humanos, sino recursos humanos.
Que no tienen cara, sino brazos.
Que no tienen nombre, sino número.
Que no figuran en la historia universal, sino en la crónica roja de
la prensa local.
Los nadies, que cuestan menos que la bala que los mata.

Fleas dream of buying themselves a dog; and nobodies dream of
escaping poverty: that one magical day good luck will suddenly
rain down on them—will rain down in buckets. But good luck
doesn't rain down yesterday, today, tomorrow, or ever. Good luck
doesn't even fall in a fine drizzle, no matter how hard the nobodies
summon it, even if their left hand is tickling; or if they begin the
new day with their right foot, or start the new year with a change
of brooms.

The nobodies: nobody's children, owners of nothing. The nobodies:
the no ones, the nobodied, running like rabbits, dying through life,
screwed every which way.
Who are not, but could be.
Who don't speak languages, but dialects.
Who don't have religions, but superstitions.
Who don't create art, but handicrafts.
Who don't have culture, but folklore.
Who are not human beings, but human resources.
Who do not have faces, but arms.
Who do not have names, but numbers.
Who do not appear in the history of the world, but in the police
blotter of the local paper.
The nobodies, who are not worth the bullet that kills them.
—Eduardo Galeano, "Los nadies" (1989)[1]

Just a few weeks ago, I attended the inauguration of President Gustavo Petro and Vice President Francia Márquez in Bogotá. It was a tremendously important day for me and many of my loved ones in Colombia. I had received a special invitation to attend along with other "nonofficial" international guests, and as I arrived at the meeting spot in the Centro de Memoria, Paz y Reconciliación, I saw the faces of many people I have collaborated with over the years—including those with whom I had worked on Francia Márquez's campaign for the previous year and a half. After an hour of animated greetings and group selfies, we were all loaded into buses and driven to the event, which was being held in the heart of the historical district, the illustrious Plaza de Bolívar.

August 7 was one of those intensely blue-sky days in Bogotá, which those who know the city know is a volatile gift. Bogotá's skies can turn an ominous gray in a heartbeat, and the temperature can plummet vertiginously, turning a tropical scene into a hostile highland landscape in seconds. But that day, the sky was perfectly clear. All day. As we navigated numerous security cordons and walked to the seating area, I was in awe of the impressive display of Afrocentric pride. Men, women, and children donning brightly colored African fabrics to match their spectacular hairstyles, despite the invitation's suggested dress code of "dark-colored casual." I found a seat across the aisle from the tireless youth who had led the communications strategy for Francia's campaign. Young people proudly crossing gender lines, young people raised by *campesinos* and domestic workers, university students, young mothers, artists, and feminists proudly wearing green scarves on their wrists. And then Francia came on stage. The crowd's enthusiasm overflowed. The audience was outspoken throughout the ceremony, unapologetically booing their less-favored guests—like the King of Spain—and wholeheartedly embracing their people with whooping and clapping. Here were the *nadies*—the nobodies—who Francia had so consistently uplifted and spoken to throughout her campaign, sitting in the area that had always remained off limits to them.

The event was a majestic celebration of the Colombian *patria* (fatherland), despite the glaring absence of the outgoing president, Iván Duque. The outgoing administration's planning committee had made sure the event was replete with national symbols and moments intended to evoke national pride and somber reflection, marveling at Colombia's cultural, historical, and natural grandeur. But among all the symbols, Bolívar's sword was the most remarkable. The sword of El Libertador, which represents the struggle for independence, stands as the most triumphant symbol of the birth of the creole Colombian nation and has been the object of bitter political controversy. In 1974, a handful of members of the M-19—the guerrilla group that President Petro once belonged to—broke into the presidential palace, stole the sword, and held it until the group demobilized in 1991.[2] Petro had asked for it to be taken out of the Casa Nariño for the inauguration, but Duque had declined. So immediately after being anointed, in a defiant first action as president, Petro ordered that the sword be brought out with *the people*. This was a well-understood gesture, a profound indication that those who had been excluded from power were finally in legitimate possession of the sword. By placing the sword within the reach of *the people*, history was being righted.

In the midst of the excitement surrounding the sword, I thought for a second that President Petro intended to entrust it to Francia Márquez, who was approaching the scene in her splendidly ruffled blue African-print dress, to be sworn in. But that didn't happen. By failing to hand Francia—a young, black woman activist who was known for fighting gold miners out of her impoverished rural hometown—the Libertador's sword, Petro missed the opportunity to make a radical statement about his government truly belonging to the nobodies. But Francia, seized the opportunity. As she held her hand up she deliberately modified the script of the oath she was expected to repeat. She included *the people* as the rightful witnesses of her oath alongside God and immediately added her *ancestros y ancestras* to the list—all of them as guardians of her relentless work to fight for those who have been historically excluded until the day "that dignity may become customary."[3]

Francia's election as vice president, her righteous occupation of a place of power in the heart of the *criollo* nation, is nothing short of astounding. It is, without a doubt, a dramatic and hopeful interruption of business of usual. Her campaign—run entirely on the grassroots fuel of those who believe in her—invigorated the masses. I had the privilege of accompanying her on the final days of her vice presidential campaign. I witnessed the power of Francia as an electrifying wave of people standing to greet her at the Pascual Guerrero stadium in Cali; as an auditorium full of young women, trans and cis, clamoring against misogyny; as a sober meeting of indigenous leaders discussing rural reform; and as the faithful protection of the Guardia Cimarrona. I had been witnessing the power of Francia for many years. And although she is truly charismatic, I dare say that her enormous appeal is not only because of who she is but also because of what she promises: *vivir sabroso.*

The promise of *vivir sabroso* is capacious and also precise. It entails living without fear: fear of untimely death, fear of precarious life, fear of being violated. The promise of *vivir sabroso* is most centrally a project to end the politics of death; and in this sense it is the fiercest iteration of the pursuit of Black Citizenship that I have seen. The right to *vivir sabroso* is a demand for inclusion in the nation; but that nation must be remade not in its colonial semblance but as something else entirely: as a project that harnesses the experiences of the marginalized and exploited and brings them front and center. With Francia and her *nadies* in power, there is a chance for the pursuit of Black Citizenship to be carried out *within* the state, as well as outside and against it. *Vivir sabroso* holds the promise of an alternative to the extractive economies of savage neoliberalism, of a reckoning with historical forms of violence, of a long-postponed attainment of peace, as the triumph of a politics of life.

And yet we must not forget that this liberatory vision is being launched from within the master's house. Is it possible to carry out a decolonial project—against the racist, patriarchal, and exploitative structures that sustain death—while occupying the very center of Colombia's most paradigmatic colonial institution? Can the nation-state be re-created from its entrails? The challenges and contradictions of this project are indeed formidable. The memory and enduring power of the creole national vision—unapologetically white, masculine, and modeled on European modernity—instilled in Bolívar's sword is omnipresent. And still, the presence of Francia and the *nadies* in government holds the promise of transformation of the very state apparatus and of the substance of the nation. Likely unaccomplishable in four years, but hopeful nonetheless. And that is the moderately conservative hope I wish to close with. With the full awareness of the persistent structures that continue to wreak death in all its ugly forms, and with the hope that we can learn from those experiences of violence. To claim the nation-state, only to transform it. Perhaps the project for Black Citizenship involves undoing the very thing that is being reclaimed.

NOTES

Introduction: Black Citizenship

1. This quote was taken from a video caught by an observer who witnessed as NTN24 news channel interviewed protesters on the street. The video was uploaded to a WhatsApp chat on the day of the events.

2. "[De]mostrarle a Colombia y al gobierno nacional que Buenaventura existe." This quote was also taken from a WhatsApp chat created by an important Afro-Colombian activist as the strike erupted to garner international support for the strikers.

3. The following quote from an article titled "Buenaventura's Metastasis" conveys the magnitude of public and private investment that has been undertaken in Buenaventura, which is commensurate with the economic profits that are generated there: "Singapore, Hong Kong, and Tokyo would envy Puerto Aguadulce [in Buenaventura]. . . . In all truth, Buenaventura's three ports evoke the most modern maritime terminals of the Asian tigers, on the other side of the Pacific. Measuring up to this level meant undertaking a 107,000 million [Colombian pesos] dredging works and a two-lane road that is still under construction. . . . It is not coincidental that half of all of Colombia's international commerce goes through there" (*Semana* 2017d). My translation. Unless otherwise noted, all translations are my own.

4. According to Colombia's governmental statistical center, DANE, Buenaventura's poverty index, known as Pobreza Multidimensional, is seventeen points higher than the national average of 49 percent. Further, the unemployment rate in Buenaventura, published by the government's planning department (Departamento Nacional de Pla-

neación) is 62 percent, while the informal employment rate is estimated at 90 percent (*Semana* 2017c).

5. While every year different towns receive recognition for having the largest average rainfall in the world, the Pacific Region of Colombia as a whole is identified as one of the world's wettest areas (Sharp 1981).

6. Quote taken from the same protester being interviewed by NTN24 on May 20, 2017. The video was taken and uploaded to social media on the same day.

7. During just its first day, the economic costs associated with the civic strike were estimated at 10 billion pesos—approximately US$3.4 million at the time (*El Espectador* 2017a). The port was privatized during the government of César Gaviria in 1994, leaving a tremendous amount of wealth in the hands of a miniscule circle of megarich, none of whom live in Buenaventura (Las2Orillas 2014).

8. President Santos received the Nobel Peace Prize in 2016 for his successful negotiation of the peace accords with the FARC.

9. Violence in Buenaventura has been endemic and persistent. Colombia's largest guerrilla group, the FARC, entered the region in the 1980s and by the 1990s had attained hegemonic status. But by the end of the 1990s, the AUC, an extreme-right paramilitary organization, had gained formidable strength and dispersed its militias across the country. In Buenaventura, the AUC's Bloque Calima terrorized the population, carrying out twenty-six massacres in four years and indiscriminately murdering civilians in what has been referred to as "the period of a thousand deaths" (Centro Nacional de Memoria Histórica 2015). Even the so-called demobilization of paramilitary groups, which formally dismantled the Bloque Calima in 2004, did not stop the murders, disappearances, and death threats that ravaged Buenaventura. Instead, the disarticulated wings of the AUC vied among themselves to maintain territorial control of the area to oversee the lucrative arms and drug trade. As a result, numerous groups of heavily armed men, whom the government bluntly called Bandas Criminales, or BACRIM, formed everywhere. While the government sought legitimation of the peace process by marking a substantive difference between the violence of the AUC and that of the BACRIM, signaling a shift away from political violence and toward common crime, the change for Bonaverenses was irrelevant. During this post-AUC period, Buenaventura became known for its infamous *casas de pique* (cutting centers)—clandestine centers where people were tortured, murdered, and subjected to unspeakable forms of bodily degradation. In the period after the formal demobilization of paramilitary groups like the Bloque Calima, the number of illegal armed groups in Buenaventura skyrocketed, accompanied by a horrific degradation of their repertoires of violence. At this time, *casas de pique* surfaced as a phenomenon associated with Buenaventura's intractable lawlessness. In them, the dismembered bodies of unidentified victims of torture were left as ghastly evidence of the city's unabated horror (Centro Nacional de Memoria Histórica 2015; Human Rights Watch 2014; *The Economist* 2014).

10. This text was written on a banner carried by a protester outside the Colombian embassy in Washington, DC. The protesters were convened by the Washington Office on Latin America, which shared photos of the event on social media on May 20, 2017.

11. The civic strike's Organizing Committee is an example of one such community of resistance. In fact, Buenaventura had two previous civic strikes in 2014 and 2016 and had organized in citizen groups for many years before that, like a group that in 2010 mobilized to demand uninterrupted water service (*Semana* 2018).

12. As I detail in chapter 1, the use of kin terms to refer to fellow Afro-descendants is common in Colombia as in other parts of the African diaspora.

13. Some of the Congress members who responded to the strike in Buenaventura through their Twitter accounts were Hank Johnson (D-GA), Gregory Meeks (D-NY), and Keith Ellison (D-MN).

14. For example, while Buenaventura had been virtually invisible in the United States, during the civic strike I was surprised to hear news of the strike make headlines five times in two weeks in the left-wing outlet *Democracy Now*: May 23 and 30, and on June 2, 5, and 7.

15. It is important to explain that the term *Chocó*—which formally refers to an administrative unit similar to a state—is used in common parlance to refer to the entire Pacific Region from the border with Panama to the border with Ecuador. Also, the term *chocoano* is often used as a euphemism for "black."

16. Elsewhere I offer a detailed overview of the place of blackness in Latin American colonial and national formations (Cárdenas 2012). Here I focus on the multicultural moment and its immediate precursor, *mestizaje*.

17. In essence, *mestizaje* is an inversion of the eugenicist idea that miscegenation—or racial mixture—results in degeneration. In efforts to cast the futures of their nations in a more favorable light vis-à-vis their European colonizers, *criollo* nationalist thinkers throughout Latin America reinterpreted miscegenation as a quintessentially Latin American contribution to humanity and as a national asset rather than a liability. Taking the indigenous, black, and European elements as constitutive building blocks, *mestizaje* extolled the virtues of each while claiming that their conjoining would result in a far improved subject that had shed the original "vices" of its components. It bears noting, however, that the mixture championed by *mestizaje* did not equally valorize the components that made up the *mestizo*. As López Rodriguez (2019) has shown in her analysis of whiteness in eighteenth-century Colombia, *mestizaje* became a compelling national project because it offered a viable route to whitening, as *mestizos* gradually became seen as white.

This positive reinterpretation of miscegenation, championed by immortalized scholars like Brazil's Gilberto Freyre (1933) and Mexico's José Vasconcelos (1925) at the beginning of the twentieth century, allowed Latin America to become a potential candidate for modernity at a time when European fascism and its eugenic ideas raised new concerns about white supremacy's global impact. Having turned scientific racism on its head, *mestizaje* made an important and provocative political contribution to the global scenario of the 1930s (Skidmore 1992). Furthermore, *mestizaje* offered a virtuous reinterpretation of Latin America's violent history of racial mixing, which was proudly propped against the United States' white supremacist values expressed in its foundational myth of manifest destiny. Thus, by solidifying a sense of nationalism that refuted accusations of racial inferiority and revalorizing Latin American cultural uniqueness (Euraque, Gould, and Hale 2005), *mestizaje* also functioned as a powerful response to US hegemony.

In the period after World War II, *mestizaje* reigned supreme across Latin America as the foundation of national identities. In some places, such as Mexico, the *mestizo* was imagined as the offspring of only European and indigenous ancestors, while in others, such as Brazil and Cuba, blackness was recognized and valorized as part of that mixture. In some places, *mestizo* nationalism was taken up by the state in both its rhetoric and its policies (Vinson and Vaughn 2004), and in others it became sedimented into common understanding as an antiestablishment revolutionary idea (Gould 1998). Despite these differences, *mestizaje* acquired a number of common characteristics that included the celebration of a homogeneous, mixed-race national subject, a rewriting of colonial history that tended to erase the memory of racial domination by emphasizing harmonious inter-racial *convivencia* (coexistence), and nurturing a profound sense of racial exceptionalism that cast Latin America in a favorable light when compared to its neighbor to the north (Segato 2007).

Most important, as revisionist critics of *mestizaje* have shown, this nationalist ideology is founded on indigenous genocide and antiblackness. By celebrating the gradual whitening of black and indigenous people through race mixture and cultural assimilation, *mestizaje*, in its elite and state-sponsored iterations, has amounted to a Latin American variety of white supremacy. Black scholars in particular have shown its deleterious effects on black subjectivities and black political mobilization across Latin America. There is a rich scholarship that shows how *mestizaje* simultaneously depreciates or erases blackness and indigeneity (Dinzey-Flores and Lloréns 2020; Lloréns 2014; López Oro 2016; Pinho 2009) while denying accusations of racism altogether (De la Cadena 2001; Moreno Figueroa and Saldívar Tanaka 2016; Twine 1997). While a deep engagement with this body of work is beyond the scope of this work, it is important to acknowledge the nuanced ways these authors have traced the gendered (Gilliam 1998; Lloréns 2013), sexual (Allen 2011), and political (Hanchard 1998; Hooker 2005a; Rahier 2003) dimensions of *mestizaje* across the region, remarking on the particularities of their specific contexts while converging on the observation that in their obsessive pursuit of whiteness, *mestizo* nationalisms have historically sought to erase blackness.

18. *Criollo*, sometimes translated as "creole," was the colonial term used for children of Spaniards born in the Americas. Although the term has a wide array of meanings across the Americas, for the purpose of this text, I use it as a racialized term that signals European descent and, by extension, whiteness.

19. The blanket ethnicization of difference was derived from a long history of ethnicizing indigeneity. By the 1900s, the *indio* was already conceived as the quintessential ethnic subject, and therefore served as the model for ethnic difference during the Constituent Assembly of 1991 that formally identified Afro-Colombians as ethnic subjects for the first time in Colombian history (Bocarejo 2008). Although an analysis of the ethnicization of indigeneity is beyond the scope of this work, it bears highlighting that this, too, has been produced and is neither natural nor necessary (Comaroff and Comaroff 2009).

20. I have chosen to capitalize *Black Communities*, because this was the legal term for the collective subject of rights designated by Law 70 in 1993. In other words, *Black Community* refers to a concept that did not exist as a juridical category prior to the passage of Law 70. Because Black Communities are legally entitled to collective territories, I have also opted to capitalize the terms *Black Territories* and *Black Territoriality.*.

21. The local government committed to immediately opening two water treatment plants to solve the city's meager water supply of fewer than ten hours every two days. A common fund of more than US$500 million was destined to be spent during the course of the incumbent governor's administration on housing, health, employment, water and sanitation, education, energy, and justice. Finally, the government committed to drafting a ten-year development plan in collaboration with members of the civic strike's Organizing Committee as well as representatives of previously existent black and indigenous governance units. The plan was to be jump-started by a seed fund of US$76 million that would be supplemented by 50 percent of all tax income generated from commercial port activities (*Semana* 2017e).

22. The Yoruba concept of *ashe* refers to the power to command authority and the ability to make things happen, to produce change.

23. This quote was taken from a video circulated by a member of PCN in the aftermath of Temístocles's murder in a private WhatsApp chat. The video depicts Don Temis's *compañeros* making a statement of grief and solidarity in front of the camera.

24. In fact, until the very recent election of Gustavo Petro in June 2022, Colombia had never had a left-wing president in power, and thus the differences in prior administrations' approaches to racial, gender, and economic equality were more of degree than substance.

25. It is beyond the scope of this work to thoroughly review the robust literature on the Colombian conflict. Instead, I point to a few scholars whose excellent works on memory and resistance I find particularly enlightening (Uribe Alarcón 1990, 2004, 2009; Riaño-Alcala 2006; Ramírez 2001; Jimeno 2010, 2011; Castillejo Cuéllar 2014 2000). For other discussions of the war, see Bejarano Ávila and Díaz Uribe (1985); Bolívar Ramirez (2003); Guzmán Campos (1963, 2005); and Sánchez G. and Aguilera Peña (2001).

26. I have chosen to maintain the term *campesino* in Spanish to signal the differing genealogies and contemporary usage of the terms *campesino* and *peasant*. While a thorough history of these terms is beyond the scope of this explanation, it is important to note that *campesino* is a current identity that signals particular relationships to land and labor relations in Colombia and in Latin America more broadly. The term has been used as a self-ascribed marker of political identity and gained further currency with the rise of transnational agrarian organizations in the 1990s. The choice is therefore not simply a matter of refusing translation but of signaling a particular genealogy and political content. For more on this, see Edelman (2013).

27. For more on the emergence of the FARC, see Tate (2007). For more on Colombia's exclusionary democracy and "failed state," see Bushnell (1993); Palacios (1983).

28. For an in-depth ethnographic account of paramilitaries, see Civico (2015).

29. The links between paramilitary forces and elected officials—in particular those allied with Uribe—have been well documented since the early 2000s thanks to the bold denunciations made by Gustavo Petro and Clara López. The phenomenon, known as *parapolítica*, or in some cases *parauribismo*, was so deep that by 2013, more than sixty members of Congress and other elected officials had been convicted for their links to these illegal groups and many more were under investigation.

30. The Asociación Campesina Integral del Atrato, or ACIA, was a coalition of *campesino* communities along the Atrato River, which was formed in 1987 in the Pacific Region to protect the area from the threat of extractivist industries such as large-scale logging. After articulating its work to protect lands with that of black activists driving the passage and implementation of Law 70, ACIA became a coalition of black community councils, Consejo Comunitario Mayor de la Asociación Campesina Integral del Atrato (COCO-MACIA) and the first recipient of a collective land title in Colombia.

31. To signal its change in structure, this national office changed its name to Asociación Nacional de Afrocolombianos Desplazados in 2009, although it kept the same acronym.

32. I have placed scare quotes around Afro-Colombian culture to distance my own conception of the diverse cultural practices of Afro-Colombians from an essentialized notion of Afro-Colombian culture, which when mobilized in formal spaces is often imagined as a monolith. The purpose is evidently not to undermine the value of Afro-Colombian cultural practices, but quite the opposite, to recognize its plurality and resist its homogenization.

33. In fact, for a brief moment they joined their international lobbying efforts and opened a joint AFRODES-PCN-USA office in Washington, DC. This was a short-lived effort because of both personal and political differences between members of the two organizations.

34. Many of these new organizations prefer the term *Afro* over the term *negro*. While sometimes used interchangeably, the two terms have different genealogies and often signal a different set of political commitments. While a detailed analysis of the difference is beyond the scope of this text, I find it important to signal that they are not entirely synonymous, and that while *negro* is most often associated with the rural movements of the late 1980s, *Afro* has become the norm after the solidification of the multicultural state apparatus that followed the passage of Law 70.

35. When I mention family I am referring to the kinship ties that I made through marriage and child rearing, as well as to the long-term relationships that I have forged over the years and are now part of my chosen family.

36. I am grateful to Anthony Dest for offering the language of "ethnographies in struggle" to think through the political and methodological entanglements of politically committed research.

37. In Colombia, *desplazados* is the colloquial term that people use to refer to internally displaced people, or IDPs. Though common, it is perceived as offensive by some, and for that reason, I try to use it only when it appears in my interlocutors own speech.

38. I learned about Geiler and AFRODES through my then-husband, the filmmaker Juan Mejía, who had begun a collaborative video project with a group of displaced youth that were affiliated to AFRODES that year. Like myself, Juan has maintained his collaboration with Afro-Colombian activists over the years and has been steadfast in his commitment to anti-racism in Colombia. Most recently, he directed a documentary on Francia Márquez's candidacy to the presidency and her subsequent triumph as vice president. This brilliant documentary, due to premiere in 2023, is entitled *Igualada*.

39. Forced confinement, which occurred primarily in rural areas, refers to community members' inability to move freely within their territories or between communities for fear of encountering armed combat or entering enemy territory. The material and symbolic consequences of this restriction on movement was very severe for Black Communities, and it is a topic that chapter 1 addresses in depth.

40. Márquez initially ran a precampaign as presidential candidate for the movement Soy Porque Somos (a Spanish translation of the concept of ubuntu), which she created and continues to lead. In the end, despite a fierce attempt at running a grassroots campaign, she joined the left-wing coalition Pacto Histórico, which had the support of more established political figures and organizations on the left. The coalition elected the presidential and vice-presidential candidates through a primary in March 2022. Although Márquez did not win the nomination as presidential candidate, she won the second highest number of votes within the Pacto Histórico coalition (and the third across the political spectrum) and secured her candidacy as vice president, running alongside Gustavo Petro later in 2022.

Chapter 1: Black Territoriality

1. *Mireños* is the term with which inhabitants of the Mira River refer to themselves. As I will explain in more detail, there are many villages along the entire course of the river, but I focus on its lower portion, the Bajo Mira, which flows into the Pacific Ocean.

2. As explained in the introduction, I refer to the multicultural turn as the moment when the Colombian government—like others across Latin America—granted special rights to ethnically differentiated groups and recognized the nation not as culturally homogeneous but as multicultural and pluriethnic.

3. The original inhabitants of the Pacific were indigenous groups that sparsely inhabited the area before the arrival of Spanish colonizers. As early as 1511 the Spaniards knew that there was gold in the Pacific Region, but topography, climate and "fierce Indians" rebuffed attempts to enter this potential El Dorado until the seventeenth century. The Spanish penetrated this region of tropical rainforests and mangrove swamps with their slave gangs only after having triggered an Indian ethnocide through disease and protracted warfare. The region's many rivers served as useful, if treacherous, ways to follow ore deposits. Their flows determined possible travel routes through the forested lowland areas, and as a result, colonial occupation took on a riverine and haphazard pattern, making permanent settlements rare. Here, scattered and provisional mining camps served the primary objective at hand: to find and extract gold using African enslaved

labor. Given the hot and humid climate, the region was believed to be unhealthy for whites, and most slave-owners preferred to send overseers to manage their business while retiring to a life of comfort with their domestic slaves in towns with established colonial administrative seats and more temperate weather.

Even during slavery, the frontier character of the Pacific Region offered enslaved people and their descendants respite from the long arm of colonial domination. This made possible the acquisition of de facto forms of freedom through a combination of widespread manumission and Maroonage. As a result, many black people joined "unpacified" Indians to practice subsistence and commercial agriculture (which they traded with miners, who were always in need of food provisions), as well as independent mining (*mazamorraje*) and contraband gold trade (Sharp 1981). Particularly during the wars of independence, black pressure through guerrilla warfare and Maroonage was relentless and helped bring about the final abolition of slavery in 1851. By this time, free blacks outnumbered the enslaved and had successfully settled in small aggregates away from centers of white power. Almost invariably, they had continued to mine as *mazamorreros*, or free laborers. Over the following century, black population aggregates expanded at a far greater rate than indigenous populations, and Afro-Colombians came to dominate the Pacific Region both numerically and in relative political terms in a process that Whitten (1974, 51) has termed *racial succession*.

4. On the Pacific in general, legal marriage is rare. The norm is common-law marriage, which is marked at the moment in which a man and a woman live in the same house. The phrase that is used to refer to this is *cogió mujer* or *cogió marido*, which can be translated as "getting a woman" or "getting a husband." Throughout when I mention marital terms such as *wife*, *husband*, or *marriage*, I am referring to this practice.

5. This term is used to refer to the swampy forests of the Colombian Pacific. These forests differ from those that are seasonally flooded due to the overflow of nearby riverbanks. *Guandal* forests remain flooded with the abundant and constant rainfall of the region (Frazier 1957; Frazier and Glazer 1966; Herskovits 1958).

6. In the rest of this chapter I alternate between the emic term *proceso* and its literal translation in English—process. However, in both cases the term refers to the historically situated process of creating ethnic consciousness among Afro-Colombians and the attaining of cultural and territorial rights.

7. This has changed somewhat since the law was passed in 1993 as a result of Afro-Colombians' insistent work to expand the interpretation of the law. In the rest of this book I trace some of these changes, such as the struggle to include black people in urban areas not as anomalies or "people out of place" (Cresswell 1996).

8. In collective territories with higher population density this is no longer possible. However, on the Mira River, which is still sparsely populated (less than ten thousand people), it is a common practice.

9. *Walking* refers to living an itinerant life with or without a concrete destination, and it is most often done by young people who are unencumbered by family responsibilities or by men who can more easily eschew them. When they refer to their walking, people

may have been following seasonal work, such as logging, fishing, or plantation farming; or they may have been on route to a specific place, such as to meet family on another river; or they may let their travels be spontaneously dictated by chance. Walking is usually not regarded as a temporary way of living but as a temporary and particularly carefree and enjoyable life stage.

10. In her work in the lower Atrato River in the Northern Pacific, Natalia Quiceno Toro (2016, 4) suggests that the concept of *vivir sabroso* entails the right balance of temperature, movement, and distance, which creates a good life. Rather than a model for an ideal life, the pursuit of *vivir sabroso* is a way to navigate the risks, dangers, and tensions of a territory steeped in conflict. I return to Quiceno in chapter 2, where I explore place-making in the midst of war.

11. For a thorough analysis of the place of blackness within Latin American nation-building projects, see Cárdenas (2010).

12. I use *creole* as the translation of *criollo*, to refer to children of Spaniards born in the Americas.

13. Furthermore, this effort responds to a call by various revisionist scholars of *mestizaje* to analyze blackness and indigeneity in Latin America jointly (Anderson, 2009; Hale and Mullings, 2020; De la Cadena, 2000; Wade, 1993) to challenge the common idea that has placed blacks in the realm of race and indigenous people in the realm of culture.

14. The language that I use is here is taken from the PCN's first three guiding principles, which speak about "the affirmation of being, the space to be, and the exercise of being." See the web page "Quiénes somos" at the PCN website (https://renacientes.net/quienes-somos/).

15. My discussion of love as an analytical category is strongly informed by Donna Haraway's (2003) theorization of interspecies relationality. In particular, I build on her suggestion that love is manifested through careful attention.

16. In a richly descriptive piece on the *tuqueros*, or loggers, of Colombia's southern Pacific, the anthropologist Eduardo Restrepo (1996) minutely lists all the terms that are locally used in the process of identifying, producing, and transporting commercial wood from the *guandal* forests.

17. Aroldo told me that whereas the going market price for a hectare of conserved forest could be as high as US$800, they were currently receiving 40,000 Colombian pesos in kind (approximately US$22) per conserved hectare. This still amounted to more than US$200,000 in income for the community council, and although the market was far more profitable, intermediaries could take as much as 50 percent of the going price. In his view, the MIDAS project was a dress rehearsal for the community council to enter the incipient global market for environmental services.

18. These three fishing methods are listed from least to most invasive. The *atarraya* is a handheld circular net that is usually operated by a single person standing on a boat or on the water's edge. The *chinchorro* is a long net with lead weights on the bottom that is dragged along a circular area, scooping up all the fish in that space. The number of people

required to operate it depends on its size. And finally, the *trasmallo* consists of several layers of woven nets that create pockets to catch fish. On the Mira River's smaller streams people sometimes place them across the entire course of the water, thereby catching everything that flows downriver.

19. There is a robust literature on indigenous notions of *buen vivir* in Latin America (Gudynas 2011; Walsh 2016; Postero 2017), which is complementary to my discussion and useful in illustrating visions of well-being that contrast with the capitalist pursuit of profit. Although there is no single notion *buen vivir*, there are several characteristics that can be distilled to approximate a definition. *El buen vivir* is fundamentally collective. It centers communities rather than individuals. It is focused on cultivating nonharmful relationships, not only with other people—within and outside a given community— but also with nonhumans. In Western parlance, this is often referred to as an ecological awareness, although I think it is important to attribute it to a distinct awareness of interspecies relationality. And finally, this notion of well-being is not prescriptive or ethnocentric, but multiple and culturally expansive. It is a vision of the world, as the Zapatistas have articulated, as "a world in which many worlds fit." This notion has many resonances among black communities in Colombia and is best captured in the notion of *vivir sabroso*, which I describe in more detail in chapter 2. Recently, and as a result of Francia Márquez's vice-presidential candidacy, this concept has exploded in usage well beyond black communities on the Pacific and has been embraced as a hopeful alternative to living in fear of poverty, war, and violence more broadly.

20. According to reports by the Diocese of Tumaco, PCN, and the human rights group Comisión Intereclesial de Justicia y Paz, Felipe Landázuri, a member of the Bajo Mira's board and a health promotor was tied behind the health post and the community was taken at gunpoint to witness his torture. After witnesses were dismissed, they heard the shots that killed him. The murder occurred just when the community council had begun a systematic survey of the territory in its efforts to keep oil palm and coca cultivation out (Diócesis de Tumaco 2008; Comisión Intereclesial de Justicia y Paz 2008).

21. Unlike their indigenous counterparts, *resguardos*, the community councils of Black Communities, do not receive cash transfers from their respective municipalities and therefore have no discretionary funds.

22. According to data collected by the UNODC (2011; 2012, 8), the municipality of Tumaco went from having no coca cultivation in 2001 to being one of the four municipalities with highest concentration of coca over the following ten years.

23. According to the latest UNODC (2020, 41) coca census, conducted in 2019, the border region of Nariño (which belongs to the municipality of Tumaco), continued to experience steady and sharp growth in coca cultivation until 2016, and the Bajo Mira's neighboring community council of Alto Mira y Frontera had one of the three highest areas of coca cultivation of all Black Communities between 2017 and 2019 (UNODC 2020, 170).

24. Plan Colombia was the massive US foreign-aid package that funded Colombia's military spending between 1999 and 2015. The plan was a major factor in escalating the

war and deepening human rights violations with the pretext of eradicating illicit crops and eliminating insurgent *guerrilla* groups.

25. However, after 2012, coca cultivation saw a sharp increase in Tumaco again and more broadly across the Pacific Region and in Black Communities specifically. Nariño, in fact, was the department with the most areas of coca cultivation in the country until 2018 (UNODC 2020).

26. A cornerstone of this struggle is the current defense of prior consultation, which in theory guarantees the participation of ethnic authorities in being informed and making decisions regarding projects or activities held in their territories. The right to prior consultation is a key provision of the Indigenous and Tribal People's Convention, 1989 (No. 169), which was passed by the International Labour Organization in 1989 and ratified by the Colombian government in 1991.

27. I use the term *community council* to refer to both the legally recognized forty-three black communities of the Lower Mira River and to the administrative unit—the board—on which they sit. For this reason, the community council can be both a beneficiary of donated goods—as I have described here—and a supplier of the same goods. As a supplier in the case above, the FAO would pay the community council's board to produce seedlings. Then the board would use that income to benefit the communities of the community council at its discretion.

28. Between 2006 and 2009, the US dollar lost significant ground to international currencies worldwide. In Colombia, this was a period of sharp decrease in the price of US dollars.

Chapter 2: Differential Reparations

1. Condoto is a municipality of the Colombian Department of Chocó along the Condoto River, a tributary of the San Juan River, one of the Chocó's three largest river basins.

2. *Monte* is a difficult Colombian term to translate into English. In general it can refer to the "wilderness" in opposition to a town or to a farm. It doesn't refer specifically to a particular ecosystem, so the *monte* can be a lowland forest or a highland plateau. In the case of guerrilla groups, their modus operandi is synonymous with hiding out in a vague and undetermined *monte*, which refers to spaces not normally inhabited by civilians.

3. I borrow this concept of *los armados* (armed men) from Natalia Quiceno Toro's (2016) ethnographic work on the Atrato River. She takes this term from her interlocutors, to note that for them the boundaries between the legal force of the state and illegal groups on both the right and the left are often blurry if not altogether irrelevant. For Black Communities on the Atrato River, all *armados* contribute to the militarization of their territories, which in turn has brought about "the transformation of life, and the imposition, even through the use of arms, of other ways of living" (Quiceno Toro 2016, 16).

4. María Elena is referring to members of Colombia's AUC, which was an illegal, nationwide coalition of extreme-right militias that consolidated in 1997 and was officially demobilized in 2005.

5. Even though Vergara-Figueroa chooses the word *deracination*, which is the English

adaptation of a French word, I have chosen to keep the Spanish term *destierro*, which is Arboleda's original term.

6. For example, in their analyses of the internal displacement of Afro-Colombians, Escobar (2008), Restrepo (2005), and Wouters (2001) have all described it as a new, unprecedented phenomenon.

7. In 2021 María Elena received the Defender of the Year Award from Colombia's annual Human Rights Prize.

8. The struggle that I outline in this chapter is specifically concerned with aid, restitution, and reparations for Afro-Colombian victims of the war. It is not, as I show in this chapter and the next, directly concerned with historical reparations for slavery. This is a very important distinction. In practice, the language that Afro-Colombian activists use simply refers to "aid, restitution, and reparations for Afro-Colombian victims," and the word *war* tends to remain implicit. I have decided to include the word *war* in parentheses to clarify that they are demanding redress for Afro-Colombian victims of the war, but also to highlight that often the distinction between victims of war and historical victims is not explicit (Arboleda Quiñones 2007; Mosquera Rosero-Labbé 2007).

9. It is important to clarify that the attack in Riosucio was not replicated in identical form across the region. In each place, the actors, interests, histories, and responses were different. These contextual details make a difference, and I do not intend to make broad generalizations that obviate these particularities. That said, I take the events in Riosucio as an important marker of the shift in forms of violence that occurred across the Pacific during this period.

10. The data on Operation Genesis were taken from the reports drafted by the human rights watchdog group Comisión Intereclesial Justicia y Paz (http://justiciaypazcolombia .com) (Colombia Plural 2016; *El Espectador* 2014, 2017).

11. Just a few days after the paramilitary entry in Riosucio, the first and largest collective land title was granted to the members of the Asociación Campesina Integral del Atrato, or ACIA, who had been organizing since the 1980s, first as *campesinos* and later as members of Black Communities who formally became an alliance of community councils called Consejo Comunitario Mayor de la Asociación Campesina Integral del Atrato (COCOMACIA). Observers have noted with suspicion the coincidence of armed violence with the strengthening of the local organizational process of Black Communities (Paschel 2016; Quiceno Toro 2016).

12. Throughout this section I use the term *IDP* because it is the emic category used category used by the state, humanitarian aid organizations, and uprooted people themselves. I engage in a further analysis of this category in chapter 3.

13. This figure is adjusted for people who since 1985 have died and for those who "have overcome housing-related vulnerability as they have started to move towards a durable solution to their displacement" (Internal Displacement Monitoring Centre 2018).

14. These calculations were done using the most updated data available at the time of writing and revising the final draft of this manuscript in October 2022.

15. It is important to note that the 2005 census data, which places the Afro-Colombian

population at approximately 11 percent of the national total, is widely regarded as ludicrously low. Also, I wish to add a clarification of the categories used in that census, which were subsequently adopted as the standard. The census question includes five racial/ethnic categories: *gitano o rom* ("Gypsy" or Romany), *indígena* (indigenous), *negro o afro-colombiano* (black or Afro-Colombian), *palenquero* (from the Maroon community of Palenque San Basilio), and *raizal* (from the Caribbean islands of San Andrés, Santa Catarina, and Providencia). There is also the option of choosing *ninguna* (none), which is a tacit way of marking whiteness or an ethnic nondistinction. For the purpose of this chapter, I combine the last three categories as "black."

16. "El río en su tejido es ahora memoria de las últimas destrucciones, los meandros son aposento donde se resguardan los despojos, las canoas partidas y los aparejos de pesca deshechos. Desde la orilla todo quiere ser camino del olvido, los rostros dolidos ante la gran avenida, y los gritos que acechan, y los cantos que lloran todos los muertos. Arriba, en el río Timbiquí y en el Saija, sus gentes en la estampida se olvidan del guazá y del tambor; los del Naya, solo tienen recuerdos de muerte; los del Napi, escuchan historias de miedo y en las noches los fantasmas acompañan su sueño. Como ola gigante llega desde muy lejos el canto de Guerra, el horizonte es apenas incendio en Sanquianga, entre los esteros se pregona la muerte, en firmes y playas se clavan las banderas del odio y en Barbacoas, la de historias doradas, el universo es ahora hecho de cascajo, ruinas y escombros."

17. The original in Spanish is "la guerra es una situación a pesar de la cual la vida sigue" (Quiceno Toro 2016, 10).

18. Most literally, this term could be translated as "a delicious life." However, I have decided to leave it in Spanish because of the difficulty of adequately translating it. *Sabroso* could loosely be translated as "delicious" to signify things, actions, people that produce pleasure. It is a sensory term in that it usually refers to at least one of the senses, but in Quiceno Toro's (2016, 5) interpretation of her interlocutors' use, it is more than that; it is an aspiration, a practice, a philosophy that searches for balance in life and it is an ethics, not simply a pursuit of pleasure.

19. It is important to recall that the official term used by government offices in Colombia is *personas en situación de desplazamiento*. The term *desplazado*, however, is the one that circulates most broadly in common parlance although it is sometimes perceived as pejorative. My own usage is meant to preserve the most broadly circulating term while economizing on words. I also use it interchangeably with *IDP*, which is the internationally circulating term in English.

20. This organization as well as the full apparatus of humanitarian aid disbursement are described in detail in chapter 3. The amounts depended on the total number of members in a family unit. From my informants' recollections, at that time the amount for a family of five was 900,000 pesos. If we use the historical exchange rate for January 1, 1999, it amounts to approximately US$512.

21. Strictly speaking, *chocoano* is the Spanish term for people from the department (state) of Chocó, the largest state along the Pacific Region. In common parlance, however, it is also a racialized term, used as a euphemism for "black."

22. In a separate piece coauthored with members of PCN, I outline the structural dimensions of antiblack racism in Colombia in detail (Cárdenas et al. 2020). For the purpose of this chapter, which focuses on interpersonal racism primarily, I provide a brief summary of recent data on racial inequality. The analyses made in the past decade show persistent gaps between the poverty rate of Afro-descendants and the white-*mestizo* populations of the country. According to a 2012 study by the Colombian National Administrative Department of Statistics (DANE), the proportion of the national population living under the poverty line was 34 percent, while the corresponding proportion for Afro-Colombians was 55 percent. The panorama is even more unequal considering statistics on extreme poverty, which show that the proportion of Afro-Colombians living in these conditions (25 percent) is almost double the percentage for the national population (13 percent) (Urrea, Viáfara, and Viveros 2014, 105). Likewise, the Afro-Colombian population, in relation to the national population that is ethnically unidentified, suffers from double the rate of hunger (DANE and CIDSE 2010). These gaps are also present in access to basic services: twice as many Afro-Colombian households lack aqueducts, sewage, and energy services compared to the corresponding rate of the overall national population (Rodríguez Garavito et al. 2009, 63). To these statistics we can add national indicators on education, which confirm the persistence of racial inequalities (Telles, Flores, and Urrea-Giraldo 2015), as well as the systematic underrepresentation of Afro-Colombians in the media, in government, and in positions of power more broadly.

23. Of course, scholars have remarked that the two are not unrelated but rather reflect and constitute one another (Bonilla-Silva 2009; Bourgois 2003), but the analytical distinction between the difference of experience is important here.

24. In Colombia, the generic form for curricula vitae includes a space for a picture. While different employers may have different requirements for a job application, it is generally assumed that the CV should include a recent photo of the applicant.

25. Rosa is implicitly referring to a common racial insult that circulates in Colombia and in Latin America more broadly, which is *negro hijueputa*. The phrase could be translated as "you black son of a bitch," but it is incredibly flexible in its usage and can be combined with practically any other insult. Because the emphasis in this phrase is on the adjective *negro* rather than whatever follows it, it is a racial slur indistinct of its use.

26. Between 2003 and 2005 I worked as a volunteer for AFRODES at the office in Bogotá. In addition to providing support with grant writing and managing the databases on affiliates, I also helped design and launch the organization's first website. Much of the information in this section is taken from unpublished documents that I compiled during this period.

27. The Conferencia Nacional Afro-Colombiana (CNOA) was initially conceived as a collective space for black organizations to come together to pursue a common political agenda in their negotiations with the state. When this initiative failed, in large part due to interpersonal conflicts and important political differences among its member organizations, CNOA turned into an independent organization of its own. Since then, numerous other national-level coalitions such as CONAFRO and the CONPA have emerged.

28. The creation of the SNAIPD was mandated by Law 387 in 1997 and conceived as a network of government offices, which together were charged with designing and implementing protection and response measures for IDPs. Along with the CNAIPD—its executive branch—it was the overarching government initiative for IDPs until 2012, when following the passage of the Victims' Law in 2011 (Law 1448), the SNAIPD was superseded by the Unidad para la Atención y Reparación Integral a las Víctimas (Center for Comprehensive Aid and Reparations for Victims).

29. Over time, they incorporated the denunciation of individual and collective human rights violations to this aspect of their work. Specifically, they documented the violation of black leaders' human rights in order to denounce them both inside and outside of Colombia and they worked to design and implement protection plans for black activists at risk.

30. This was echoed later in their active involvement in the passage of the 2011 Victims Law, which had specific provisions for reparations for Afro-Colombians and which I discuss in greater detail in chapter 5.

31. This is not exclusively Geiler's idea, but a product of the ethno-territorial process that I outlined earlier in this book.

32. I am referring to the well-known disagreement between Franklin Frazier and Melville Herskovits regarding cultural loss or retentions of African Americans, and in Colombia to a heated debate between those who locate the essence of Afro-Colombians' difference in their *huellas de africanía* (footprints of Africanness) (Friedemann 1992) and those who understand black identity as shifting and overdetermined (Restrepo 2003).

33. For García, as for his countless informants, the international border that separates these two nation-states is simply a line (*una raya*) that cuts across a single territory and its people.

34. The participants of this project—CNOA, PCN, ORCONE, AFRODES, and Asomujer y Trabajo—included all but one of Colombia's main national black organizations and was by no means an exclusive product of AFRODES's initiative. However, AFRODES appropriated the document that was produced as its public policy proposal for black IDPs because its members were the most active participants in its design. In fact, in subsequent interorganizational spaces with fellow Afro-Colombians, AFRODES attempted to introduce the document as common ground, but it was often not wholeheartedly embraced even by the organizations that participated in its design. For this reason, I take this document to be mainly representative of AFRODES's views.

35. The language in the law was vague and failed to delineate concrete steps for ethnicity-specific reparations. Instead, it charged the government with designing these measures by including the following injunction: "The measures for assistance, aid and reparations for indigenous people and Afro-Colombian communities will be part of a specific set of norms that will be elaborated for each of these ethnic groups, and which will be previously consulted in order to respect each group's customs and collective rights" (Ley 1448 del 2011).

36. This rerouting was not exclusive to AFRODES and has also been characteristic of

PCN in recent years. In fact, for a few years, AFRODES and PCN established a partnership to coordinate their international political efforts. Together they presented human rights reports at the Inter-American Commission on Human Rights, lobbied key Congress members to intervene on behalf of specific issues (e.g., implementation of Auto 005, against passage of the Free Trade Agreement), and built a robust network of allies that stood ready to write letters and make phone calls to denounce human rights violations abroad. Although this partnership was short-lived due to long-standing political differences between the two organizations, both of them continue to do much international lobbying work with partners and allies in the United States.

37. In fact, AFRODES's report is one of only two independent shadow reports presented by Colombian civil society organizations. The other was the result of a joint effort of three organizations: the Observatorio de Discriminación Racial, the Comisión Colombiana de Juristas, and the Organización Nacional Indígena de Colombia (ONIC). In addition to these, two international observers presented reports: the organization Afrocolombia XXI, and the Internal Displacement Monitoring Centre. Unlike AFRODES, none of the organizations listed are led or staffed by Afro-Colombians.

Chapter 3: Beyond Victimized Citizenship

1. I wish to draw attention to the fact that *Afro* has been taken up as the most common term for ethno-racial identification in the past twenty years. It is sometimes used interchangeably with the term *negro* (black) but often replaces it as a more politically correct choice. However, some activists insist on maintaining the use of *negro*. For a discussion of the history and politics of these racial terms, see Restrepo (2021).

2. The process to become an official IDP requires individuals to give a declaration at a state-sanctioned post. Then, the declaration is verified and a notification of acceptance or rejection is given. The criteria for determining whether the testimonies rendered are legitimate are inconsistent and opaque. Sometimes the determining factor is mostly a bureaucratic issue; sometimes the veracity of the story is called into question. In any case, in 2009 if the declaration was deemed legitimate, the individual and their designated family unit were entered into the national IDP database that existed then (Registro Único de Población Desplazada, or RUPD) and became eligible for state aid.

3. For the small minority of people who were employed, the two most common occupations were in construction and domestic service. Although I can't pause to analyze formal sources of employment for residents of Cazucá, I cannot overlook the fact that these are highly gendered and racialized occupations.

4. As discussed in chapter 2, estimates of IDPs in general and black IDPs specifically, vary. Despite this variability, it is safe to assert that a disproportionately large number of displaced people in Colombia are black.

5. The magnitude and tragedy of forced displacement in Colombia is difficult to overstate. For over two decades, approximately 250,000 people have been violently uprooted from their homes and forced into extremely precarious and dangerous circumstances every year (CODHES 2013). Although this number may not be as dramatic as that of

other countries such as Syria, the accumulated number of IDPs places Colombia among the five countries that together account for more than 60 percent of the number of IDPs around the world, along with Sudan, Nigeria, and the Democratic Republic of Congo (IDMC 2016). Another way to look at the astounding scale of this humanitarian crisis is to consider that this number accounts for nearly 15 percent of the total Colombian population.

6. In chapter 2, I analyze this in detail by looking at the work of AFRODES and its shifting strategies over the past twenty years.

7. To distinguish the two pursuits, I consistently qualify the word *reparations*. I use *war reparations* to refer to the contemporary efforts to incorporate ethno-racial specific demands to state-administered programs for victims of Colombia's civil war. By *historical reparations*, I refer to movements to repair the harm done by slavery, the transatlantic slave trade, and their accumulated effects.

8. In Wilson's case, the monthly stipend was 500,000 pesos (US$239) for food and 300,000 pesos (US$143) for rent. The lump sum transfer was $1.5 million pesos (US$714). The average exchange rate in 2000 was 2,088 pesos to the US dollar.

9. Elsewhere I describe in detail how both Wilson's sister and Isaías were active leaders in ABCUN, the local chapter of AFRODES, and as such they key brokers in the recognition of *afro-desplazados* (Cárdenas 2018).

10. In an earlier article, I coined this convergence "green multiculturalism." There, I looked at the case of small-scale oil-palm cultivation in the collective territory of the Lower Mira River. By analyzing that case, I corroborated what I already suspected: that state-sanctioned land titles are not sufficient to protect territorial autonomy for Black Communities. But more surprisingly and certainly most perversely, that the granting of rights themselves can end up jeopardizing Black Communities' pursuit of autonomous livelihoods (Cárdenas 2012c).

11. More precisely, although the RSS had been operating since 1994, it was officially created as a national public entity in 1997 (through Law 368). It also bears noting that the idea of a government office dedicated to vulnerable population groups and the eradication of poverty had two antecedents in prior administrations: President Betancur's Secretaría de Integración Popular and President Barco's Plan Nacional de Rehabilitación (BID 2011).

12. Interestingly, although the United Nations has never established an agency charged specifically with overseeing internal displacement, in some cases such as in Colombia, it has granted the UNHCR—whose mission is to deal with refugees—the necessary authority to intervene on behalf of IDPs. This responds to an attempt to respect states' sovereignty by not meddling in their internal affairs.

13. See Meertens (2010) on the central role of the Constitutional Court in creating "positive discrimination" mechanisms to distinguish gendered and racialized victims.

14. The complete name of this office is Unit for Attention and Integral Reparation for Victims, but it is often referred to simply as "La Unidad."

15. This conflation tends to flatten the distinctions not only between the two cate-

gories but also internal to each, such that the risk factors that indicate that a person is "vulnerable" can include poverty, drug traffic, or armed violence, obviating the profound differences in the political contexts and needed resolutions to each of these cases.

16. This is not to say that slaves and their descendants in the Americas have never been recognized as victims. However, for historical reasons beyond the scope of this analysis, these recognitions have been marginal in comparison to those for indigenous people. Restrepo (2008), for example, traces the arduous work of Padre Alonso de Sandoval to baptize African slaves in Cartagena to save their souls. In many ways, Sandoval's work could be seen as parallel to that of Bartolomé de Las Casas with indigenous people in Mexico. However, Sandoval's work to draw attention to the colonial victimization of African descendants has not remained vivid in Colombian history and has certainly not been incorporated into regnant views of blackness. According to Restrepo, Sandoval's work and that of others like him constitute what Foucault (1980) would call a subjugated knowledge, which has not yet become dominant or even fully audible but whose roots have been effectively planted and which can emerge as a full-fleshed discourse in the future. The same can be said of Pedro Claver, the Jesuit priest who became known as the "slaves' slave" for his Christianizing work in Cartagena de Indias.

17. For a comparative history of struggles for reparations in the Americas, see Araujo (2017). Most noteworthy to the discussion at hand, Araujo posits that demands for reparations for slavery and the slave trade in the Americas are deeply shaped by the way in which "former slaves and their descendants achieved or at least attempted to achieve citizenship in former slave societies" (4).

18. Several scholars of the African diaspora have placed victimization at the center of their definitions of blackness. Du Bois, Fanon, and Gilroy, just to name a few, have all theorized that black subjectivity is a direct result of the experience of slavery, dislocation, and ineffable violence. For each of them, this original victimization is at the heart of the black experience everywhere in the African diaspora. However, as I have shown elsewhere (Cárdenas 2010), until very recently, the literature of the African diaspora had not contemplated Colombia as a part of this black community of belonging. In fact, the recognition of racial sameness across the African diaspora has been historically asymmetrical; with black Colombians tending to be aware of black struggles elsewhere but not the reverse (Cárdenas 2012a). These diasporic fractures in conjunction with the strong national formations of blackness in Colombia (which been more strongly associated with culturalism than racial difference) had effectively obstructed the full incorporation of the notion of historical victimization as an inherent part of blackness in Colombia.

19. See Araujo (2017) for a historical overview of movements for reparations across the Americas.

20. While reparations for Holocaust and Japanese internment survivors are also examples of war reparations, they provide the most solid precedents of broad, material reparations carried out in the name of historical reckoning.

21. For a full explanation of CARICOM's plan, see (CARICOM 2014).

22. Note that in Latin America the first and clearest endorsement of the plan came from Cuba.

23. For the final communiqué of the 2015 CARICOM/NAARC summit, see National African-American Reparations Commission (2015).

24. This position was articulated by Mireille Fanon Mendes-France (daughter of Frantz Fanon), who has consistently remarked that "the future of the world cannot ignore the history of enslavement" as a system, and that to do so, "we have to deal with European culpability" (AIDC 2016).

25. By Durban, I am not only referring to the ten days during which representatives of UN member states and civil society organizations worldwide discussed the global manifestations of racism. I use *Durban* as shorthand to refer to the political effervescence that preceded it—for example, at the regional preconference in Santiago—as organizations and activists prepared for the conference; to the conference itself and the encounters that took place there; and to the commitments and relationships—both formal and informal—that followed from it.

26. Because he is a well-known public figure I use his real name.

27. After the inaugural event at the National University in Bogotá, Davis flew to Cali and then traveled by land to La Toma, Cauca, where she witnessed the dispossession of communities of artisanal miners at the hands of multinational gold mining corporations. This invitation was extended by Francia Márquez, a native of La Toma, who had met Davis on a political tour earlier that year. In planning her visit to La Toma, PCN activists were both reciprocating the hospitality that Francia had received abroad and visibilizing the effects of Colombia's deepened neoliberal policies on black communities. While not exactly framed as a result of the war, they clearly wanted to showcase the land struggle of miners in La Toma as a consequence of black communities' historical dispossession. La Toma was also upheld as a proud example of resistance and therefore an occasion to share in joyful diasporic exchanges. For more on La Toma's struggle against large-scale gold mining, see Paola Mendoza's documentary by the same name, *La Toma.* (Mendoza 2010).

28. These decisions included two main foreign policy initiatives of the US government, stalling the approval of the Free Trade Agreement and spending decisions for Plan Colombia monies. The first of these was thought to be important because, if approved, PCN believed that the economic effects of the agreement would have particularly detrimental consequences for Black Communities' rural economies. The second foreign policy issue was important for two reasons that had direct bearing on black Colombians: because military spending from Plan Colombia was disproportionately generating violence in the Pacific Region, and because Plan Colombia money could be earmarked for development projects for Afro-Colombians.

29. In fact, during her entire visit in Colombia, Davis was recognized first and foremost as a black leader. This, despite the fact that she was initially invited to the inaugural event of the Universidad Nacional's master's program in gender studies. At every single event in which people flocked to hear her speak, it was clear that they were there to see a black celebrity. This was repeatedly made clear by the sale of Afro wigs outside her keynote speech, the Black Panther salute that members of CADHUBEV rehearsed, the stickers with the outline of her figure with a prominent Afro printed on occasion of her

visit, and the giant mural of a Black Power fist painted outside the venue of her talk at the university to commemorate her visit.

30. This forum was virtual as a result of the COVID-19 pandemic, which also significantly slowed down the work of the burgeoning commission.

31. For a full analysis of the decolonizing possibilities of Afro-Colombians' participation in transitional justice, see Ojulari (2022).

32. Ojulari paused to stress the shift from ethnic demands to ethno-racial demands, and to emphasize the importance of that difference.

33. The people in attendance were Ron Daniels from the National African-American Reparations Commission, Verene Shephard, Earl Bousquet, and Mireille Fanon.

34. As a white Latin American, I include myself among those of "us" who have benefited from colonialism and enslavement.

Chapter 4: Black Visions of Peace

1. This number was taken from Indepaz's cumulative report since the peace accords and is available on their website at https://indepaz.org.co.

2. *Nos están matando*, or "they are killing us," has become a common and politicized phrase used by organizers and human rights workers in Colombia. It is also the title of a short documentary released in 2018 to document the persecution of activists and community leaders. The documentary traces the life and work of Feliciano Valencia, a prominent indigenous leader, and Héctor Marino Carabalí, an Afro-descendant activist. See Laffay (2018).

3. There are many difficulties in identifying who among the victims are Afro-Colombian, if nothing else, because I often do not have access to victims' ethno-racial self-identification and because organizations who are separating by race/ethnicity often use overlapping terms such as *Afro* and *campesino* (farmer), which may invisibilize black farmers, for example. To address this difficulty, I developed a makeshift methodology of identifying black victims. First, I searched for their institutional affiliations and included anyone who was working for black organizations. Then, I used geographical cues and internet searches to learn more about individual cases. This is admittedly an imprecise method, but one that I'm hoping is better able to identify black victims when explicit data is unavailable. Because I tracked this data for several years, the data available and my methodology also changed over time. Beginning in 2020, Indepaz began including a category called *calidad* (loosely translated as "type") in its data sets. Indigenous and Afro-descendant were two of the newly incorporated types, along with "environmentalist," "cultural," "communal," "social," "civic," and "campesino." With these new categories I incorporated only those marked as "Afro-descendant" to my list, recognizing, again, that this is an imperfect accounting method.

4. Following Bourdieu (2001), I understand symbolic violence to be the imposition (of values, institutions, practices) on subordinated groups, which legitimates and naturalizes the status quo. It includes not only the monopoly of legitimate violence (e.g., the police, the army) but also the monopoly of symbolic violence that legitimates physical violence.

This happens within the state (e.g., as expressed in the law) and within civil society (e.g., through the media) and on an everyday basis in ordinary acts such as finding housing, going to school, and watching TV. Symbolic violence has the power to universalize dominant practices and renders its Others provincial, particular, and exceptional. This is how the state and dominant classes more broadly produce hierarchies that are internalized by everyone—including those who rebel against them. It is the metafield of the state. Bourdieu's concept overcomes the dichotomy of coercion-consent by pointing to three components: ignorance of the arbitrariness of domination, recognition of the domination as legitimate, and internalization of domination by the dominated.

5. Anthropologists have added a cultural lens to the analysis of structural violence, illuminating how cultural difference enables the exoticization of suffering or can render it incomprehensible or naturalized (Bourgois 2003; Holmes 2013; Scheper-Hughes 1993).

6. For example, I am finishing this chapter in the midst of the powerful protest movement that followed George Floyd's assassination by a police officer in Minneapolis in 2020, which spread across the United States and globally to denounce antiblackness. As I hope to clarify in the following section, I cast doubt on the idea that Colombia's civil war is over. This is why I call the period after the 2016 peace accords an "alleged aftermath."

7. As early as November 2012, when the negotiations had just begun, President Santos stated publicly that "the economic and political model is not up for debate with the FARC" (*Semana* 2012).

8. It is important to acknowledge that white supremacy devalues all nonwhite forms of life and that indigenous people, too, have been victims of its genocide. In Colombia indigenous leaders are also working tirelessly (and sometimes alongside Afro-Colombians) to further anti-genocidal visions of peace. For the purpose of this chapter, however, I zoom in on Afro-Colombians to highlight the entrenchment of antiblackness in Latin American societies and to underscore the value of mobilizing the history of the black experience with violence as an essential contribution to build an anti-genocidal vision of peace.

9. Dest (2019) is responding to Holloway and Sitrin's suggestion (2007) that movements tend to shift from working "in and against the state" to operating "against and beyond it." Like Dest, I agree that these two do not constitute an either-or position but are often engaged alternately or simultaneously.

10. The Observatorio de Memoria y Conflicto is a data collection mechanism of the Centro Nacional de Memoria Histórica, a government-funded but autonomous entity established by decree following the 2011 passage of the Victims' Law.

11. In the efforts to implement the peace agreement, the Santos administration created an enormous institutional structure to manage land reform, justice, and reparations. These include the Agency for Rural Development (ADR), the National Agency of Lands (ANT), the Integral System for Truth, Justice, Reparation and No Repetition (SIVJRNR), and the Special Jurisdiction for Peace (JEP).

12. Since Duque assumed the presidency, the government's apparatus has effectively obstructed the peace process by numerous mechanisms. For example, by slowing down

the implementation of land reform through bureaucratic inefficiency, by failing to guarantee alternative incomes to the families that committed to eradicating coca from their farms (through the PNIS), and by delegitimizing the authority of the JEP—the transitional justice system set up during the previous administration to administer justice through the peace process.

13. One of the notable successes of this shift was the establishment of a gender subcommission, which worked to ensure that each of the points in the accords incorporated a gender-sensitive focus.

14. For example, activists from PCN used the hashtag #SinNegrosNoHayPaz, which translates as "No peace without black people," to pressure the government to include a permanent seat for Afro-Colombians at the negotiating table during the peace talks.

15. The figure given in Spanish as "19 billones de pesos" was equivalent to approximate US$5.5 million at the time of the PND's writing.

16. This body, known as the High-Level Consultative Commission, sits in the Ministry of Interior and serves as ethnic adviser to the government. After a seven-year hiatus in its activities, it was reconstituted in late 2018. However, the *consultiva* (as it is widely known) has lost legitimacy over the years. On the one hand, the degree to which elected members of the *consultiva* represent significant sectors of civil society has been questioned by many reputable black activists. On the other hand, the government's recent attempt to limit members to representatives of community councils exclusively, unleashed an uproar because it resulted in the de facto exclusion of a large percentage of the Afro-Colombian population.

17. Although COMADRE was established with that name in 2016, AFRODES has been working with grassroots groups of displaced Afro-Colombian women since 2006, when Luz Marina spearheaded the creation of the Coordinación de Mujeres following a nationwide meeting of AFRODES affiliates.

18. The literal translation of the title of this section is "a stick in the wheels," to signify an obstacle to progress.

19. There is a small body of work that has insisted on keeping Latin America in the same frame of analysis as the rest of the continent. In particular, I want to highlight the work of Sharlene Mollett (2021a), who, along with others like Bianet Castellanos (2017), Shannon Speed (2017), Chris Loperena (2017), and Richard Gott (2007) have noted that the framework of white settler colonialism is just as useful for Latin America as it is for the United States and Canada; and that in fact, when we analyze the whole continent together we bring into focus some of the shortcomings of settler-colonial theory while shedding new light on analyses of race in Latin America that too often insist on the region's exceptionalism and difference from the United States due to its history of *mestizaje*.

20. In gauging the scope of this, I find Appadurai's (1990, 1996) notion of five scapes of modern life useful: mediascapes, technoscapes, ethnoscapes, financescapes, and ideoscapes.

21. I translate *el cuidado de la vida* throughout this chapter as "care for life" and sometimes as "care for all life" to highlight that it is extended to nonhuman life. However, the

use of the word *all* should not be interpreted as an association with the antiblack statement "all lives matter," which so often circulates to delegitimize the Black Lives Matter movement and to erase the particular insidiousness of the attack on black life.

22. In 2015 Francia received the National Prize for the Defense of Human Rights; in 2018 she received the Goldman Environmental Prize; and in 2019 the BBC identified her as one of the hundred most influential women in the world.

23. "Luchamos para sobrevivir o nos morimos, nos morimos de tristeza, de enfermedades o porque nos declaran objetivo militar."

24. For protection of their identity, I use pseudonyms for Francia's family members.

25. *Paisa* is a complex term with shifting and contextual meanings in Colombia. It can refer to a person's place of origin—Antioquia and the neighboring areas where *antioqueños* settled as *colonos*. *Paisas* are known throughout Colombia as having a very strong regional identity; for example, they have a particularly distinctive accent and a local cuisine. However, in parts of Colombia that are predominantly black, the term *paisa* is used to refer to white people, so it is a racial rather than a regional term (see Londoño-Vega 2004; Roldán 2003; Twinam 1985; Wade 1993).

26. I recount some of this history in chapter 1, albeit focusing on another part of the Pacific, the Lower Mira River.

27. According to the confessions of demobilized paramilitaries, members of the AUC collaborated with members of the armed forces and the police in April 2001 in a massacre of over one hundred *campesinos*, indigenous, and black people. Allegedly, the paramilitaries were advancing to the Pacific Coast to establish a paramilitary *bloque* there and were eliminating their enemies—local *campesinos* and community organizers—along the way. This was a harrowing episode that marked the memories of everyone who was living in the area at that time.

28. This statistic was taken from the website of AngloGold Ashanti on March 29, 2020 (AngloGold Ashanti n.d.).

29. Héctor Sarria is a white man with known links to an infamous figure—La Monita Retrechera—who facilitated ties between ex-president Samper and the Cali Cartel. This was discovered during the investigation known as Proceso 8,000, carried out from 1995 to 1996.

30. Colombia's government is organized in the following territorial units, from the largest to the smallest: *departamento, municipio, corregimiento*, and *vereda*. *Veredas* are located inside *corregimientos*; *corregimientos* inside *municipios*, and *municipios* inside departments—which are equivalent to US states. The *vereda* of Yolombó belongs to the *corregimiento* of La Toma, which in turn belongs to the municipality of Suárez, and the department of Cauca—in a national region known as Northern Cauca.

31. Angela Davis's visit to La Toma came after her sessions in Cali with UniValle and CADHUBEV, which I described in chapter 3.

32. As in so many disasters in which the disregard for human life is rampant, the exact death toll from this tragedy is unknown, and the numbers vary greatly depending on the source of the report.

33. Although she has returned to visit many times, Francia was unable to live in her community for many years. More recently, since her presidential precampaign and vice-presidential candidacy, she has had to split her time between Cali and Bogotá to advance her political work.

34. This delegation was cosponsored by PCN and Afro-Resistance and was coordinated by myself and Janvieve Williams Comrie.

35. ASOMUAFROYO, the Association of Afro-Descendant Women of Yolombó, is a grassroots organization whose stated objective is "to build a space for the strengthening and recognition of the ancestral, ethnic and territorial rights of black women and their communities" ("Asomuafroyo" n.d.).

36. It is important to clarify that Law 70 did not grant Black Communities rights to the subsoil, which is technically still owned by the state. However, Black Communities with collective land titles do have a right to prior and informed consent, which gives them the right to participate in decisions that directly affect their territory, including use of the subsoil.

37. To provide this proof, community members from La Toma collaborated with a group of scholars from the University of Cauca on a research project that culminated in the publication of a book titled *La Toma: Historias de resistencia y autonomía.* The book, published in 2013, provides the archival evidence of their historical presence in the area (Ararat et al. 2013). On a separate note, unfortunately, violations of prior and informed consent are rampant across Latin America, despite it being an internationally recognized right through ratification of ILO 169. Often, communities face rigged consultation processes and weak to no enforcement mechanisms to oversee that their will is respected.

38. For more on the women's march, see Hernández Reyes (2019).

Epilogue

1. Although I took this English version from *The Book of Embraces* by Eduardo Galeano, translated by Cedric Belfrage with Mark Schafer, it is my understanding that the phrase "corriendo la liebre" means something loosely translated as "chasing a living." The concept of *los/las nadies* was a central to Francia's campaign and was printed on the materials of the inauguration to celebrate them as the newly empowered political subjects.

2. When they stole it, the M-19 left behind a note that read: "Bolívar is not dead. His sword cuts through the cobwebs of the museum and launches into the battles of the present. It is now transferred into our hands and aimed against the people's exploiters."

3. This phrase, in Spanish, "hasta que la dignidad se haga costumbre," was one of the mottos of her campaign.

REFERENCES

Achiume, Tendayi. 2019. "Report of the Special Rapporteur on Contemporary Forms of Racism, Racial Discrimination, Xenophobia and Racial Intolerance." United Nations General Assembly.

AFP. 2020. "UN Human Rights Chief Calls for Reparations to Make Amends for Slavery." *The Guardian*, June 17, 2020. https://www.theguardian.com/world/2020/jun/17/un-human-rights-chief-calls-for-reparations-to-make-amends-for-slavery.

AFRODES. 1998. "Reporte alternativo al noveno informe del Estado colombiano ante el Comité para la Eliminación de la Discriminación Racial." Bogotá: AFRODES

———. 2009. "Los derechos humanos en los afrocolombianos en situación de desplazamiento forzado." Bogotá: AFRODES.

AFRODES and Global Rights. 2007. "Luces y contraluces sobre la exclusión: Informe desde una perspectiva afrocolombiana." Bogotá: AFRODES and Global Rights.

Agier, Michel, Manuela Álvarez, Odile Hoffman, and Eduardo Restrepo, eds. 1999. *Tumaco: Haciendo ciudad*. Bogotá: Instituto Colombiano de Antropología, Institut de Recherche pour le Developpement, Universidad del Valle.

Agudelo, Carlos. 2005. *Retos del multiculturalismo en Colombia: Política y poblaciones negras*. Medellín: La Carreta Editores, IRD, ICANH, and IEPRI.

Alexander, Michelle. 2012. *The New Jim Crow: Mass Incarceration in the Age of Colorblindness*. New York: New Press.

Allen, Jafari. 2011. *¡Venceremos? The Erotics of Black Self-Making in Cuba*. Durham, NC: Duke University Press.

233

Almario, Óscar. 2002. "Desesclavización y territorialización: El trayecto inicial de la diferenciación étnica en el Pacífico Sur colombiano, 1749–1810." In *Afrodescendientes en las Américas: Trayectorias sociales e identitarias. 150 años de la abolición de la esclavitud en Colombia*, edited by Claudia Mosquera, Mauricio Pardo, and Odile Hoffman, 45–75. Bogotá: Universidad Nacional de Colombia, ICANH, IRD, and ILSA.

————. 2004. "Dinámica y consecuencias del conflicto armado colombiano en el Pacífico: Limpieza étnica y desterritorialización de afrocolombianos e indígenas y 'multiculturalismo' de Estado e indolencia nacional." In *Conflicto e invisibilidad: Retos en los estudios de la gente negra en Colombia*, edited by Eduardo Restrepo and Axel Rojas. Popayán, Colombia: Universidad del Cauca.

Alternative Information & Development Centre. 2016. "Reparation, Remembering the Past, Shaping the Future." https://aidc.org.za/reparation-remembering-past-shaping-future/.

Alves, Jaime Amparo. 2018. *The Anti-Black City: Police Terror and Black Urban Life in Brazil*. Minneapolis: University of Minnesota Press.

————. 2020. "Biopólis, Necrópolis, 'Blackpolis': Notas para un nuevo léxico político en los análisis socio-espaciales del racismo." *Geopauta* 4 (1): 5. https://doi.org/10.22481/rg.v4i1.6161.

Anderson, Benedict. 1983. *Imagined Communities: Reflections on the Origin and Spread of Nationalism*. London: Verso.

Anderson, Mark. 2009. *Black and Indigenous: Garifuna Activism and Consumer Culture in Honduras*. Minneapolis: University of Minnesota Press.

AngloGold Ashanti. N.d. "AngloGold Ashanti Home." https://www.anglogoldashanti.com.

Aparicio, Juan Ricardo. 2010. "Gobernando a la persona internamente desplazada: Problemas y fricciones de un nuevo problema mundial." *Tabula Rasa*, no. 13 (July): 13–44.

Appadurai, Arjun. 1990. "Disjuncture and Difference in the Global Cultural Economy." *Theory, Culture & Society* 7 (2–3): 295–310. https://doi.org/10.1177/026327690007002017.

————. 1996. *Modernity at Large: Cultural Dimensions of Globalization*. Minneapolis: University of Minnesota Press.

Appelbaum, Nancy P. 2003. *Muddied Waters: Race, Region, and Local History in Colombia, 1846–1948*. Durham, NC: Duke University Press.

Ararat, Lisifrey, Eduar Mina, Axel Rojas, Ana María Solarte, Gildardo Vanegas, Luis Armando Vargas, and Aníbal Vega. 2013. *La Toma: Historias de territorio, resistencia y autonomía en la Cuenca del Alto Cauca*. Popayán: Consejo Comunitario Afrodescendiente del Corregimiento de La Toma, Observatorio de Territorios Étnicos.

Araujo, Ana Lucía. 2017. *Reparations for Slavery and the Slave Trade: A Transnational and Comparative History*. London: Bloomsbury Academic.

Arboleda, Santiago. 2004. "Negándose a ser desplazados: Afrocolombianos en Buenaventura." In *Conflicto e (in)visibilidad: Retos en los estudios de la gente negra en Colombia*, edited by Eduardo Restrepo and Axel Rojas, 121–38. Colección Políticas de La Alteridad. Popayán: Universidad del Cauca.

————. 2007. "Conocimientos ancestrales amenazados y destierro prorrogado: La encrucijada de los afrocolombianos." In *Afro-reparaciones: Memorias de la esclavitud y justicia reparativa para negros, afrocolombianos y raizales*, edited by Claudia Mosquera Rosero-Labbé and Luiz Claudio Barcelos, 467–86. Bogotá: Universidad Nacional de Colombia.

Arias Vanegas, Julio. 2005. *Nación y diferencia en el siglo XIX colombiano: Orden nacional, racialismo y taxonomias poblacionales*. Bogotá: Universidad de Los Andes.

Asher, Kiran. 2009. *Black and Green: Afro-Colombians, Development, and Nature in the Pacific Lowlands*. Durham, NC: Duke University Press.

Asociación de Afrocolombianos Desplazados, Asociación Organización de Comunidades Negras, and Conferencia Nacional Afrocolombiana. 2008. "Política pública con enfoque diferencial para población afrocolombiana en situaciones de desplazamiento forzado o confinamiento: Propuestas para la construcción."

"Asomuafroyo." n.d. https://www.asomuafroyo.com/.

Banco Internacional de Desarrollo. 2011. *Diálogo regional de política: Red para la Reducción de la Pobreza y la Protección Social*. Washington, DC: Banco Internacional de Desarrollo.

Bejarano Ávila, Jesus Antonio, and Alberto Díaz Uribe. 1985. *Historiografía de la violencia en Colombia*. Bogotá: Cerec Centro Gaitán.

Beltrán, Cristina. 2020. *Cruelty as Citizenship: How Migrant Suffering Sustains White Democracy*. Minneapolis: University of Minnesota Press.

Bledsoe, Adam, and Willie Jamaal Wright. 2019. "The Anti-Blackness of Global Capital." *Environment and Planning D: Society and Space* 37 (1): 8–26. https://doi.org/10.1177/0263775818805102.

Bocarejo, Diana. 2008. "Reconfiguring the Political Landscape after the Multicultural Turn: Law, Politics, and the Spatialization of Difference in Colombia." PhD diss., University of Chicago.

Bolívar Ramírez, Ingrid Johanna. 2003. *Violencia política y formación del Estado: Ensayo historiográfico sobre la dinámica regional de la violencia de los cincuenta en Colombia*. Bogotá: Centro de Investigación y Educación Popular, Facultad de Ciencias Sociales, Universidad de los Andes.

Bonilla-Silva, Eduardo. 2009. *Racism without Racists: Color-Blind Racism and the Persistence of Racial Inequality in America*. 3rd ed. Lanham, MD: Rowman & Littlefield Publishers.

Bourdieu, Pierre. 2001. *Masculine Domination*. Stanford, CA: Stanford University Press.

Bourgois, Philippe. 2003. *In Search of Respect: Selling Crack in El Barrio*. Cambridge: Cambridge University Press.

Bushnell, David. 1993. *The Making of Modern Colombia: A Nation in Spite of Itself*. Berkeley: University of California Press.

Butler, Kim D. 2001. "Defining Diaspora, Refining a Discourse." *Diaspora: A Journal of Transnational Studies* 10 (2): 189–219. https://doi.org/10.1353/dsp.2011.0014.

Caracol Radio. 2018. "'Paras' mataron más de 100.000 personas y guerrillas 35.000:

CNMH." August 6, 2018. http://caracol.com.co/programa/2018/08/02/6am_hoy_por_hoy/1533213673_640453.html.

Cárdenas, Roosbelinda. 2010. "Trayectorias de negridad: Disputas sobre las definiciones contingentes de lo negro en América Latina." *Tabula Rasa* 13: 147–89.

———. 2012a. "Articulations of Blackness: Journeys of an Emplaced Politics in Colombia." Santa Cruz: University of California, Santa Cruz.

———. 2012b. "Multicultural Politics for Afro-Colombians: An Articulation 'without Guarantees.'" In *Black Social Movements in Latin America: From Monocultural Mestizaje to Multiculturalism*, edited by Jean Muteba Rahier, 113–33. New York: Palgrave Macmillan.

———. 2012c. "Green Multiculturalism: Articulations of Ethnic and Environmental Politics in a Colombian 'Black Community.'" *Journal of Peasant Studies* 39 (2): 309–33. https://doi.org/10.1080/03066150.2012.665892.

———. 2018. "'Thanks to My Forced Displacement': Blackness and the Politics of Colombia's War Victims." *Latin American and Caribbean Ethnic Studies* 13 (1): 72–93. https://doi.org/10.1080/17442222.2018.1416893.

———. 2019. "For Afro-Colombians, the 2016 Peace Treaty Brought No Peace." *The Nation*, May 23, 2019. https://www.thenation.com/article/archive/colombia-francia-marquez-human-rights-defender/.

Cárdenas, Roosbelinda, Charo Mina Rojas, Eduardo Restrepo, and Antonio Rosero Eliana. 2020. "Afro-Descendants in Colombia: Anti-Racist Struggles and the Accomplishments and Limits of Multiculturalism." In *Black and Indigenous Resistance in the Americas: From Multiculturalism to Racist Backlash*, edited by Juliet Hooker, 93–122. London: Rowman & Littlefield.

Caribbean Community (CARICOM). 2014. *CARICOM Ten Point Plan for Reparatory Justice*. https://caricom.org/caricom-ten-point-plan-for-reparatory-justice/. Georgetown, Guyana: CARICOM.

Carrillo, Karen Juanita. 2018. "Colombia's Peace Process Witnesses Another Death: Temístocles Machado." *Amsterdam News*, February 16, 2018. http://amsterdamnews.com/news/2018/feb/16/colombias-peace-process-witnesses-another-death-te/.

Castellanos, M. Bianet. 2017. "Introduction: Settler Colonialism in Latin America." *American Quarterly* 69 (4): 777–81. https://doi.org/10.1353/aq.2017.0063.

Castillejo Cuéllar, Alejandro. 2000. *Poética de lo otro: Para una antropología de la guerra, la soledad y el exilio interno en Colombia*. Bogotá: Instituto Colombiano de Antropologia e Historia.

———. 2014. "Historical Injuries, Temporality and the Law: Articulations of a Violent Past in Two Transitional Scenarios." *Law and Critique* 25 (1): 47–66.

Centro Nacional de Memoria Histórica. 2015. *Buenaventura: Un puerto sin comunidad*. Bogotá: Centro Nacional de Memoria Histórica, Departamento para la Prosperidad Social "Prosperidad para Todos."

Chu, Julie Y. 2006. "To Be 'Emplaced': Fuzhounese Migration and the Politics of Destination." *Identities* 13 (3): 395–425. https://doi.org/10.1080/10702890600839504.

————. 2010. *Cosmologies of Credit: Transnational Mobility and the Politics of Destination in China*. Durham, NC: Duke University Press.

Civico, Aldo. 2015. *The Para-State: An Ethnography of Colombia's Death Squads*. Oakland: University of California Press.

Clifford, James. 1994. "Diasporas." *Cultural Anthropology* 9 (3): 302–38. https://doi.org/10 .1525/can.1994.9.3.02a00040.

CNN en Español. 2016. "Así se vivió la multitudinaria marcha por la paz en Colombia." *CNN*, October 6, 2016. https://cnnespanol.cnn.com/2016/10/05/asi-se-vivio-la-marcha -por-la-paz-en-colombia/.

Coates, Ta-Nehisi. 2014. "The Case for Reparations." *The Atlantic*, May 22. https://www .theatlantic.com/magazine/archive/2014/06/the-case-for-reparations/361631/.

CODHES. 2013. *La crisis humanitaria en Colombia persiste: El Pacífico en disputa. Informe de desplazamiento forzado en 2012*. CODHES No. 26. Bogotá: CODHES.

Cohen, Roseann. 2010. "Uprooted Ecologies: Rebuilding Relations between People, Plants and Land in Times of Ongoing Dispossession at the Urban Fringe of Cartagena, Colombia." PhD diss., University of California, Santa Cruz.

Colombia Plural. 2016. "1996–2016: Las heridas de Riosucio." December 18. https:// colombiaplural.com/te-contamos-comienza-una-guerra/.

Comaroff, John L., and Jean Comaroff. 2009. *Ethnicity, Inc*. Chicago: University of Chicago Press.

Combahee River Collective. 1977. "The Combahee River Collective Statement."

Comisión Intereclesial de Justicia y Paz. 2008. "En el bajo Mira, en Tumaco y en Buenaventura." June 30. https://www.justiciaypazcolombia.com/en-el-bajo-mira-en-tu maco-y-en-buenaventura/.

Comité Municipal de Prevención y Atención Integral a la Población en Situación de Desplazamiento. 2010. "Plan integral único Municipio de Tumaco."

Craven, Christa, and Dána-Ain Davis. 2013. *Feminist Activist Ethnography: Counterpoints to Neoliberalism in North America*. Lanham, MD: Lexington Books.

Cresswell, Tim. 1996. *In Place/Out of Place: Geography, Ideology, and Transgression*. New ed. Minneapolis: University of Minnesota Press.

————. 1999. "Embodiment, Power and the Politics of Mobility: The Case of Female Tramps and Hobos." *Transactions of the Institute of British Geographers*, n.s., 24 (2): 175–92.

De la Cadena, Marisol. 2000. *Indigenous Mestizos: The Politics of Race and Culture in Cuzco, Peru, 1919–1991*. Durham, NC: Duke University Press.

————. 2001. "Reconstructing Race: Racism, Culture and Mestizaje in Latin America." *NACLA Report on the Americas* 34 (6): 16–23. https://doi.org/10.1080/10714839.2001.11 722585.

Democracy Now! 2017. "Daily Show," May 30. https://www.democracynow.org/shows/ 2017/5/30.

Dest, Anthony. 2019. "After the War: Violence and Resistance in Colombia." PhD diss., University of Texas at Austin.

———. 2020. "'Disenchanted with the State': Confronting the Limits of Neoliberal Multiculturalism in Colombia." *Latin American and Caribbean Ethnic Studies*, June, 1–23. https://doi.org/10.1080/17442222.2020.1777728.

Dinzey-Flores, Zaire, and Hilda Lloréns. 2020. "The Replay: White Passes and Black Exclusions in Latinidad." *Black Latinas Know.* https://www.blacklatinasknow.org/post/the-replay-white-passes-and-black-exclusions-in-latinidad.

Diócesis de Tumaco. 2008. "Comunicado público de la diócesis de Tumaco sobre la grave situación de la población afronariñense del Gran Consejo Comunitario del Río Sanquianga del municipio Olaya Herrera y Candelilla de la Mar, municipio de Tumaco."

The Economist. 2014. "Butchery in Buenaventura: Colombia's Most Violent City," March 25. https://www.economist.com/americas-view/2014/03/25/butchery-in-buenaventura.

Escobar, Arturo. 2001. "Culture Sits in Places: Reflections on Globalism and Subaltern Strategies of Localization." *Political Geography* 20 (2): 139–74. https://doi.org/10.1016/S0962-6298(00)00064-0.

———. 2008. *Territories of Difference: Place, Movements, Life, Redes.* Durham, NC: Duke University Press.

Escobar, Arturo, and Sonia E. Álvarez. 1992. *The Making of Social Movements in Latin America: Identity, Strategy, and Democracy.* Series in Political Economy and Economic Development in Latin America. Boulder, CO: Westview Press.

El Espectador. 2014. "'Operación Génesis' al desnudo," January 9, 2014. https://www.elespectador.com/opinion/operacion-genesis-al-desnudo-columna-467580.

———. 2016. "La cuestionable estrategia de campaña del No," October 6. https://www.elespectador.com/noticias/politica/la-cuestionable-estrategia-de-campana-del-no/.

———. 2017a. "Buenaventura grita 'el pueblo no se rinde carajo,'" May 21. https://www.elespectador.com/noticias/nacional/valle/buenaventura-grita-el-pueblo-no-se-rinde-carajo-articulo-694855.

———. 2017b. "El costo del paro en Buenaventura," May 17. https://www.elespectador.com/economia/el-costo-del-paro-en-buenaventura-articulo-694259.

———. 2017c. "La herencia paramilitar a 20 años de la operación Génesis," February 19, 2017. https://www.elespectador.com/noticias/judicial/la-herencia-paramilitar-20-anos-de-la-operacion-genesis-articulo-680751.

———. 2017d. "Toque de queda en Buenaventura," May 20. https://www.elespectador.com/noticias/nacional/en-medio-de-toque-de-queda-buenaventura-marcha-de-blanco-en-quinto-dia-de-paro-articulo-694713.

———. 2018. "Los líderes del El Naya están secuestrados," May 10. https://www.elespectador.com/colombia-20/conflicto/los-lideres-de-el-naya-estan-secuestrados-article/.

Euraque, Darío A., Jeffrey L. Gould, and Charles R. Hale. 2005. *Memorias del mestizaje: Cultura política en Centroamérica de 1920 al presente.* Antigua, Guatemala: CIRMA.

Fanon, Frantz. 1967. *Black Skin, White Masks.* London: Pluto Press.

Feld, Steven, and Keith H. Basso, eds. 1996. *Senses of Place.* Santa Fe, NM: School for Advanced Research Press.

Foucault, Michel. 1980. *Power/Knowledge: Selected Interviews and Other Writings, 1972–1977.* Edited by Colin Gordon. New York: Knopf Doubleday.

Franke, Katherine. 2019. *Repair: Redeeming the Promise of Abolition*. Chicago: Haymarket Books.

Frazier, Edward Franklin. 1957. *Race and Culture Contacts in the Modern World*. New York: Knopf.

Frazier, Edward Franklin, and Nathan Glazer. 1966. *The Negro Family in the United States*. Chicago: University of Chicago Press.

Freyre, Gilberto. 1933. *Casa-grande e senzala: Formação da família brasileira sob o regime de economia patriarcal*. Río de Janeiro: Record.

Friedemann, Nina S. de. 1984. "Estudios de negros en la antropología colombiana." In *Un siglo de investigación social: Antropología en Colombia*, edited by Jaime Arocha and Nina S. de Friedemann, 507–72. Bogotá: Etno.

———. 1992. "Huellas de africanía en Colombia." *Thesaurus: Boletín del Instituto Caro y Cuervo* 47 (3): 543–60.

Frontline Defenders. 2017. *Annual Report on Human Rights Defenders at Risk in 2017*. https://www.frontlinedefenders.org/en/resource-publication/annual-report-human -rights-defenders-risk-2017.

Ghassem-Fachandi, Parvis. 2009. *Violence: Ethnographic Encounters*. Oxford: Berg Publishers.

Gilliam, Angela. 1998. "The Brazilian Mulata: Images in the Global Economy*." *Race & Class* 40 (1): 57–69. https://doi.org/10.1177/030639689804000105.

Gilmore, Ruth Wilson. 2007. *Golden Gulag: Prisons, Surplus, Crisis, and Opposition in Globalizing California*. Berkeley: University of California Press.

Gilroy, Paul. 1995. *The Black Atlantic: Modernity and Double-Consciousness*. Cambridge, MA: Harvard University Press.

Goett, Jennifer. 2016. *Black Autonomy: Race, Gender, and Afro-Nicaraguan Activism*. Stanford, CA: Stanford University Press.

Goldstein, Daniel M. 2014. "Laying the Body on the Line: Activist Anthropology and the Deportation of the Undocumented." *American Anthropologist* 116 (4): 839–42.

Gordon, Edmund T. 1998. *Disparate Diasporas: Identity and Politics in an African Nicaraguan Community*. Austin: University of Texas Press.

Gott, Richard. 2007. "Latin America as a White Settler Society." *Bulletin of Latin American Research* 26 (2): 269–89.

Gould, Jeffrey L. 1998. *To Die in This Way: Nicaraguan Indians and the Myth of Mestizaje, 1880–1965*. Durham, NC: Duke University Press.

Gregory, Steven. 1999. *Black Corona*. Princeton, NJ: Princeton University Press.

Griffin, Farah Jasmine. 2003. "Para las chicas cubanas." *Callaloo: A Journal of African-American and African Arts and Letters* 26 (1): 74–82.

Gros, Christian. 2000. *Políticas de la etnicidad: Identidad, Estado y modernidad*. Bogotá: Instituto Colombiano de Antropología e Historia.

Gudynas, Eduardo. 2011. "Buen vivir: Germinando alternativas al desarrollo." *América Latina en Movimiento ALAI* (462): 1–20.

Gupta, Akhil, and James Ferguson. 2008. "Más allá de la 'cultura': Espacio, identidad y las políticas de la diferencia." *Antípoda*, no. 7: 233–76.

Gutiérrez, Gustavo. 1988. *A Theology of Liberation: History, Politics, and Salvation.* Translated by Caridad Inda and John Eagleson. Maryknoll, NY: Orbis Books.

Gutmann, Amy. 1993. "The Challenge of Multiculturalism in Political Ethics." *Philosophy & Public Affairs* 22 (3): 171–206.

Guzmán Campos, Germán. 1963. *La violencia en Colombia: Estudio de un proceso social.* Bogotá: Ediciones Tercer Mundo.

Hale, C. R. 2005. "Neoliberal Multiculturalism." *PoLAR: Political and Legal Anthropology Review* 28 (1): 10–19.

———. 2008. *Engaging Contradictions: Theory, Politics, and Methods of Activist Scholarship.* Berkeley: University of California Press.

Hale, Charles, and Leith Mullings. "A Time to Recalibrate: Analyzing and Resisting the Americas-Wide Project of Racial Retrenchment." In *Black and Indigenous Resistance in the Americas: From Multiculturalism to Racist Backlash.* New York: Lexington Books, 2020.

Hall, Stuart. 1997. "Old and New Identities, Old and New Ethnicities." In *Culture, Globalization and the World-System: Contemporary Conditions for the Representation of Identity,* edited by Anthony King, 42–68. Minneapolis: University of Minnesota Press.

———. 1999. "Thinking the Diaspora: Home-Thoughts from Abroad." *Small Axe* 6: 1–18.

———. 2001. *The Multicultural Question.* Milton Keynes, UK: Pavis Centre for Social and Cultural Research, Open University.

———. 2021. "Cultural Identity and Diaspora." 1990. In *Identity: Community, Culture, Difference,* edited by Jonathan Rutherford, 222–36. London: Lawrence & Wishart. https://doi.org/10.1215/9781478021223-016.

Hanchard, Michael George. 1998. *Orpheus and Power: The Movimento Negro of Rio de Janeiro and Sao Paulo, Brazil, 1945–1988.* Princeton, NJ: Princeton University Press.

Haraway, Donna J. 2003. *The Companion Species Manifesto: Dogs, People, and Significant Otherness.* Chicago: Prickly Paradigm Press. https://press.uchicago.edu/ucp/books/book/distributed/C/bo3645022.html.

Harney, Stefano, and Fred Moten. 2013. *The Undercommons: Fugitive Planning & Black Study.* Wivenhoe, UK: Minor Compositions.

Harrison, Faye V. 1997. *Decolonizing Anthropology: Moving Further toward an Anthropology for Liberation.* Arlington, VA: American Anthropological Association.

Hart, Gillian. 2006. "Denaturalizing Dispossession: Critical Ethnography in the Age of Resurgent Imperialism." *Antipode* 38 (5): 977–1004.

Hartman, Saidiya V. 1997. *Scenes of Subjection: Terror, Slavery, and Self-Making in Nineteenth-Century America.* New York: Oxford University Press.

———. 2008. *Lose Your Mother: A Journey along the Atlantic Slave Route.* New York: Farrar, Straus, and Giroux.

Hernández Reyes, Castriela Esther. 2019. "Black Women's Struggles against Extractivism, Land Dispossession, and Marginalization in Colombia." *Latin American Perspectives* 46 (2): 217–34. https://doi.org/10.1177/0094582X19828758.

Herskovits, Melville J. 1958. *The Myth of the Negro Past.* Boston: Beacon Press.

Hill Collins, Patricia. 2008. *Black Feminist Thought: Knowledge, Consciousness, and the Politics of Empowerment.* New York: Routledge.

Hoffman, Odile. 2002. "Conflictos territoriales y territorialidad negra: El caso de las comunidades afrocolombianas." In *Afrodescendientes en las Américas: Trayectorias sociales e identitarias, 150 años de la abolición de la esclavitud en Colombia,* edited by Claudia Mosquera Rosero-Labbé, Mauricio Pardo, and Odile Hoffman, 351–68. Bogotá: Universidad Nacional de Colombia, ICANH, IRD, ILSA.

———. 2007. *Comunidades negras en el Pacífico colombiano: Innovaciones y dinámicas étnicas.* Quito: Editorial Abya Yala.

Holloway, John, and Marina Sitrin. 2007. "Against and Beyond the State: An Interview with John Holloway." *Upside Down World* (blog), May 29. http://upsidedownworld.org/archives/international/against-and-beyond-the-state-an-interview-with-john-holloway/.

Holmes, Seth. 2013. *Fresh Fruit, Broken Bodies: Migrant Farmworkers in the United States.* Berkeley: University of California Press.

Holston, James. 2009. *Insurgent Citizenship: Disjunctions of Democracy and Modernity in Brazil.* Princeton, NJ: Princeton University Press.

Holt, Thomas C. 1995. "Marking: Race, Race-Making, and the Writing of History." *American Historical Review* 100 (1): 1–20. https://doi.org/10.2307/2167981.

Hooker, Juliet. 2005a. "'Beloved Enemies': Race and Official Mestizo Nationalism in Nicaragua." *Latin American Research Review* 40 (3): 14–39.

———. 2005b. "Indigenous Inclusion/Black Exclusion: Race, Ethnicity and Multicultural Citizenship in Latin America." *Journal of Latin American Studies* 37 (2): 285–310. https://doi.org/10.1017/S0022216X05009016.

———, ed. 2020. *Black and Indigenous Resistance in the Americas: From Multiculturalism to Racist Backlash.* Translated by Giorleny Altamirano Rayo, Aileen Ford, and Steven Lownes. London: Rowman & Littlefield.

hooks, bell. 2000. *Feminist Theory: From Margin to Center.* Cambridge, UK: South End Press.

Human Rights Watch. 2014. *The Crisis in Buenaventura: Disappearances, Dismemberment, and Displacement in Colombia's Main Pacific Port.* London: Rowman & Littlefield. https://www.hrw.org/report/2014/03/20/crisis-buenaventura/disappearances-dismemberment-and-displacement-colombias-main.

infobae. 2022. "1327 líderes sociales y firmantes de paz han sido asesinados tras la firma del acuerdo en Colombia." March 18, 2022. https://www.infobae.com/america/colombia/2022/03/18/1327-lideres-sociales-y-firmantes-de-paz-han-sido-asesinados-tras-la-firma-del-acuerdo-en-colombia/.

Internal Displacement Monitoring Centre. 2016. "IDP Country Profiles." Internal Displacement Monitoring Centre. https://www.internal-displacement.org/countries/colombia.

———. 2018. "IDP Country Profiles." http://www.internal-displacement.org/countries/colombia.

Izagirre, Ander. 2014. "Así se fabrican guerrilleros muertos." *El País*, March 26. https://elpais.com/elpais/2014/03/06/planeta_futuro/1394130939_118854.html.

Jacobson, Matthew Frye. 1999. *Whiteness of a Different Color: European Immigrants and the Alchemy of Race*. Cambridge, MA: Harvard University Press.

Jaramillo, Pablo. 2014. *Etnicidad y victimización*. Bogotá: Universidad de Los Andes, Colombia.

Jaramillo Buenaventura, Enrique. 2009. "Políticas espaciales y comunidades negras en el Pacífico colombiano." In *Poblaciones y territorios en disputa*, 5:45–81. Cali: Universidad ICESI.

———. 2018. "Landscapes of Extraction: Labor, Belonging, and Social Policy in Northern Cauca, Colombia." PhD diss., Rutgers University. https://doi.org/10.7282/T3BK1GT0.

Jimeno, Myriam. 2011. "Después de la masacre: La memoria como conocimiento histórico." *Cuadernos de Antroplogía Social*, no. 33: 39–52.

Jimeno, Myriam, Ángela Castillo, and Daniel Varela. 2010. "A los siete años de la masacre del Naya: La perspectiva de las víctimas." *Anuário Antropológico*, no. 2: 183–205.

Kane, Patrick. 2014. "Why Did 22 Afro-Colombian Women Occupy the Colombian Interior Ministry for Five Days?" *HuffPost UK* (blog), December 3. https://www.huffingtonpost.co.uk/patrick-kane/colombia-women_b_6255064.html.

Kymlicka, Will. 1996. *Multicultural Citizenship: A Liberal Theory of Minority Rights*. Oxford: Clarendon Press.

Laó-Montes, Agustín. 2005. "Afro-Latinidades and the Diasporic Imaginary." *Iberoamericana* 5 (17): 117–30.

Las2Orillas. 2014a. "Marcha de mujeres afro del Norte del Cauca llegó a Bogotá." *Las2Orillas* (blog), November 27. https://www.las2orillas.co/marcha-de-afrocolombianas-del-norte-del-cauca-llego-bogota/.

———. 2014b. "Los verdaderos dueños de Buenaventura," April 21. https://www.las2orillas.co/los-multimillonarios-duenos-del-puerto-de-buenaventura/.

Latin American and Caribbean Solidarity Network. 2017. "Recent News from Buenaventura, Valle." http://lacsn.weebly.com/colombia.html.

Leal, Claudia. 2004. "Black Forest: The Pacific Lowlands of Colombia, 1850–1930." Berkeley: University of California Press.

Leal Buitrago, Francisco. 1986. "Estado y política en Colombia." *Anuario Colombiano de Historia Social y de la Cultura* 13–14: 350–53.

Lehmann, David, ed. 2016. *The Crisis of Multiculturalism in Latin America*. New York: Palgrave Macmillan.

Linscott, Charles "Chip" P. 2017. "All Lives (Don't) Matter: The Internet Meets Afro-Pessimism and Black Optimism." *Black Camera: An International Film Journal* 8 (2): 104–19.

Lloréns, Hilda. 2013. "Latina Bodies in the Era of Elective Aesthetic Surgery." *Latino Studies* 11 (4): 547–69. https://doi.org/10.1057/lst.2013.32.

———. 2014. *Imaging The Great Puerto Rican Family: Framing Nation, Race, and Gender during the American Century*. New York: Lexington Books.

Londoño-Vega, Patricia. 2004. *Religión, cultura y sociedad en Colombia: Medellín y Antioquia, 1850–1930*. Bogotá: Fondo de Cultura Económica.

Loperena, Christopher A. 2017. "Settler Violence? Race and Emergent Frontiers of Progress in Honduras." *American Quarterly* 69 (4): 801–7. https://doi.org/10.1353/aq.2017.0066.

López Oro, Paul Joseph. 2016. "'Ni de aquí, ni de allá': Garífuna Subjectivities and the Politics of Diasporic Belonging." In *Afro-Latin@s in Movement: Critical Approaches to Blackness and Transnationalism in the Americas*, edited by Petra R. Rivera-Rideau, Jennifer A. Jones, and Tianna S. Paschel, 61–83. Afro-Latin@ Diasporas. New York: Palgrave Macmillan. https://doi.org/10.1057/978-1-137-59874-5_3.

López Rodríguez, Mercedes. 2019. *Blancura y otras ficciones raciales en los Andes colombianos del siglo XIX*. Madrid: Iberoamericana; Frankfurt: Editorial Vervuert.

Lorde, Audre. 1984. *Sister Outsider: Essays and Speeches*. Crossing Press Feminist Series. Trumansburg, NY: Crossing Press.

Malkki, Liisa. 1995. "Refugees and Exile: From 'Refugee Studies' to the National Order of Things." *Annual Review of Anthropology* 24: 495–523.

Massey, Doreen B. 1994. *Space, Place, and Gender*. Minneapolis: University of Minnesota Press.

Mbembe, Achille. 2019. *Necropolitics*. Durham, NC: Duke University Press Books.

McDowell, Linda. 1999. *Gender, Identity, and Place: Understanding Feminist Geographies*. Minneapolis: University of Minnesota Press.

McKittrick, Katherine. 2011. "On Plantations, Prisons, and a Black Sense of Place." *Social & Cultural Geography* 12 (8): 947–63. https://doi.org/10.1080/14649365.2011.624280.

McLean, Phillip. 2002. "Colombia: Failed, Failing, or Just Weak?" *Washington Quarterly* 25 (3): 123–34. https://doi.org/10.1162/016366002260046280.

Meertens, Donny. 2010. "Forced Displacement and Women's Security in Colombia." *Disasters* 34 (2): S147–64.

Mendoza, Paola, dir. 2010. *La Toma*. Documentary. Rola Productions.

Moghnieh, Lamia. 2017. "'The Violence We Live in': Reading and Experiencing Violence in the Field." *Contemporary Levant* 2 (1): 24–36.

Mollett, Sharlene. 2014. "A Modern Paradise: Garifuna Land, Labor, and Displacement-in-Place." *Latin American Perspectives* 41 (6): 27–45. https://doi.org/10.1177/0094582X13518756.

———. 2016. "The Power to Plunder: Rethinking Land Grabbing in Latin America." *Antipode* 48 (2): 412–32. https://doi.org/10.1111/anti.12190.

———. 2021a. "Hemispheric, Relational, and Intersectional Political Ecologies of Race: Centring Land-Body Entanglements in the Americas." *Antipode* 53 (3): 810–30. https://doi.org/10.1111/anti.12696.

———. 2021b. "Resistance against the Land Grab: Defensoras and Embodied Precarity in Latin America." In *The Routledge Handbook of Critical Resource Geography*, edited by Matthew Himley, Elizabeth Havice, and Gabriela Valdivia, 93–102. London: Routledge.

Moreno Figueroa, Mónica G., and Emiko Saldívar Tanaka. 2016. "'We Are Not Racists,

We Are Mexicans': Privilege, Nationalism and Post-Race Ideology in Mexico." *Critical Sociology* 42 (4–5): 515–33. https://doi.org/10.1177/0896920515591296.

Morris, Courtney Desiree. 2012. "To Defend This Sunrise : Race, Place, and Creole Women's Political Subjectivity on the Caribbean Coast of Nicaragua." PhD diss., University of Texas at Austin. https://repositories.lib.utexas.edu/handle/2152/ETD -UT-2012-08-5944.

——. 2016. "Toward a Geography of Solidarity: Afro-Nicaraguan Women's Land Activism and Autonomy in the South Caribbean Coast Autonomous Region." *Bulletin of Latin American Research* 35 (3): 355–69. https://doi.org/10.1111/blar.12490.

Morris, Hollman. 2013. "Suárez Gold: Afro-Colombian Miners Defending Their Heritage." *Minority Rights*, April 22. https://stories.minorityrights.org/afro-descendants/ chapter/film-suarez-gold-afro-colombian-miners-defending-their-heritage/.

Mosquera Rosero-Labbé, Claudia. 2007. "Reparaciones para negros, afrocolombianos y raizales como rescatados de la trata negrera trasatlántica y desterrados de la guerra en Colombia." In *Afro-reparaciones: Memorias de la esclavitud y justicia reparativa para negros, afrocolombianos y raizales*, edited by Claudia Mosquera Rosero-Labbé and Luiz Claudio Barcelos, 213–76. Bogotá: Universidad Nacional de Colombia.

Moten, Fred. 2013. "The Subprime and the Beautiful." *African Identities* 11 (2): 237–45. https://doi.org/10.1080/14725843.2013.797289.

Munn, Nancy D. 1986. *The Fame of Gawa: A Symbolic Study of Value Transformation in a Massim (Papua New Guinea) Society*. Cambridge: Cambridge University Press.

National African-American Reparations Commission. 2015. "Final Communiqué, the National/International Reparations Summit," April 22. https://reparationscomm.org /naarc-news/press-releases/final-communique-the-national-international-reparations -summit/.

Nembhard, Jessica Gordon. "Theorizing and Practicing Democratic Community Economics: Engaged Scholarship, Economic Justice, and the Academy." In *Engaging Contradictions*, edited by Charles R Hale, 265–96. University of California Press, 2008.

Ng'weno, Bettina. 2007. "Can Ethnicity Replace Race? Afro-Colombians, Indigeneity and the Colombian Multicultural State." *Journal of Latin American and Caribbean Anthropology* 12 (2): 414–40. https://doi.org/10.1525/jlat.2007.12.2.414.

Nordstrom, Carolyn, and Antonius C. G. M Robben. 1995. *Fieldwork under Fire: Contemporary Studies of Violence and Survival*. Berkeley: University of California Press.

Noticias ONU. 2019. "La cifra global de desplazados se dispara al nivel más alto en 70 años," June 19. https://news.un.org/es/story/2019/06/1458001.

Ojulari, Esther Yemisi. 2021. *Decolonising Transitional Justice: A Framework for Historical Reparations for the Afro-Descendant People in Colombia*. London: Institute of Commonwealth Studies, School of Advanced Study, University of London.

——. 2022. *Decolonising Transitional Justice: A Framework for Historical Reparation for Afro-Descendant Peoples in Colombia*. London: Institute of Commonwealth Studies, School of Advanced Study, University of London.

Oslender, Ulrich. 2008a. "Another History of Violence: The Production of 'Geographies of

Terror' in Colombia's Pacific Coast Region." *Latin American Perspectives* 35 (5): 77–102.

———. 2008b. *Comunidades negras y espacio en el Pacífico colombiano: Hacia un giro geográfico en el estudio de los movimientos sociales.* Colección Antropología en la Modernidad. Bogotá: ICANH.

———. 2016. *The Geographies of Social Movements: Afro-Colombian Mobilization and the Aquatic Space.* Durham, NC: Duke University Press.

Palacios, Marco. 1983. *El café en Colombia 1850–1970: Una historia económica, social y política.* Mexico City: Colegio de México; Bogotá: Ancora Editores.

Paschel, Tianna S. 2010. "The Right to Difference: Explaining Colombia's Shift from Color Blindness to the Law of Black Communities." *American Journal of Sociology* 116 (3): 729–69. https://doi.org/10.1086/655752.

———. 2016. *Becoming Black Political Subjects: Movements and Ethno-Racial Rights in Colombia and Brazil.* Princeton, NJ: Princeton University Press.

La Paz en el Terreno. N.d. "Líderes asesinados desde la firma del acuerdo." https://lapazenelterreno.com/lider-social/emilsen-manyoma.

Pécaut, Daniel. 1988. *Crónica de dos décadas de política colombiana: 1968–1988.* Bogotá: Siglo XXI.

Perry, Keisha-Khan Y. 2013. *Black Women against the Land Grab: The Fight for Racial Justice in Brazil.* Minneapolis: University of Minnesota Press.

Pinho, Patricia de Santana. 2009. "White but Not Quite: Tones and Overtones of Whiteness in Brazil." *Small Axe: A Caribbean Journal of Criticism* 13 (2): 39–56. https://doi.org/10.1215/07990537-3697250.

Postero, Nancy. 2017. *The Indigenous State: Race, Politics and Performance in Plurinational Bolivia.* Oakland: University of California Press. https://doi.org/10.1525/9780520967304-007.

Povinelli, Elizabeth A. 2007. *The Cunning of Recognition: Indigenous Alterities and the Making of Australian Multiculturalism.* Durham, NC: Duke University Press.

Proceso de Comunidades Negras. 2017. "Llamado urgente a la comunidad internacional y organismos multilaterales: ¡Presidente Santos detenga la respuesta violenta al paro cívico en Buenaventura!" *Renacientes* (blog), May 20. https://renacientes.net/blog/2017/05/20/llamado-urgente-a-la-comunidad-internacional-y-organismos-multilaterales-presidente-santos-detenga-la-respuesta-violenta-al-paro-civico-en-buenaventura/.

Quiceno Toro, Natalia. 2016. *Vivir sabroso: Luchas y movimientos afroatrateños, en Bojayá, Chocó, Colombia.* Bogotá: Universidad del Rosario.

Rahier, Jean Muteba. 2003. "Introduction: Mestizaje, Mulataje, Mestiçagem in Latin American Ideologies of National Identities." *Journal of Latin American Anthropology* 8 (1): 40–50. https://doi.org/10.1525/jlca.2003.8.1.40.

———, ed. 2012. *Black Social Movements in Latin America: From Monocultural Mestizaje to Multiculturalism.* New York: Palgrave Macmillan.

———. 2020. "From the Transatlantic Slave Trade to Contemporary Ethnoracial Law in Multicultural Ecuador: The 'Changing Same' of Anti-Black Racism as Revealed by

Two Lawsuits Filed by Afrodescendants." *Current Anthropology* 61 (S22): S248–S259. https://doi.org/10.1086/710061.

Ramírez, María Clemencia. 2001. *Entre el Estado y la guerrilla: Identidad y ciudadanía en el movimiento de los campesinos cocaleros del Putumayo.* Bogotá: Instituto Colombiano de Antropología e Historia, Colciencias.

Ramírez Baquero, Santiago. 2019. "'Mantenerme viva es una victoria': Francia Márquez." *Semana Rural*, May 9. https://semanarural.com/web/articulo/entrevista-con-francia -marquez-mantenerme-viva-es-una-victoria/947.

Registro Único de Víctimas. 2018. Unidad para las Víctimas. https://www.unidadvictimas .gov.co/es/registro-unico-de-victimas-ruv/37394.

Reiter, Bernd. 2013. *The Dialectics of Citizenship: Exploring Privilege, Exclusion, and Racialization.* East Lansing: Michigan State University Press.

———. 2018. "Recognition, Reparations and Political Autonomy of Black and Native Communities in the Americas." In *Comparative Racial Politics in Latin America*, 2nd ed., 44–63. New York: Routledge.

Restrepo, Eduardo. 1996. "Los tuqueros negros del Pacífico Sur colombiano." In *Renacientes del guandal: "Grupos negros" de los ríos Satinga y Sanquianga*, edited by Jorge Ignacio del Valle and Eduardo Restrepo, 245–348. Bogotá: Universidad Nacional de Colombia.

———. 2003. "Entre arácnidas deidades y leones africanos. Contribución al debate de un enfoque afroamericanista en Colombia." *Tabula Rasa*, no. 1 (December): 87–123. https://doi.org/10.25058/20112742.189.

———. 2004. "Ethnicization of Blackness in Colombia." *Cultural Studies* 18 (5): 698–753. https://doi.org/10.1080/0950238042000260405.

———. 2005. "De 'refugio de paz' a la pesadilla de la guerra: Implicaciones del conflicto armado en el proceso organizativo de 'comunidades negras' del Pacífico nariñense." Bogotá.

———. 2013. *Etnización de la negridad: La invención de las "comunidades negras" como grupo étnico en Colombia.* Popayán, Colombia: Universidad del Cauca.

———. 2021. "¿Negro o afrodescendiente? Debates en torno a las políticas del nombrar en Colombia." *Perspectivas Afro* 1 (1): 5–32. https://doi.org/10.32997/pa-2021-3541.

Revista Diners. 2019. "'Seguiré luchando hasta el día en que me muera,' Francia Márquez," November 18. https://revistadiners.com.co/tendencias/73317_no-voy-a-parar-de -luchar-francia-marquez/.

Riaño-Alcala, Pilar. 2006. *Jóvenes, memoria y violencia en Medellín: Una antropología del recuerdo y el olvido.* Medellín: Universidad de Antioquia; Bogotá: ICANH.

Robinson, Randall. 2001. *The Debt: What America Owes to Blacks.* New York: Plume.

Rocha, Luciane de Oliveira. 2012. "Black Mothers' Experiences of Violence in Rio de Janeiro." *Cultural Dynamics* 24 (1): 59–73. https://doi.org/10.1177/0921374012452811.

Rodríguez Garavito, César A., Tatiana Alfonso Sierra, Isabel Cavelier Adarve, and Universidad de los Andes (Bogotá Sociojurídicas Colombia) Centro de Investigaciones. 2009. *El desplazamiento afro: Tierra, violencia y derechos de las comunidades negras en Colombia.* Bogotá: Universidad de los Andes, Facultad de Derecho, CIJUS.

Rojas, Axel. 2014. "De la salvación al desarrollo: Gente negra, evangelización y extractivismo en el suroccidente colombiano." *Revista de História Comparada* 8 (1): 59–95.

Roldán, Mary. 2003. *A sangre y fuego: La violencia en Antioquia, Colombia, 1946–1953.* Bogotá: Instituto Colombiano de Antropología e Historia, Fundación para la Promoción de la Ciencia y la Tecnología.

Saito, Natsu Taylor. 2015. "Race and Decolonization: Whiteness as Property in the American Settler Colonial Project." *Harvard Journal on Racial & Ethnic Justice* 31: 31–68.

Sánchez G., Gonzalo, and Mario Aguilera Peña. n.d. *Memoria de un país en guerra: Los mil días, 1899–1902.* Bogotá: IEPRI, Unidad de Investigaciones Jurídicos-Sociales Gerardo Molina, Universidad Nacional, Planeta.

Scheper-Hughes, Nancy. 1993. *Death without Weeping.* Berkeley: University of California Press.

Segato, Rita Laura. 2007. *La nación y sus otros: Raza, etnicidad y diversidad religiosa en tiempos de políticas de la identidad.* Buenos Aires: Prometeo Libros.

Semana. 2012. "Santos: 'El modelo económico y político no está en discusión con las FARC,'" November 16. https://www.semana.com/nacion/articulo/santos-el-modelo-economico-politico-no-esta-discusion-farc/267919-3.

———. 2016a. "Ideología de género: Una estrategia para ganar adeptos por el 'no' al plebiscito," August. https://www.semana.com/nacion/articulo/ideologia-de-genero-una-estrategia-para-ganar-adeptos-por-el-no-al-plebiscito/488260.

———. 2016b. "'Las mentiras' de las campañas del No, según el Consejo de Estado." December 19. https://www.semana.com/nacion/articulo/el-consejo-de-estado-dice-que-se-le-mintio-al-electorado-en-campanas-del-no/510040.

———. 2017a. "Buenaventura, entre disturbios y saqueos," May 19. https://www.semana.com/Item/ArticleAsync/525876?nextId=525913.

———. 2017b. "La furia de Buenaventura," May 20. https://www.semana.com/nacion/articulo/detenidos-y-heridos-por-protestas-en-buenaventura/525913.

———. 2017c. "La metástasis de Buenaventura," May 25. https://www.semana.com/nacion/articulo/paro-en-buenaventura-estalla-cuando-mas-se-ha-invertido-en-la-ciudad/526610.

———. 2017d. "Paro en Buenaventura llega a su fin," June 6. https://www.semana.com/nacion/articulo/paro-en-buenaventura-acuerdo-entre-gobierno-y-comunidad/527628.

———. 2017d. "Las seis deudas históricas por las que protestan en Buenaventura," May 22. https://www.semana.com/nacion/articulo/buenaventura-cifras-de-pobreza-desempleo-inseguridad/526149.

———. 2018a. "Asesinan a uno de los líderes del paro cívico de Buenaventura," January 27. https://www.semana.com/nacion/articulo/asesinan-a-temistocles-machado-uno-de-los-lideres-del-paro-civico-de-buenaventura/555146.

———. 2018b. "En memoria de Bernardo Cuero," December 11. https://www.semana.com/contenidos-editoriales/derechos-humanos-viven/articulo/en-memoria-de-bernardo-cuero/594665/.

Serna, Sonia. 2011. "Vivir de los imaginarios del mar: Restaurantes y estereotipos sobre el Pacífico en Bogotá." *Tabula Rasa*, no. 14: 265–94.

Sexton, Jared. 2008. *Amalgamation Schemes: Antiblackness and the Critique of Multiracialism*. Minneapolis: University of Minnesota Press.

———. 2011. "The Social Life of Social Death: On Afro-Pessimism and Black Optimism." *InTensions Journal*, no. 5: 1–47.

———. 2012. "Ante-Anti-Blackness: Afterthoughts." *Lateral* 1 (1). https://csalateral.org/issue/1/ante-anti-blackness-afterthoughts-sexton/.

Sharp, William Frederick. 1981. *Slavery on the Spanish Frontier: The Colombian Chocó, 1680–1810*. Norman: University of Oklahoma Press.

La Silla Vacía. 2017. "El asesinato anunciado de Bernardo Cuero," June 11. https://www.lasillavacia.com/historias/silla-nacional/el-asesinato-anunciado-de-bernardo-cuero/.

Skidmore, Thomas E. 1992. *Black into White: Race and Nationality in Brazilian Thought*. Durham, NC: Duke University Press.

Smith, Christen A. 2016a. *Afro-Paradise: Blackness, Violence, and Performance in Brazil*. Urbana: University of Illinois Press.

———. 2016b. "Facing the Dragon: Black Mothering, Sequelae, and Gendered Necropolitics in the Americas." *Transforming Anthropology* 24 (1): 31–48. https://doi.org/10.1111/traa.12055.

———. 2017. "Battling Anti-Black Genocide in Brazil." *NACLA Report on the Americas* 49 (1): 41–47. https://doi.org/10.1080/10714839.2017.1298243.

Speed, Shannon. 2017. "Structures of Settler Capitalism in Abya Yala." *American Quarterly* 69 (4): 783–90. https://doi.org/10.1353/aq.2017.0064.

Stavenhagen, Rodolfo. 2009. "Indigenous Peoples as New Citizens of the World." *Latin American and Caribbean Ethnic Studies* 4 (1): 1–15. https://doi.org/10.1080/1744222080 2681373.

Tate, Winifred. 2007. *Counting the Dead*. Berkeley: University of California Press.

———. 2013. "Proxy Citizenship and Transnational Advocacy: Colombian Activists from Putumayo to Washington, DC." *American Ethnologist* 40 (1): 55–70. https://doi.org/10.1111/amet.12005.

Taussig, Michael. 1987. *Shamanism, Colonialism, and the Wild Man: A Study in Terror and Healing*. Chicago: University of Chicago Press.

TeleSur. 2017. "Hallan fosa común con 2.000 cadáveres sin registrar en Colombia," November 7. https://www.telesurtv.net/news/Hallan-fosa-comun-con-2.000-cadaveres -sin-registrar-en-Colombia-20171107-0015.html.

———. 2018. "Denuncian asesinato de 4 líderes comunitarios en Naya, Colombia," June 5. https://www.telesurtv.net/news/colombia-naya-asesinato-lideres-comunitarios -20180605-0041.html.

Telles, Edward, René D. Flores, and Fernando Urrea-Giraldo. 2015. "Pigmentocracies: Educational Inequality, Skin Color and Census Ethnoracial Identification in Eight Latin American Countries." *Research in Social Stratification and Mobility* 40 (June): 39–58. https://doi.org/10.1016/j.rssm.2015.02.002.

El Tiempo. 2014. "Mineros en Cauca quedaron a 20 metros de profundidad tras derrumbe," May 1. https://www.eltiempo.com/archivo/documento/CMS-13916575.

Trouillot, Michel-Rolph. 2002. "The Otherwise Modern: Caribbean Lessons from the Savage Slot." In *Critically Modern: Alternatives, Alterities, Anthropologies*, edited by Bruce M. Knauft, 220–37. Bloomington: Indiana University Press.

———. 2003. "Anthropology and the Savage Slot: The Poetics and Politics of Otherness." In *Global Transformations: Anthropology and the Modern World*, edited by Michel-Rolph Trouillot, 7–28. New York: Palgrave Macmillan US. https://doi.org/10.1007/978-1-137-04144-9_2.

Tsing, Anna. 2000. "The Global Situation." *Cultural Anthropology* 15 (3): 327–60.

———. 2004. *Friction: An Ethnography of Global Connection*. Princeton, NJ: Princeton University Press.

Twinam, Ann. 1985. *Mineros, comerciantes y labradores: Las raíces del espíritu empresarial en Antioquia: 1763–1810*. Medellín: Fondo Rotatorio de Publicaciones FAES.

Twine, Francine Winddance. 1997. *Racism in a Racial Democracy: The Maintenance of White Supremacy in Brazil*. New Brunswick, NJ: Rutgers University Press.

Unidad de Atención y Reparación Integral a Víctimas. 2015. "Informe del Gobierno nacional a las Comisiones primeras del Congreso de la República: Unidad para las Víctimas." https://www.unidadvictimas.gov.co/es/informe-del-gobierno-nacional-las-comisiones-primeras-del-congreso-de-la-rep%C3%BAblica/442.

UNODC (Oficina de las Naciones Unidas contra la Droga y el Delito). 2011. *Colombia: Monitoreo de cultivos de coca 2010*. Bogotá: UNODC.

———. 2012. *Cultivos de coca: Estadísticas municipales censo 31 de diciembre de 2011*. Bogotá: UNODC.

———. 2020. *Colombia: Monitorea de territorios afectados por cultivos ilícitos 2019*. Bogotá: UNODC.

Uribe Alarcón, María Victoria. 1990. *Matar, rematar y contramatar. Las masacres de La Violencia en Tolima 1948–1964*. Bogotá: Universidad del Rosario.

———. 2004. *Antropología de la inhumanidad: Un ensayo interpretativo del terror en Colombia*. Bogotá: Norma.

———. 2009. "Memory in Times of War." *Public Culture* 21 (1): 3–7. https://doi.org/10.1215/08992363-2008-017.

Van Cott, Donna Lee. 2000a. *The Friendly Liquidation of the Past: The Politics of Diversity in Latin America*. Pitt Latin American Series. Pittsburgh, PA: University of Pittsburgh Press.

Vargas, João H. Costa. 2008. *Never Meant to Survive: Genocide and Utopias in Black Diaspora Communities*. Lanham, MD: Rowman & Littlefield Publishing.

———. 2018. *The Denial of Antiblackness: Multiracial Redemption and Black Suffering*. Minneapolis: University of Minnesota Press.

Vasconcelos, José. 1925. *The Cosmic Race / La raza cósmica*. Translated by Didier T. Jaén. Baltimore: Johns Hopkins University Press.

Vélez-Torres, Irene. 2014. "Governmental Extractivism in Colombia: Legislation, Securitization and the Local Settings of Mining Control." *Political Geography* 38 (January): 68–78. https://doi.org/10.1016/j.polgeo.2013.11.008.

Veracini, Lorenzo. 2011. "Introducing: Settler Colonial Studies." *Settler Colonial Studies* 1 (1): 1–12.

Verdad Abierta. 2012. "Los orígenes de la masacre de El Naya," June 19. https://verdadabierta.com/los-origenes-de-la-masacre-de-el-naya/.

———. 2018. "'Buenaventura es una contradicción': Temístocles Machado," January 29. https://verdadabierta.com/buenaventura-es-una-contradiccion-temistocles-machado/.

Vergara-Figueroa, Aurora. 2011. "Ripped from the Land, Shipped Away and Reborn: Unthinking the Conceptual and Socio-Geo-Historical Dimensions of the Massacre of Bellavista." PhD diss., University of Massachusetts, Amherst. http://scholarworks.umass.edu/theses/570/.

———. 2017. *Afrodescendant Resistance to Deracination in Colombia: Massacre at Bellavista-Bojayá-Chocó*. New York: Springer.

Villa, William. 2001. "El Estado multicultural y el nuevo modelo de subordinación." In *Seminario de Evaluación: 10 años de la Constitución colombiana*, 89–101. Bogotá: Universidad Nacional, Facultad de Derecho, Ciencias Políticas y Sociales.

Vinson, Ben, and Bobby Vaughn. 2004. *Afroméxico: El pulso de la población negra en México, Una historia recordada, olvidada y vuelta a recordar*. Mexico City: Fondo de Cultura Económica.

Wade, Peter. 1993. *Blackness and Race Mixture: The Dynamics of Racial Identity in Colombia*. Baltimore: Johns Hopkins University Press.

———. 2000. *Music, Race & Nation: Música Tropical in Colombia*. Chicago: University of Chicago Press.

———. 2005. "Rethinking Mestizaje: Ideology and Lived Experience." *Journal of Latin American Studies* 37 (2): 239–57. https://doi.org/10.1017/S0022216X05008990.

Waldmann, Peter. 2007. "Is There a Culture of Violence in Colombia?" *Terrorism and Political Violence* 19 (4): 593–609. https://doi.org/10.1080/09546550701626836.

Walsh, Catherine. 2016. "¿Comunicación, decolonización y buen vivir? Notas para enredar, preguntar, sembrar y caminar." In *Comunicación, decolonialidad y buen vivir*, edited by Francisco Sierra Caballero and Claudio Maldonado, 39–58. Quito: Ediciones CIESPAL.

Walters, Ronald W. 2008. *The Price of Racial Reconciliation*. Politics of Race and Ethnicity. Ann Arbor: University of Michigan Press.

Whitten, Norman E. 1974. *Black Frontiersmen: A South American Case*. New York: Schenkman Pub.

Wilderson, Frank B., III. 2010. *Red, White & Black: Cinema and the Structure of US Antagonisms*. Durham, NC: Duke University Press.

Wolfe, Patrick. 2006. "Settler Colonialism and the Elimination of the Native." *Journal of Genocide Research* 8 (4): 387–409. https://doi.org/10.1080/14623520601056240.

Wolford, Wendy. 2010. *This Land Is Ours Now: Social Mobilization and the Meanings of Land in Brazil*. Durham, NC: Duke University Press.

Wouters, Mieke. 2001. "Ethnic Rights under Threat: The Black Peasant Movement against Armed Groups' Pressure in the Chocó, Colombia." *Bulletin of Latin American Research* 20 (4): 498–519. https://doi.org/10.1111/1470-9856.00027.

————. 2002. "Comunidades negras, derechos étnicos y desplazamiento forzado en el Atrato Medio: Respuestas organizativas en medio de la guerra." In *Afrodescendientes en las Américas: Trayectorias sociales e identitarias, 150 años de la abolición de la esclavitud en Colombia*, edited by Claudia Mosquera Rosero-Labbé, Mauricio Pardo, and Odile Hoffman, 369–97. Bogotá: Universidad Nacional de Colombia, ICANH, IRD, and ILSA.

WRadio. 2011. "'El país está en deuda con su población afro': Presidente Santos," May 21. https://www.wradio.com.co/noticias/actualidad/el-pais-esta-en-deuda-con-su-poblacion-afro-presidente-santos/20110521/nota/1476313.aspx.

Ybarra, Megan. 2018. *Green Wars: Conservation and Decolonization in the Maya Forest.* Berkeley: University of California Press.

Zuleta, Mónica. 2005. "Genealogía de la moral predominante en la literatura académica sobre la violencia política colombiana del siglo XX." *Nómadas*, no. 22: 282–86.

Zuluaga, Pedro Adrián. 2018. "'Tenemos un gran desafío: Transformar las políticas de muerte en políticas para la vida.'" *Contexto y Acción*, September. http://ctxt.es/es/2018 0905/Politica/21487/Pedro-Adrian-Zuluaga-Francia-Elena-Marquez-activismo-Colombia-transformacion-politico.htm.

INDEX

Page numbers in italics denote figures, and endnotes are indicated by "n" followed by the endnote number.

The authorized representative in the EU for product safety and compliance is:
Mare Nostrum Group
B.V Doelen 72
4831 GR Breda
The Netherlands

www.ingramcontent.com/pod-product-compliance
Lightning Source LLC
Chambersburg PA
CBHW030353270326
41926CB00009B/1091